To my wife, Lois,
and sons, Clay and Adam

Contents

v

Preface

The value of training in managerial communications is indisputable. Edward Radding, Vice President of Media Services for the Milton Bradley Company, stated in a recent letter to the author:

> I believe the ability to communicate both orally and in written form is one of the most important assets a student can bring to the business world. . . . No business problems can be solved, however, if the recommended solution cannot be persuasively communicated. My business school training involved constant written and oral communication. It is this training in effective communicating that I have drawn upon most often in my business experience. A brilliant recommendation for a selected action is useless if you are unable to convince the other party of the value of your thinking.

Years ago, business communications courses stressed content alone and were essentially applied English courses, limited to one aspect of communications, writing. Some courses were appropriately entitled "Business Letters and Reports." More recently, attention has been given to other communicative skills, such as speaking and listening.

Presently, the demands for increased office productivity are paramount. Attention must also be given to communication systems and procedures as well as basic content. Technological breakthroughs, coupled with computer wizardry, have revolutionized modern communications systems and procedures.

A business executive told the author: "I took a course in business communications and then had to learn everything else I needed to know in communications on my own—word processing concepts, micrographics, electronic communications, reprographics, and so on." Another executive said: "It seems impossible to keep up with the dazzling breakthroughs in technology. A revolution in modern communications is taking place. The thing that is frightening is that many schools are ten years behind—and the students will never catch up!"

Of necessity, the director of managerial communications must be a master of content, systems, and procedures. The ability to communicate accurately and quickly is essential in the modern business world. In the near future, voice, image, video, data, and hard-copy printed material will be integrated, as will office systems, such as word processing, data processing, printing, phototypesetting, and telecommunications.

Goals

The goals of the author are to provide basic theory and content information and to review modern office communication systems and procedures. These goals will be achieved by:

1. Presenting a solid background in communication theory (Part I).
2. Introducing the varied written communications utilized in the modern business office (Part II).
3. Explaining nonwritten communications (Part III).
4. Providing basic information about the new electronic/technological revolution in communications (Part IV).

Features

Although this book has been designed as a one-semester college textbook, business managers can use it as a handy guide to communication in the modern business world. Special learning features of the book designed to assist the student are:

1. A logical, systematic presentation with ample headings and enumerations that highlight key ideas, definitions, information, and the like.
2. Learning goals at the beginning of each chapter.
3. End-of-chapter summaries, discussion and study questions, and activities.

4. Checklists at the ends of chapters to measure the achievement of learning goals.
5. A *complete*, model formal report.
6. Numerous illustrations of equipment, format, and documents that serve as visual aids to comprehension.
7. Guidelines for nonsexist discrimination in communications.

Performance objectives

The student completing this program of instruction should be able to:

1. Communicate effectively.
2. Understand basic communication theory.
3. Master basic communicative skills (writing, speaking, listening, reading).
4. Conduct basic research from secondary and primary sources.
5. Manage the new technology in the field of communication.
6. Use modern communication systems and procedures effectively.
7. Acquire essential technical skills in order to utilize verbal and non-verbal communication processes.
8. Write effective business documents (letters, reports, memorandums, news releases, and so on) at an acceptable level of comprehensibility for the business world.
9. Develop sound, basic principles relating to business communications.
10. Apply up-to-the-minute information about new procedures and systems in office communications.
11. Pursue personal career goals expeditiously and effectively—write letters of application and resumés, prepare for interviews, and so on.

Students who have completed the course of study in this textbook should be able to assume their roles as business executives with confidence in their communicating expertise.

Acknowledgments

I am indebted to numerous individuals in education, business, and industry for their invaluable contributions to this book. Connecticut General Corporation allowed me to tour their modern administrative offices, take numerous photographs for illustrative purposes, gather photographs from files, and discuss modern communicating systems and procedures with employees. Mr. Hal

Rives, Director of Public Relations, and his staff were particularly helpful and solicitous. Various documents and forms used in this textbook were obtained from the Connecticut General Corporation. Mr. Rives reviewed the section on press releases and made constructive suggestions for improvement.

I am also grateful to Mrs. Carol C. Jonic, formerly with the IBM Corporation, for reviewing the chapter on Word Processing and making many invaluble suggestions. Mrs. Jonic is a recognized leader in the field of word processing, and her suggestions enhanced the chapter immeasurably.

Mr. Edward Radding, Vice President of Media Services at the Milton Bradley Company, provided significant information about electronic communications at his company. Mr. Radding evinced practical, progressive thinking about managerial communications that convinced me that I was on the right track writing an innovative textbook in the field.

Mr. Richard Jackson, Manager of Corporate Communications at Aetna Life & Casualty provided important information about electronic teleconferencing. Several other executives from major corporations reviewed sections of the manuscript but requested anonymity. I am indebted to all these individuals for their significant contributions.

I wish to extend special appreciation to my colleagues in the School of Business at Central Connecticut State University for sharing materials and giving useful suggestions. Also, thanks are extended to my students who communicated the need for a new publication in the field. This encouraged me to pursue this project.

Illustrations and/or materials were obtained from the following businesses: Aetna Life & Casualty, Bell & Howell, Milton Bradley Company, CIGNA Corporation, Connecticut Natural Gas Corporation, Exxon Office Systems Company, IBM Office Products Division, AM Jacquard Systems, Eastman Kodak Company, Motorola Inc., Norelco (Philips Business Systems, Inc.), Olympia USA, Inc., Prentice-Hall, Inc., Royal Business Machines, Inc., Sage-Allen & Co. Inc., Satellite Business Systems, Service Merchandise Company, Inc., Southern New England Telephone Company, 3M, The Travelers Insurance Companies, Wang, Western Electric Co., Inc., Western Union, Xerox Corporation.

I am particularly indebted to the editorial staff of the College Division of Prentice-Hall, Inc. Mr. John Duhring, editor, enthusiastically accepted the challenge of publishing a modern, innovative text and was extremely cooperative. Mr. Duhring made many constructive suggestions for improving the manuscript. His assistant, Ruth Weadock, was particularly helpful and assistive. It was very pleasant associating with Mr. Fred Dahl, who coordinated the various illustrations and designed the layout. He made important suggestions for improving the content and format.

Finally, I wish to express my sincere appreciation to my wife, Lois, and sons Clay and Adam, for their invaluable moral support and assistance.

NATHAN KREVOLIN

I

COMMUNICATION THEORY

The Communication Process

LEARNING GOALS

1. Identify the manager's role in the communication process.
2. Comprehend the communication process and basic communication theory.
3. Detect communication breakdowns.
4. Understand the importance of feedback or verification in the communication process.
5. Define ascendant, descendant, and lateral communication.
6. Recognize communication networks found in a business organization.
7. Improve your ability to communicate.

The manager's role

A modern business organization is a complex association of individuals striving towards common goals. If the organization is to function effectively, and earn a profit, the actions of the individuals must be coordinated and controlled by effective communication. Even the most competent and intelligent person's effectiveness will be limited, if thoughts cannot be communicated clearly and precisely. This entails the formation and transmission of messages that are understandable.

The successful manager is usually the successful communicator—the individual who can read and listen well, write effectively, and speak fluently. The manager persuades, directs, and informs. The successful manager understands the complexities of the communication process.

The communication process

STIMULUS-RESPONSE

Organisms respond to stimuli (Figure 1–1).
The word "stimulus" is derived from the Latin word meaning "goad." The stimulus is some form of energy that incites or rouses an organism to respond.

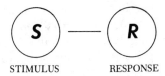

STIMULUS   RESPONSE   **FIGURE 1–1.** Stimulus and response

Our sensory receptors (eyes, ears, skin, nostrils, tongue) detect stimuli in the environment; nervous impulses travel to the spinal column and/or brain, and the organism responds. When a telephone rings, the sound waves stimulate the ear and the brain interprets the sound. The response is to pick up the telephone receiver.

Because the receiving mechanisms of human beings are limited—a cat's sense of smell is one hundred times sharper than ours, an eagle flying high in the sky can see a mouse crossing a field, a dog can hear sounds that we cannot—we supplement our sensory receptors with instruments (microscopes, telescopes, etc.).

Nevertheless, our limited capacity as receptors of stimuli can cause communication problems. Also, there are psychological factors, such as readiness and attention, that inhibit communication. An individual can actually tune out or tune in messages.

The stimulus to action in the communication process may come from within the individual (intrapersonal) or from an external source (interpersonal).

COMMUNICATION DEFINED

The word "communicate" is from the Latin *cummunicatus* (pp. of *communicare*), to impart, share. Communication involves the transmission and reception of thoughts, feelings, and ideas between two or more points. Modern business communications may involve manifold integrated systems, such as word processing, data processing, microfilming, reprographics (photocopying or duplicating), phototypesetting, and telecommunications (radio, television, facsimile, and so on). The new systems often entail new office procedures.

Ideally, if the communication system is working effectively, the communicator will have conveyed thoughts and ideas precisely, efficiently, and rapidly to the receiver. Communication has not taken place if the message is incomprehensible to the receiver. The objectives of communication are understanding and, in some cases, directed response.

BUSINESS COMMUNICATION SYSTEMS

Business communication systems provide the means for effective internal and external interchanges of ideas, facts, information, and instructions. Sound and sight are the primary senses used for sending and receiving messages in the business world; however, other senses are also utilized.

5

Verbal and Nonverbal Communication. Business communications fall into two broad classifications, *verbal* and *nonverbal*. Verbal communication involves the use of words (speaking, writing, listening). Nonverbal communication involves gestures, body language, sign language, and the display of objects.

Business communication skills are specialized adaptations of the communicative skills acquired for everyday life. An effective business communicator needs a solid background in English skills, as well as training in current techniques of communication. Social communications are often rambling, imprecise and subjective. Generally, business communications should be rapid, precise, and objective.

Himstreet, Porter and Maxwell list some of the most common activities in business communications:

Oral	*Written*
Listening to instructions.	Writing letters.
Giving instructions.	Writing memorandums.
Using the telephone.	Writing telegrams.
Dealing with visitors.	Writing reports.
Requesting information.	Writing orders.
Listening while taking dictation.	Making notes of telephone calls, interviews, and so forth.
Listening to a transcribing machine.	Transcribing shorthand notes.
Proofreading (one person reads, the other checks copy).	Transcribing machine dictation.
Dictating to a machine.	Filling in printed forms.
Explaining about a product or service.	Writing postal cards.
Introducing new workers.	Abstracting minutes of meetings and conferences.
Interviewing job applicants.	Writing copy for advertising, news releases, and so forth.
Speaking at meetings.	Writing data for office manuals, sales manuals, and so forth.
Participating in conventions, conferences, and so on.	Drawing up outlines.[1]

[1] William C. Himstreet, Leonard J. Porter, and Gerald W. Maxwell, *Business English in Communications* (Englewood Cliffs, N.J.: Prentice-Hall, Inc. 1975), p. 4.

A communicator, a message, and a receiver are needed if communication is to occur. The communicator's role in this relationship is to:

1. *Formulate* the message.
2. *Encode* the message in transmissible form.
3. *Select* the channel of communication (air, paper, electronic, etc.).
4. *Transmit* the message.

The receiver's role is to:

1. *Receive* the message (perceive it accurately).
2. *Decode* and interpret the message (translate the symbols).
3. *Understand* the message (comprehension). Take action if desirable.
4. *Feedback* (response) to the communicator that the message has been received completely and accurately.

The communication process is illustrated in Figure 1–2.

on Test questions →

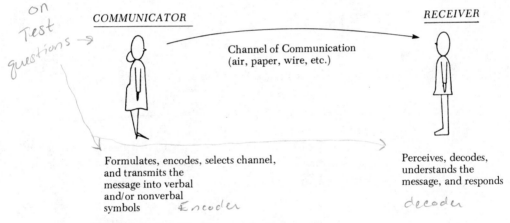

COMMUNICATOR

Channel of Communication
(air, paper, wire, etc.)

RECEIVER

Formulates, encodes, selects channel, and transmits the message into verbal and/or nonverbal symbols   *Encoder*

Perceives, decodes, understands the message, and responds

decoder

FIGURE 1–2.   The communication process

COMMUNICATION BREAKDOWNS   *Faults in Communication*

Breakdowns in communication can take place when:

1. The communicator does not formulate, encode, or transmit the message well;
2. There is a failure within the channel of communication (technical breakdowns, etc.); and   *telephone*

3. The receiver does not perceive or comprehend the message.

"Noise" Defined. The term *noise* is used in the field of communication to denote any interference, physical or psychological, preventing communication. Noise, therefore, is not limited to sound or noise in the usual sense. A radio making sounds in the background, a broken wire, an incorrect or misinterpreted gesture, a smudge on a manuscript, poor diction, language difficulties, and so on are examples of noise (Figure 1–3). Ideally, all noise should be eliminated in communications because it may totally or partially block the communication process.

Test question →

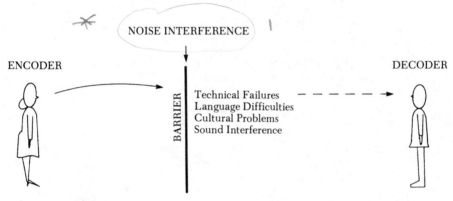

FIGURE 1–3.   Breakdowns in communications from noise interference

In addition to noise interference, communication breakdowns can occur at the point of origination (encoder) and at the point of reception (decoder). (See Figures 1–4 and 1–5.)

FEEDBACK   *Study   fill ins*

If the message has been received and an accurate response has been sent back to the encoder, acknowledgment is called *feedback*. Feedback enhances the communication process, for it verifies the effectiveness of the communication process. For example, a college instructor (the encoder) lectures (transmits a message orally) to his or her students (decoders) and at a later date gets feedback (test results). Feedback can be received more rapidly if the instructor asks questions orally during the lecture. Instantaneous feedback results when the instructor observes the students' reactions.

Another question on Test

study

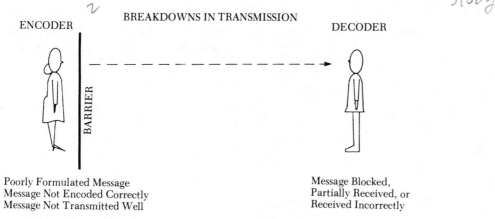

ENCODER   BREAKDOWNS IN TRANSMISSION   DECODER

BARRIER

Poorly Formulated Message
Message Not Encoded Correctly
Message Not Transmitted Well

Message Blocked,
Partially Received, or
Received Incorrectly

FIGURE 1–4. Breakdowns in transmission of the message

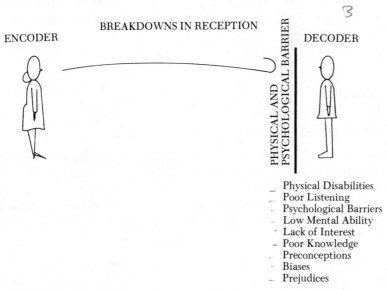

ENCODER   BREAKDOWNS IN RECEPTION   DECODER

PHYSICAL AND
PSYCHOLOGICAL BARRIER

Physical Disabilities
Poor Listening
Psychological Barriers
Low Mental Ability
Lack of Interest
Poor Knowledge
Preconceptions
Biases
Prejudices

FIGURE 1–5. Physical and psychological barriers of the decoder
(breakdowns in reception)

        Feedback is essential, for it allows correction. Hopefully, the instructor
will learn if the lecture was effective and make modifications for improvement if needed.

9

CLOSED SYSTEM *[handwritten: Test question]*

When the message has been formulated, transmitted, decoded by the receiver, and acknowledgment has been sent to the sender, we say that the system is *closed*. (See Figure 1–6.)

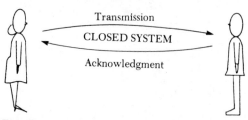

FIGURE 1–6. Closing the system

Closing the system may occur very rapidly in person-to-person conversations. The system may be closed many times in a conversation. When writing to an associate at a long distance, it may take days or weeks to receive a reply and close the system.

Communication direction *[handwritten: almost all communication go ascendant (upward)]*

ASCENDANT, DESCENDANT, AND LATERAL *[handwritten: (upward) (downward) (sideways)]*

[handwritten margin note: on Test — Knowledge going upward]

Communication within a business organization moves in three directions: upward (ascendant), downward (descendant), and sideways (lateral). A report by a department manager to the president is upward communication; a directive by a vice-president to a production worker is downward communication; a memo from one department head to another is lateral communication. (Figure 1–7).

INTERNAL AND
EXTERNAL COMMUNICATION

If communication flows from a home office to a distant branch office, this is called internal communication. External communication is communication outside a business organization. The media used for communication are often relative to whether the communication is external or internal. For example, the letter is used primarily for external communication; the memorandum form for internal communication.

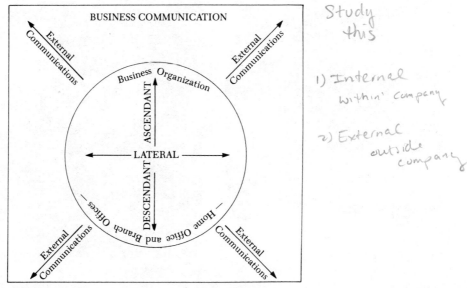

FIGURE 1–7. Direction of communications

[handwritten: Study this]

[handwritten: 1) Internal within company]

[handwritten: 2) External outside company]

Personal communication

[handwritten: gift for the employees company picnic]

Social or personal communication is an ancillary activity; it occurs both internally and externally. For example, within an office there may be exchanges about a company picnic. Externally, a condolence letter may be sent to a company supplier. Personal communication is vital if morale and goodwill are to be engendered. Some companies provide for personal communication by having a company newsletter or newspaper. However, most personal exchanges arise when the need exists.

GRAPEVINE *[handwritten: Heard it through the grapevine]*

An informal communication network, known as the *grapevine,* exists in many organizations in addition to formal, structured organizational networks. Often, the grapevine carries gossip and false rumors. Effective managers are aware of this informal network and learn to use it effectively.

11

Personal communication

Three communication networks

There are three intricate communication networks found in a business organization: *personal, internal,* and *external*. The communication networks carry the lifeblood of the business organization. Data, information, directions, statements, reports, letters, memos, and news releases travel continuously, for communications are a continual process in the business organization.

factors → *Time, space,* and *cost,* are important considerations in this communication process. Communicating quickly may be essential when meeting deadlines or obligations. Distance may have to be surmounted. In many American companies, managers are physically isolated from workers. The president may be in his penthouse suite, individuals lower in the hierarchy may be twenty floors below. Cost is an important consideration both in internal and external communication. The cost of a telegram is more than the cost of a letter. The importance of the message will determine whether it is oral or in written form. A record of agreements, transactions, findings, and so on, may be necessary.

Suggestions for improving communications

AVOIDING BREAKDOWNS

Since the process of communication is complex, there are many points at which breakdowns can occur. These are some suggestions for improving communication:

1. The communicator must *formulate* the message clearly before transmitting it. For example, it is wise to outline the content of a letter before dictating it. *Visualize person who is going to receive message*
2. The communicator should *visualize* the receiver and structure the level of vocabulary and psychology accordingly. Since communication is generally a social process, receptiveness, the right tone, courtesy, and sincerity should prevail in business communications.
3. The method of *transmission* should be appropriate, effective, and economical. If speed is essential, a telephone call is better than a letter. However, if speed is not essential and a record of a transaction is needed, a letter is more appropriate. If both speed and a written record are needed, a telegram or Mailgram could be used. When speed is a factor, the expense of a long distance call must be considered. In many cases, proper office procedure will dictate the

method of transmission. For communications within a company, a memo is generally used instead of a letter.

4. Try to *eliminate noise* (all interference). Some of the noise problems are mechanical and correctable (smudges, defective communication equipment, background noise, etc.).

5. The receiver must, of necessity, be a good receptor of stimuli—read well, *listen attentively*, be observant. The decoder may have difficulties when deciphering a message. There may be physical disabilities (poor hearing, poor vision, etc.). Semantics are a major consideration. What connotations are implied by the words? Perhaps additional training or reinforcement of language skill is required. What are the motives of the communicator? Are there ancillary, nonverbal communications along with the verbal? If so, are they in agreement? The person is suspect who states while smiling, "I am sorry your business lost money during the past quarter." The full play of intelligence and psychology are critical if accurate perception is to take place. Determine what action, if any, is desired by the communicator. Analyze the message for content and meaning, stated or implied.

6. When appropriate, *feedback* should be conveyed as soon as possible. For example, if a letter is received requiring a response, reply as soon as possible, within a twenty-four hour period, if possible. Answer telephone calls promptly. Procrastination is the nemesis of rapid communication. *You should reply to a letter in 24 hours* *on test*

Summary

The successful manager is usually an effective communicator—an individual who can listen well, write effectively, and speak fluently. The manager persuades, directs, and informs.

Communication involves the transmission and reception of thoughts, feelings, and ideas between two or more points. Modern business systems are complex and involve many integrated systems, such as word processing, data processing, microfilming, reprographics, phototypesetting, and telecommunications. These systems often entail new office procedures.

Business communications fall into two broad classifications: verbal and nonverbal. Business communication skills are specialized adaptations of the communicative skills acquired for everyday life.

There are eight steps in the communication process: formulation, encoding, selecting the channel of communication, transmission, reception, decoding, understanding, and feedback. Breakdowns in the communication process are caused by noise, any interference, physical or psychological, preventing communication.

If the message has been received and an accurate response has been sent back, acknowledgment is called "feedback." Communication within a business is ascendant, descendant, and lateral.

There are three intricate communication networks found in a business organization: internal, external, and personal. Social or personal communication is an ancillary activity; it occurs both internally and externally. An informal communication network, known as the grapevine, exists in many organizations.

Communications can be improved by:

1. Formulating the message clearly before transmitting it;
2. Structuring the vocabulary and psychology used accordingly;
3. Selecting the most appropriate, effective, and economical method of transmission;
4. Eliminating interference;
5. Receiving stimuli correctly;
6. Transmitting feedback rapidly.

Discussion

1. Relate the manager's role in the communication process.
2. Explain briefly the communication process.
3. Speak about the relationship between business communication skills and English skills.
4. Give several examples of interference in communication.
5. Explain briefly the importance of acknowledgment in the communication process.
6. Give examples of how the process of communication can be improved.

Study questions

1. Differentiate between intrapersonal and interpersonal stimuli. *within the individual , external source*
2. What is communication? *Latin word for share*
3. What are the objectives of communication? *pg 6, 7, 8 understanding directed response*
4. What are the two primary senses used for communicating in the business world? *Verbal and Nonverbal*
5. What is verbal communication? *Involves the use of words, letters, lists*
6. What is nonverbal communication? *Involves gestures, body language, sign language*

7. Breakdowns in communication can take place at three points—list them. PG. 7   Encoder place of transmission
   Decoder   channel

8. In the field of communication, what does noise mean? PG. 8

9. What is the acknowledgment that a message has been received accurately called? Feedback

10. When the message has been formulated, transmitted, and decoded, what do we call this? Transmission acknowledgment
    closed system

11. What are the three communication directions within a business organization? Ascendant, Descendant, and Lateral

12. What is the informal communication network that exists in many organizations called? Grapevine,

Activity

1. Assess the effectiveness of communications in a collegiate, business, or social situation. Describe the method of communication, any barriers, and feedback.

ACHIEVEMENT OF LEARNING GOALS

Check the appropriate boxes to determine whether you have or have not achieved the learning goals of this chapter.

I Can:

	YES	NO
1. Identify the manager's role in the communication process.	☑	☐
2. Comprehend the communication process and basic communication theory.	☐	☐
3. Detect communication breakdowns.	☑	☐
4. Understand the importance of feedback or verification in the communication process.	☑	☐
5. Define ascendant, descendant, and lateral communication.	☑	☐
6. Recognize communication networks found in a business organization.	☑	☐
7. Communicate more effectively.	☑	☐

If any of your responses were "no," it is suggested that you review pertinent chapter parts.

II

WRITTEN COMMUNICATIONS

Writing for Business

LEARNING GOALS

1. Master the basic techniques of effective business writing.
2. Eliminate bias in writing.

The English skills used when writing business papers are taught in standard English classes. Employees who are proficient in using the English language are highly valued by business executives. Management disapproves of poor grammar, spelling errors, punctuation and capitalization errors, inadequate vocabulary, faulty sentence structure, and so on.

Writing instruction in standard English classes often emphasizes the subjective style, which is usually wordy. Romanticism and emotionalism are prized in this type of writing. *Writing effectively for business entails a specialized style.*

Style of writing

In the business world, *time is money*. Few businesses can afford the luxury of long, involved passages. The following basic techniques are suggested for business writing:

- Accuracy
- Clarity
- Completeness

- Conciseness
- Consideration
- Courtesy
- Logical organization
- Positiveness

ACCURACY

Accuracy is essential in business communications because writing errors can be costly; a misquoted estimate or price could have serious repercussions. Recently, the members of a town council in Connecticut asked for estimates to repair a building. A very low estimate of $10,000 was received and accepted. By mistake, the contractor's typist dropped a zero when typing the estimate— the $10,000 estimate should have been $100,000! Fortunately for the contractor, the town council released the contractor from the obligation.

Check and Recheck. The executive cannot slough off responsibility for inaccuracies. It is the executive's fault if a letter that contains an error goes out with his or her signature. Messages must be checked and, at times, rechecked for accuracy. Pay particular attention to the accuracy of figures. Search for omissions. Be certain sentences are complete.

Be Precise. Correct grammar, punctuation, and spelling are very important. A misplaced comma can change the meaning of a sentence. Be precise in the use of words. If in doubt, use a good dictionary. Keep a dictionary and a thesaurus on your desk for reference purposes—and use them! The names of individuals should be spelled correctly. Most people are very annoyed when their names are misspelled.

To ensure accuracy, check your sources of information carefully. Consult with specialists if there are questions about content. Be specific. Mistakes in writing tend to distract. The person reading the message may have thoughts beyond those intended by the content of the message. For example, the reader, upon seeing a careless error in spelling, punctuation, or grammar, may think that the writer is incompetent and/or uneducated.

CLARITY

Be Concrete. Clarity in business communications refers to the clearness or understandability of messages. Avoid abstract, ambiguous words. Exaggerated language is difficult to understand. Instead, select concrete nouns whenever possible. Concrete words relate to tangible, real things. Abstract words are vague and difficult to understand; their meanings are imprecise. Words such as typewriter, computer, and desk are concrete; truth, justice, and equality are examples of abstract words.

Abstract Statements	Concrete Statements
the business	the partnership
many replied	70 percent replied
several months ago	August
large profit	$2-million profit
metal bowl	sterling silver bowl
the college	University of California

Use Appropriate Words. To make yourself clear, use familiar, simple words whenever possible. Carefully select words that the reader will understand. A vocabulary appropriate for one person may not be appropriate for another. For example, you may want to use the word "criterion" when corresponding with Worker A, and the word "standard" when corresponding with Worker B.

Use Visual Aids. Important points are usually more understandable when displayed visually. So whenever possible, use visual aids. It is easier to locate information in visual displays than it is to "plow through" masses of typewritten copy.

Avoid Jargon. Proper word choice is critical if precise meaning is to be communicated. Jargon, technical language that is familiar within a particular profession or field, may be difficult for outside people to comprehend. For example, if you are an accounting major, technical terms, such as participating preferred stock, contingent liabilities, amortization, and so on, may be meaningful to you, but not to others. If possible, substitute understandable words for technical language. If you must use a word that may not be understood, define the word.

The following statement, made by a microbiologist, is loaded with technical terms:

Diagnostic laboratory examination indicates a gram-negative, polar monotrichous, rod in short chains. The organism is oxidase positive, utilizing glucose oxidatively in O–F medium, ornithine decarboxylase reactions are negative while arginine dihydrolase produces positive tests. Causitive organism is *Pseudomonas aeruginosa*.

The following version has been simplified for the layman:

Laboratory examination reveals a common bacterium found in water.

In the business world, short words with clear meanings are *generally* preferred. Pretentious language may not be understandable. The readability level of the material should be at a level appropriate for the recipient.

Gunning's Readability Index. Robert Gunning is known for the Gunning Fog Index, a formula he devised to determine the grade level of written material. The more complex the readability, the higher the grade level assigned the material. A Fog Index score of 9 indicates that the material is at a ninth-grade level. Many popular magazines and newspapers are written at a junior or senior high school level. Writing at a college level, grade 13 and above, is usually too high for most business communications. If the vocabulary level *is too high* for the reader, it will not be understood.

Polysyllabic Words. Words that contain three or more syllables, polysyllabic words, make reading comprehension difficult. Gunning cautioned about the use of these "hard words." The following list suggests the type of words suitable for business writing:

Instead of...	*Use*
acquiesce	accept or comply
advantageous	favorable
ameliorate	improve
analyze	study
ancillary	side
approximately	about
ascertain	find out
cognizant	aware
consummate	complete
corroborate	confirm
criteria	standard
delectable	delicious
discrepancy	difference
disproportionate	unfair
disseminate	spread
effectuate	carry out
effete	worn out
embellish	adorn
endeavor	try

Test question

Fog index
grade level
9

Instead of. . .	*Use*
evince	show
exorbitant	excessive
fabrication	lie
initiate	begin
innocuous	harmless
institute	start
interrogate	question
jeopardize	imperil
neophyte	beginner
optimum	best
promulgate	proclaim
remunerate	pay
subsequent to	after
terminate	end

Avoid Oversimplification and Irrelevancies. A word of caution—oversimplification can also be a problem. Complete information is needed for clarity. Be careful about omitting important ideas and essential details when trying to simplify your writing.

Irrelevancies may also contribute to confusion by distracting the reader. Try to stay on target when writing. The following statement contains an irrelevant remark, which is in italics:

> The firm has decided to build its new corporate headquarters in Bloomfield. The tax rate is low, and adequate land is available at a reasonable price. *Also, Bloomfield has a long history. It once was part of Farmington, Windsor, and Simsbury.* Public transportation is available for employees.

Avoid Unintentional Connotations. Denotation is the *specific* meaning a word has; connotation is its *personal* meaning. A word may suggest an idea apart from its explicit denotation. For example, the word "executive," as used in the business world, pertains to a person who administers or manages (denotation); however, the word may connote toughness and determination to one person while another may think of an executive in terms of friendship, shared responsibility, and cordiality.

Since the connotations of words vary, clarity is imperiled if words are indiscriminately or carelessly used. Saying an individual is a crafty businessperson can convey manifold connotations. Some individuals may interpret that the individual is devious; others that the individual is clever.

COMPLETENESS

Business communication should be complete and give all the necessary information. Pertinent details, instructions, prices, and so on should not be omitted.

When replying to correspondence, be sure to answer *all* questions. It is very frustrating to receive a letter that contains incomplete information, for it entails writing a follow-up letter. This costs money and creates a delay that may be a critical factor in a business transaction.

Enclosure Reminder. Always add an enclosure reminder at the bottom of a letter when something extraneous is included in the envelope: a pamphlet, carbon or photocopy, graph. (See Figure 2–1.)

Cordially yours,

Susan J. Foster

Susan T. Foster
President

lct
Enclosure

FIGURE 2–1.
Closing section of a letter

ENCLOSURE REMINDER

Many executives write notes directly on correspondence received; this practice ensures a response to all pertinent points. The original communication with handwritten comments serves as a visual guide for dictation (Figure 2–2).

FIGURE 2–2. Making notes on a letter

Specifically, may I have some additional information about your credit card calculator.   *square root key, memory*

Does the calculator come complete with batteries and a case?   *yes pouch*

Be sure that instructions are specific and complete. Instead of directing an employee to "write a report about traffic problems," say, "write a formal, analytical report about the flow of traffic in B lot at Center Street." Encourage personnel to write down specific instructions.

Complete information is very important when ordering items: quantity, description, size, catalog number, color, weight, price, pattern, and so on. The illustrated order form from Service Merchandise Catalog Showrooms (Figure 2–3) reveals the many items required when ordering information.

CONCISENESS

Avoid Rambling Discourses. In the business world, few can afford the luxury of long-winded, rambling discourses that tend to obscure thought. Avoid extra words, if possible. Brevity of expression, rather than superfluous elaboration, is generally preferred. Conciseness is an important key to readability.

Include a Summary. A corporation president may have over one hundred reports to respond to during an average week! To keep from being overwhelmed by the time-consuming task of reading each of them, an executive prefers that a concise summary be placed at the front of each report. Usually, only the summary statement is read to get the main ideas of the report. Only when supporting details are needed, is the body of the report read. Some executives request that a separate *abstract* of reports be written. The report proper is read only when deemed necessary by the harried administrator.

Avoid Trite Expressions. Precision in writing—selecting the right words—is essential. Avoid unnecessary words, trite expressions, and redundancies. A trite expression is one that is used frequently. The following are outworn expressions:

- We are in receipt of your letter dated December 10.
- Thank you for your recent letter.
- I regret to inform you. . .

Avoid Redundancies. A redundancy is a superfluous repetition. The following expressions are redundancies (see Table 2–1):

- each and every day
- a big, huge elephant
- true facts
- cooperate together
- each individual person
- important essentials
- exact same
- close proximity

TOLL FREE ORDERING SERVICE 8 A.M. - 6 P.M. CST FOR CHARGE TO YOUR VISA OR MASTERCARD

NO C.O.D.
ORDERS
ACCEPTED

NASHVILLE RESIDENTS	251-6707
TENNESSEE RESIDENTS	1-800-342-8398
ALL OTHERS CALL	1-800-251-1212

CUSTOMER SERVICE FOR NON-TENNESSEE RESIDENTS IS TOLL FREE: 1-800-251-3508

SOLD TO:

NAME _____
ATTENTION _____
ADDRESS _____
CITY & STATE _____ ZIP _____
TELEPHONE _____ Area Code _____

SHIP TO: COMPLETE ONLY IF DIFFERENT ADDRESS

NAME _____
ATTENTION _____
ADDRESS _____
CITY & STATE _____ ZIP _____
TELEPHONE _____ Area Code _____

CATALOG NUMBER	HOW MANY	DESCRIPTION	WEIGHT	PAGE	COLOR OR SIZE	PRICE EACH	TOTAL

NO COD ORDERS ACCEPTED - DO NOT SEND STAMPS OR CASH

MULTIPLY TOTAL WEIGHT BY AMOUNT SHOWN BELOW FOR ZONE TO WHICH ORDER WILL BE SHIPPED:

_____ X _____ = _____

CHECK METHOD OF PAYMENT:

☐ CHECK OR MONEY ORDER ☐ VISA ☐ MASTERCARD ☐ COMMERCIAL ACCOUNT

_____ BANKCARD NUMBER _____ EXPIRATION DATE

X _____
COMMERCIAL ACCOUNT NO. _____ PURCHASE ORDER

_____ AUTHORIZED SIGNATURE FOR CHARGE

_____ IF EXEMPT FROM STATE TAX PRINT NAME & NUMBER

ZONE 1 $ .20 PER POUND	ZONE 2 $ .30 PER POUND	ZONE 3 $ .40 PER POUND
*AL *NC	*CT *NH	AK NM
*AR *OH	DE *NE	AS NV
DC SC	*FL *NJ	AZ OR
*GA *TN	*IA *NY	*CA PR
*IL VA	KS *OK	CO SD
*IN WV	*MA *PA	GU UT
*KY	*ME RI	HI VI
LA	*MI TX	ID WA
*MO	MD *VT	MT WY
*MS	MN WI	ND

SALES TAX MUST BE PAID IF THIS ORDER IS SHIPPED TO A STATE MARKED * ABOVE.

MERCHANDISE TOTAL		
SHIPPING CHARGE		
HANDLING CHARGE	1	20
SALES TAX		
JEWELRY ORDER		
RING SIZING		
TOTAL		
AMOUNT ENCLOSED		

IF YOUR ORDER IS ALL JEWELRY OR CONTAINS A JEWELRY ITEM ADD $ .75 FOR JEWELRY ORDER. EXAMPLE: WATCHES, RINGS, CHAINS, PENDANTS, ETC.

ADD $9.00 PER SIZE & $4.50 PER ½ SIZE FOR ALL RINGS THAT NEED TO BE ADJUSTED. THIS APPLIES TO MEN'S RINGS OVER SIZE 12 AND LADIES' RINGS OVER SIZE 8.

I WILL BE RESPONSIBLE FOR COLLECT FREIGHT CHARGES ON ITEMS TOO LARGE OR HEAVY TO BE MAILED BY PARCEL POST OR UPS.

CUSTOMER SIGNATURE X

ALL CODED CATALOG PRICES ARE SUBJECT TO CHANGE WITHOUT NOTICE. TYPOGRAPHIC, CLERICAL, & PHOTOGRAPHIC ERRORS ARE SUBJECT TO CORRECTION.

A7

SEND ORDER TO: SERVICE MERCHANDISE CO., INC. • P.O. BOX 25130 • NASHVILLE, TENN. 37202

FIGURE 2–3. Order form (Courtesy of Service Merchandise Catalog Showrooms)

TABLE 2–1. Avoid needless repetitions

Long-Winded	Concise
There will be a meeting tomorrow afternoon, December 15, at 3:15 p.m.	The meeting will be held at 3:15 p.m. on December 15.
Each and every member of the Advertising Department will submit a duplicate copy of the report.	Members of the Advertising Department will submit a copy of the report.
Henceforth, starting today, only true factual information should be logged.	Starting today, only factual information should be logged.
In the event that you want to refer back, follow the same identical procedure.	If you want to refer, follow the same procedure.
Enclosed please find the same identical folder.	Enclosed is the same folder.
Your invoice in the amount of $25 was, needless to say, a great deal more than I thought the invoice would ever happen to be.	Your invoice for $25 was more than anticipated.
He said over and over again that about three employees would go to the conference.	He repeated that several employees would attend the conference.
If we cooperate together, we can terminate and end the complete control and power of the agency.	If we cooperate, we can end the power of the agency.

One of the hazards of being concise is the tendency to omit relevant details or ideas. Review your plan of organization to insure the inclusion of important information.

Avoid Long Sentences and Paragraphs. Long, involved sentences tend to be difficult to comprehend. In business writing, short sentences are generally preferred. Rudolf Flesch, an expert on readability, suggests that sentences average seventeen words.[1] This does not mean, of course, that every sentence will be the same length. A variety of sentence lengths should be employed.

Paragraphs should also be short. Paragraphs averaging nine lines seem adequate for reports; six line paragraphs are about right for letters. At times, the length of a paragraph is relative to its location; for example, the opening and closing paragraphs of a typical business letter are usually brief, in some instances, only one sentence in length.

Numbering Paragraphs. Numbering paragraphs tends to keep them concise.

[1]Rudolf Flesch, *The Art of Plain Talk* (New York: Harper & Row, 1946), p. 38.

Each numbered paragraph usually contains one idea or topic. The Administrative Management Society has suggested a letter style in which main ideas in the message are numbered.

A word of caution—suggestions for an efficient writing style consisting of short words, sentences, and paragraphs should not be misconstrued as an open invitation to choppy, childish writing. Readability and understandability are critical in the business world. Ideas must be expressed with precision and variety.

CONSIDERATION

possible test question

A general aim of business communication is to sustain and enhance good relations. The successful executive conducts business associations in a friendly manner. Effective business writers convey a tone of cordiality in their communications. Be considerate, understanding, and tactful.

Avoid Ill-tempered Remarks. Ill-tempered remarks often generate hostile replies. For example: a student purchased a defective battery for his calculator and was very upset because the calculator went dead during an examination. The student mailed a nasty letter with the defective battery enclosed to the manufacturer. The defective battery was promptly returned by mail with no apology, offer of replacement, compensation, or adjustment! A more cordial letter to the manufacturer would have probably brought better results.

Remember that in your communications there is another human being receiving your messages. Your communications may well be an exercise in futility if you fail to take the recipient's feelings into account.

"You" Attitude. Try to view your writing from the reader's standpoint. A *you attitude* in writing is an indication of your consideration for others. Avoid using "I," "we," and "my." For example:

ask question

Inconsiderate	Considerate
I want to make it crystal clear that *we* expect a response.	Will *you* please respond?
I have the complaint in *my* file.	Thank *you* for *your* letter requesting an adjustment.
We mailed two pamphlets a week ago.	Two pamphlets were mailed to *you* recently.
I and *my* staff are working on the transfer request.	*Your* transfer request is receiving consideration.

COURTESY

Creating and Sustaining "Goodwill." A goal of business communication is fostering "goodwill," for this promotes business success. Courteous behavior entails being thoughtful and cooperative. It is very important, when writing for business, to be polite. For example, most business letters start with a friendly greeting or salutation—Gentlemen, Dear Miss Jones, Dear Sir, etc.—and end with a warm closing—Cordially yours, Yours truly, Sincerely, and so on.

Use Courteous Language. Sprinkle your writing with courteous words, such as "please," "appreciate," and "thanks."

Polite	*Impolite*
Thank you for your suggestions for improving customer service.	Don't send us any suggestions. We can do without them!
Your special consideration of our request is very much appreciated.	It's about time you paid attention to our request.
Please send to me the catalog as soon as possible.	Send the catalog out immediately and don't dawdle.

Avoid Sexism. Since sexism is both insidious and pervasive, special attention to this form of discrimination is given here. An awareness of sexism in business writing is very important, for many people are sensitive to masculine or feminine portrayals of roles. Sexism in writing is offensive to many and should be avoided. The guidelines in Appendix A will aid the writer in identifying those expressions or practices that should be avoided.

Reply Promptly. Promptness in replying is an indication of good manners. Keeping a correspondent waiting a long period of time for a reply is rude. If possible, make it a policy to respond within one day.

Be Tactful. When granting special requests where a buyer has been at fault, be tactful. Avoid rude remarks that ruffle feelings. The tone of business writing should be friendly. To cite a specific example, the closing paragraph of a letter of transmittal accompanying a report should be courteous, pleasant:

> Thank you very much for the opportunity to research this challenging subject. If you have any questions, please ask. Additional details are available.

Using An Outline. Written business communications, such as letters, memos, reports, and so on, should be structured in a cogent, well-organized fashion. Reports are usually outlined as follows:

1. Introduction
2. Findings
3. Summary
4. Conclusions
5. Recommendations

An outline helps to structure ideas in a unified fashion. A typical outline for a business report looks like this:

   I. Introduction
     A. Definition of Terms
     B. Statement of Problem
     C. Historical Background
     D. Sources of Information
     E. Limitations

  II. Findings
     A. California Plants
        1. Los Angeles
        2. San Diego
     B. Massachusetts Plants
        1. Boston
        2. Springfield
     C. New York Plants
        1. Albany
        2. Syracuse
     D. Texas Plants
        1. Austin
        2. El Paso
        3. Houston
        4. San Antonio

 III. Summary

 IV. Conclusions

  V. Recommendations

Two Organizational Plans. An orderly presentation tends to be a comprehensive one. Before replying to a memo or letter, jot down the main ideas, minor points, supporting data, and so on. The systematic listing of ideas and information to be communicated makes an orderly presentation possible. An organized presentation aids in sustaining the interest and attention of the recipient.

Learn difference between two

Two Logical Plans of Organization

1. Deductive Plan (psychological and direct patterns)
   - Main ideas first
   - Details next

   Example: A letter granting a request is usually in deductive order. First, the request is granted; next, reasons are presented.

2. Inductive Plan (logical and indirect patterns)
   - Details presented first
   - Main ideas next

   Example: If a request is not granted, a letter usually starts with the reasons for the refusal; next, the refusal (stated or implied) would follow.

Be Coherent. Business writing should be coherent. Sentences should be linked to convey an idea or information; groups of sentences create paragraphs. Paragraphs subdivide a composition. Each paragraph has a point or idea that is stated in a topic sentence. In business writing, the topic sentence is usually found at the beginning of the paragraph; subsequent sentences provide details. (See Figure 2–4.)

An organizational aid in business writing is enumerating (numbering) items. Enumerating contributes to coherence. An example of enumerating follows:

Please direct the administrative assistant to:

1. Collect the necessary data.
2. Interpret the data.
3. Write a preliminary report.
4. Edit the report.
5. Draft a final report.

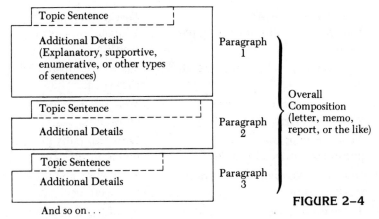

(handwritten top right) Deductive / Main idea / Details   Inductive / Details / main idea

FIGURE 2–4

POSITIVENESS

(handwritten left margin) ★

Be Positive. Business communication should *convey a feeling of* confidence and a positive attitude. *Avoid negative expressions*, such as no, not, never, cannot, will not, and so on. If you must say no to a request, try to present the reasons for the refusal, but do not use the word "no." The refusal is implied, not stated. The following is an example of a letter with an implied, but not stated, refusal:

(handwritten left margin) no should / be implied / but not / stated / never say / "NO"

Dear Dr. Keiter:

Your cordial letter, dated January 9 requesting a contribution has been received.

The Delta Corporation has already budgeted monies for specific charitable organizations for the year. During this period of retrenchment, the company must, unfortunately, maintain a strict budget.

You are to be commended for your charitable interests and efforts. Please contact us again next year. Perhaps, when we formulate our new budget, we can make provision for your worthwhile charity.

Thank you for contacting the Delta Corporation.

Cordially yours,

Trigger Words. Some words, such as "biased," "unreasonable," and "failed" should be used with caution in business writing since they can trigger hostile emotions. An awareness of the negative connotations of certain words has caused department stores to change the name of their complaint departments to customer service departments or adjustment departments.

(handwritten left margin) negative statements

The negative words italicized in the following statements should be avoided by employing the positive statements.

Negative Statements	*Positive Statements*
You *misled* us with *untrue* statements.	Your statements are being considered.
You *cannot* purchase on a credit basis.	There are substantial discounts for cash purchases.
Your *offensive* remarks are *unacceptable.*	Your remarks are being considered.
No one except company personnel can be admitted.	Only company personnel can be admitted.
Your *false complaint* about our service has been received.	Your letter about our service has been received.
There is *not* a free typewriter.	All of the typewriters are in use.
We are *displeased* by your *failure* to operate the car correctly.	Please warm up the engine of your car first.
You will *never* be promoted.	Prospects for promotion are limited.
Your complaint is *offensive* and *unreasonable.*	Your request for an adjustment is being considered.
Your *negligence* caused the problem with the engine.	Please oil the engine twice a month.
You *don't* realize you made a *mistake.*	The error was made inadvertently.

Summary

The English skills used when writing business papers are those taught in standard English classes; however, writing effectively for business entails a specialized style. All of the following are important when writing for business: accuracy, clarity, completeness, conciseness, consideration, courtesy, logical organization, and positiveness.

   Accuracy is essential in business communications. The writer must have high qualitative standards. Messages must be checked and at times rechecked for accuracy. Correct grammar, punctuation, and spelling are very important.

   Clarity refers to the clearness or understandability of messages. Avoid abstract, ambiguous words. Instead, select concrete nouns whenever possible. As a further aid to clarity, use familiar, simple words. Proper word choice is critical if precise meaning is to be communicated. Jargon may be difficult for

FIGURE 2-5. Do's and don'ts when writing for business

Be	Avoid
Accurate	Abstract statements
Clear	Ambiguities
Coherent	Bias
Complete	Illogical statements
Concise	Inaccuracies
Concrete	Incomplete statements
Considerate	Involved sentences, paragraphs
Conversational	Irrelevancies
Courteous	Jargon
Empathetic	Negative language
Friendly	Omissions
Logical	Oversimplifications
Objective	Polysyllabic words
Original	Prejudice
Positive	Profanity
Sincere	Redundancies
Sympathetic	Repetition
Tactful	Rudeness
Unbiased	Subjectivity
Understandable	Typographical errors
Vivid	Wordiness

people outside the particular area of expertise to comprehend. The readability level of the material should be at an appropriate level for the recipient.

Business communication should be *complete,* giving all the necessary information. Pertinent details, instructions, prices, and so on should not be omitted.

Conciseness is an important key to readability. Avoid long-winded, rambling discourses that tend to obscure thought. Brevity of expression is generally preferred. Avoid unnecessary words, trite expressions, and redundancies. Keep sentences short, if possible. Avoid involved phrases that do not contribute to understanding. Numbering paragraphs tends to keep them concise.

Consideration helps sustain and enhance goodwill through business communications. The successful executive conducts business in a friendly manner. Ill-tempered remarks should be avoided. Also, avoid sexist, ethnic, or religious expressions. Try to view your writing from the reader's standpoint. A *you attitude* in writing is an indication of your consideration for others. *Politeness* is important. Sprinkle your writing with courteous words, such as please, appreciate, and thanks. Promptness in replying is an indication of consideration.

Written business communications should be *structured logically,* in a cogent, well-organized fashion. An outline helps to structure ideas in a unified fashion. There are two logical plans of organization, deductive and inductive.

Business communication should convey a feeling of confidence and a *positive attitude*. Avoid negative expressions whenever possible. Try to write positively.

Discussion

1. Differentiate between writing for business and writing in standard English classes.
2. Explain what is meant by bias in writing.

Study questions

1. Are basic English skills used in business communications different from those taught in standard English classes? *contains specialized style*
2. What are the eight basic techniques for business writing?
3. Who is ultimately responsible for inaccuracies, the secretary or the executive? *the executive*
4. What are concrete words? *has distinct meaning*
5. What are abstract words? *personal meaning hard to define*
6. What is the Gunning Fog Index?
7. Define the following words:

   - Diction - *choice of words*
   - Jargon - *tech. language*
   - Denotation - *specific meaning of word*
   - Connotation - *what word means to you*
   - Redundancy - *repetitiveness*

[handwritten left margin notes:]
Accuracy
Clarity
Completeness
Conciseness
Consideration
Courtesy
Logical organization
Positiveness

Activity

Rewrite the following message, using effective business communication techniques.

Dear Ms. Napolitano:

Attached please find a copy of the credit terms you insisted that we mail to you. I am sure your careless negligence in paying your bill caused the extra added interest charge.

I feel your problems with future billing next month will be terminated if and when you follow simple directions about payment.

The J. R. Owens Company is cognizant of customer problems and hopes the enclosed copy of its credit terms will help you to see the light. We can disseminate literature not as complicated if you cannot comprehend the enclosed literature.

Sincerely yours,

ACHIEVEMENT OF LEARNING GOALS

Check the appropriate boxes to determine whether you have or have not achieved the learning goals of this chapter.

I Can:

	YES	NO
1. Understand the basic techniques of effective business writing.	☑	☐
2. Eliminate bias in writing.	☐	☐

If any of your responses were "no," it is suggested that you review pertinent chapter parts.

3

Report Planning and the Research Process

LEARNING GOALS

1. *Comprehend* the role of reports in the decision-making process.
2. *Plan* an effective business report.
3. *Investigate* a problem by using secondary and/or primary research.

Reports defined

[handwritten: report – oral, written objective presentation of ideas thoughts]

[handwritten: Test question]

A report is an objective oral or written presentation structured to communicate information, investigate a problem, record ideas and facts, interpret and/or provide solutions to a problem. Some reports contain conclusions and recommendations relating to the problem under consideration. Under this broad definition, such diverse communications as credit reports, memo and letter reports, oral report presentations, corporate annual reports, computer printouts, and formal written reports are included.

Although a command of standard English is required for effective business report writing, there are other specialized skills required which may be omitted in English courses.

Need for reports

FOUR C's OF REPORT WRITING

[handwritten: Clear, Concise, Correct, Comprehensive]

Since reports are vital to the communication process, it is important that they follow a prescribed format and be well written. The reader of the report must

clear
con cise
correct
comprehensive

Know these

be able to make interpretations from data presented, so the report must be *clear, concise, correct,* and *comprehensive.*

This chapter explains the procedures for effective business report writing; similar procedures can be followed when writing college term papers. Therefore, expertise in report writing will help you succeed on the job and in school as well.

REPORTS AID DECISION MAKING

Although written reports move upward, downward, and sideways in an organization, the main direction of motion is upward. Reports provide a continuous flow of information vital for management decision making.

FIGURE 3-1.   The main direction of reports is upward

Reports that flow downward to subordinates are usually called *directives.* Very often, these reports provide information to elicit the support of employees.

In addition to upward, downward, and sideways movement within an organization, reports travel outside the company to customers, stockholders, and other individuals.

FIGURE 3-2.   Five steps in the report process

Step 1   Planning
Step 2   Investigating
Step 3   Outlining
Step 4   Writing
Step 5   Presentation

Steps 1 and 2 are discussed in this chapter. Steps 3 and 4 appear in Chapters 4 and 5, and Step 5 is discussed in Chapter 6.

Planning the report (step 1)

There are various determinations the writer will have to make during the planning stage:

- What is the problem?
- Is the purpose of the report to inform, persuade, compare, interpret, or analyze?
- What are the basic factors to be considered?
- What is the scope of the report?
- Are there any delimitations (cost, time, etc.)?
- What arrangement will be used (direct, indirect)?
- Will secondary and/or primary research be used?
- How will data be collected?
- Are progress reports needed?
- Is an abstract needed?
- What is the degree of formality?
- What format should be used?
- How should the completed report be presented?

FIVE CONSIDERATIONS

Five basic actions that the writer must take before writing the report are:

1. State the problem;
2. Determine the purpose of the report;
3. List the factors (areas to be investigated);
4. Specify the delimitations; and
5. Plan an orderly presentation.

Statement of the Problem. First, the writer must clearly identify the problem and state it precisely. It would be a waste of time and money to investigate the wrong problem! The following is a statement of a problem:

> What kind of airplane should the Beta Corporation purchase for executive use?

Determine the Purpose. The report originator should identify the purpose the report is to serve, either in writing (letter of authorization) or orally. The writer must determine if the purpose is to provide information, persuade, compare, analyze, or interpret. A report may encompass a combination of these purposes. The purpose can be stated as follows:

> To conduct a comparative analysis of airplanes and to recommend one plane to be purchased by the Beta corporation.

List the Factors. Next, the basic factors should be identified and listed. A company planning to purchase an airplane might review the following factors:

1. Price
2. Seating capacity
3. Range
4. Maintenance
5. Safety
6. Luxury
7. Operational expenses

Specifying the Delimitations. There are delimitations to achieving the objectives of a report, such as time, money, available data, and assistance.

Because of delimitations, it may be necessary to restrict the scope of a report. For example, instead of writing an international report, it may be necessary to confine the geographic area to the United States, to a section of the country, or to a state.

Planning the Presentation. There are manifold arrangements of content; however, the direct (deductive) and indirect (inductive) are most common. In direct order, the main ideas are presented first (summary, conclusions, recommendations) and the details follow. In indirect order, details are presented first and the main ideas (summary, conclusion, recommendation) follow.

Direct Order	*Indirect Order*
(Deductive)	*(Inductive)*
Main Ideas	Introduction
Summary	Findings
Conclusions	*Main Ideas*
Recommendations	Summary
Introduction	Conclusions
Findings	Recommendations

The indirect order is the traditional plan of arrangement, and it is commonly used by report writers. Some harried executives prefer a modified indirect order; that is, the summary appears first:

Modified Indirect Order

Main Ideas $\Big\{$
- Summary
- Introduction
- Findings

Main Ideas $\Big\{$
- Conclusions
- Recommendation

WORKING OUTLINE

A preliminary, informal, *working outline* may be drawn up prior to the investigation of the problem. The writer jots down the main sections of the report and helpful guides.

- Summary
- Introduction
    Definition—Air Transportation
    Problem—Need for an Executive Airplane
    Sources—Secondary and Primary
    Scope—United States
- Findings or Text
    Sources of Information:
        Review of Company Records and Library Sources
        Questionnaire to Corporations and Manufacturer's Brochures
    Comparative Analysis
- Conclusions
- Recommendations

This tentative outline should not be confused with the formal, comprehensive outline prepared after the investigation is completed.

THE BODY OF THE REPORT

The following is a brief overview of the body of a report: summary, introduction, research findings, conclusions, recommendations.

Summary. The summary is a condensation of the substance or main ideas of the report. A major summary is usually an integral part of the report. In addition, minor summaries may also appear at the ends of sections to facilitate comprehension. As stated previously, busy executives may prefer the summary at the beginning of the report, where it can be located quickly and easily.

Introduction. The introduction should contain a clear statement of the problem, objectives, and delimitations: sources, time, etc. An experimental study states the hypothesis in the introduction. The introduction may also contain historical backgrounds and the definition of terms used.

Research Findings. The research findings section follows the introduction and is called the text. Data collected are listed, graphic aids are presented, and interpretations and analyses are made. This section contains the bulk of the report; it usually comprises about 75 percent of the content.

Conclusions. Conclusions are derived from the interpretations and analyses in the text. It is important to base the conclusions on the facts presented in the study, not on the opinions of the researcher. The conclusions are frequently numbered to aid the reader.

Recommendations. It is common practice for the originator of the report to request a statement of recommendations. The recommendations, which follow the conclusions, suggest specific actions to be taken. The writer develops the recommendations based on interpretations of the findings. This requires a great deal of thought and the ability to reason logically.

Investigating (step 2)

After the initial planning (Step 1) has been completed, the next major step in the creative process is undertaken: the investigation of the problem. This entails the collection of data that will provide the information needed to solve the problem.

Generally, research findings are classified as either *secondary* or *primary.* A report may contain either secondary or primary information, or it may utilize both. Secondary research is discussed first in this textbook since experienced researchers engage in it first, before conducting primary research in order not to duplicate existing research.

SECONDARY RESEARCH   books, articles

Secondary research is the review of research others have conducted; that is, sources other than the researcher. Secondary research materials are often found in libraries; however, other sources, such as governmental agencies and

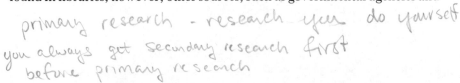

business services (Moody's, Standard & Poor's, Gale Research, Predicasts, Inc., etc.), company publications, encyclopedias, dictionaries, handbooks, and almanacs are used. The investigator reports on the recorded findings of others by examining books, magazines, periodicals, journals, research studies, and so on.

Modern Library Use. Today's library contains books, other textual materials, microforms, records or audiotapes, and films or videocassettes. However, modern technology is restructuring the traditional library. Books have some obvious shortcomings as a primary medium for the storage of information. They take considerable time to locate and they take up a great deal of storage space because of their bulk.

Computer Use. The computer provides a better medium for the storage and retrieval of information. Information recorded on computer tapes is used as the data base or memory of a computer. Large quantities of information can be stored in relatively little space and retrieved in microseconds. Retrieved information is printed on paper or displayed on a cathode ray tube (television-like screen). Since computers can communicate or be linked to other computers, the storage and retrieval capabilities are mind boggling.

At the present time, the cost of computer based information is too high for most public libraries. To reduce costs, publishers will create computer tapes (in addition to printed materials).

Librarian working on the periodicals records. The terminal is connected to a main frame IBM computer, which replaces the Kardex file system. (Courtesy of CIGNA Corp.)

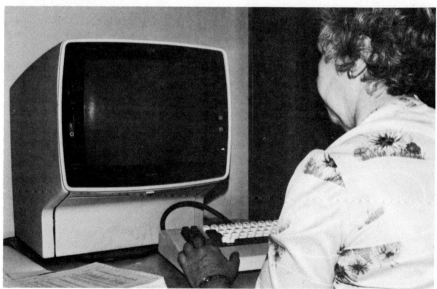

Since books are widely used at the present time as the primary medium of library information, researchers must, of necessity, learn how to locate and use textual information rapidly and efficiently.

Researching with a System. To be effective and to avoid wasting time, library research should be conducted systematically. First, the investigator should look for an appropriate library (company, university and college, public, state, specialized, private, Library of Congress, and so on). Next, the researcher must select the best sources of information:

Almanacs	Encyclopedias
Annual reports	Guides
Articles	Handbooks
Atlases	Indexes
Bibliographical guides	Journals
Biographical directories or dictionaries	Leaflets
	Magazines
Books	Manuals
Brochures	Newspapers
Bulletins	Pamphlets
Dictionaries	Periodicals
Directories	Reports
Documents	Yearbooks

Using Library Resources. To assist the researcher, information contained in a library is classified by either the Dewey Decimal System or the Library of Congress method.

The Dewey Decimal System classifies all books into ten major categories:

000 General Works
100 Philosophy
200 Religion
300 Social Sciences
400 Philology
500 Pure Science
600 Useful Arts—Applied Science
700 Fine Arts
800 Literature
900 History

The Library of Congress classification system is preferred by larger libraries since it is more expansive. Letters of the alphabet are used to provide twenty major classifications:

20 letters of alphabete

- A General Works—Polography
- B Philosophy—Religion
- C History—Auxiliary Sciences
- D History and Topography (Except America)
- E, F America
- G Geography—Anthropology
- H Social Sciences
- J Political Science
- K Law
- L Education
- M Music
- N Fine Arts
- P Language and Literature
- Q Science
- R Medicine
- S Agriculture—Plant and Animal Industry
- T Technology
- U Military Science
- V Naval Science
- Z Bibliography and Library School

Additional indexing is accomplished by the use of numbers and letters.

The Card Catalogue. Usually, the first step in conducting library research is to refer to the card catalog, where the material in the library (reference works, books, films) is indexed three ways: by author, title, and subject matter. Figure 3–3 presents a bibliography card written by the researcher.

Referring to Indexes. Besides consulting the card catalog, the researcher can locate current information in periodicals by referring to indexes, such as the *Reader's Guide to Periodical Literature, Business Periodicals Index, The Education Index,* the *New York Times Index, The Wall Street Journal Index,* and others. Another excellent source of secondary information is company publications. Many companies have their own libraries and a staff of librarians.

Recording Data. The researcher should collect data and information in an organized fashion. Information should be recorded on note cards or photo-

```
Awad, Elias M.

Introduction to Computers in Business

Englewood Cliffs, N. J.:  Prentice-Hall, Inc.

1977

pp. 243-244
```

FIGURE 3–3. Sample bibliography

copied. The information card, if used, should indicate the source. Figures 3–4 and 3–5 show two examples of the information that should appear on these cards.

```
VOICE RESPONSE

        Voice response in use since 1964 by banking in-
dustry (checking information, balance in account).
        Drawbacks to voice response:

1.   Psychological reservations--some people do not
     like machine conversation.
2.   Time-consuming.
3.   Computer's vocabulary limited (few hundred words).
4.   Output is slow.
5.   No hard copy of information received.

Elias M. Awad, Introduction to Computers in Business,
(Englewood Cliffs, N.J.: Prentice-Hall, Inc., 1977),
p. 244.
```

FIGURE 3–4. Information card with paraphrasing

When photocopying material, it is wise to make a copy of the table of contents of a periodical or title page of a book; be sure to jot down the copyright date on the photocopy for future reference.

Make a second card containing bibliography information. The bibliography is an alphabetical listing of sources of information; therefore, the cards should be arranged alphabetically and *numbered to correspond with the information card.* The bibliography card provides information needed for typing footnotes.

```
VOICE RESPONSE

    "One of the latest breakthroughs in computer tech-
nology has been the development of the computer's ability
to 'talk' with the user, called audio response or voice
output."
```

Source:
Author, Title,
Page Number

```
Elias M. Awad, Introduction to Computers in Business,
(Englewood Cliffs, N.J.: Prentice-Hall, Inc., 1977),
p. 243.
```

FIGURE 3–5. Information card with direct quotation

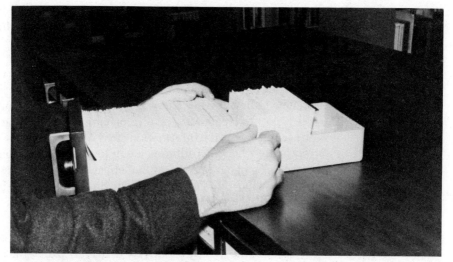

Using a card file (Courtesy of CIGNA Corp.)

Plagiarism. The researcher should give credit to the original source of information; otherwise the researcher will be accused of plagiarism, literary theft. Not only is plagiarism unethical, it is also illegal.

Plagiarism began in early times and, unfortunately, exists today. John Greenway states:

> Plagiarism was so common in the churches by the time of King James that he had to order at least one sermon a month be original. . . . But it

didn't start with Christendom. Vergil, Demosthenes, Sophocles, Aeschines, Isocrates, and Plutarch did not let the comparative lack of sources prevent them from filching the best of their predecessors....

Every one of Shakespeare's plays was worked up from someone else's genius except *Love's Labour's Lost,* and the odds are 37 to 1 that this is an exception only because the source has not yet been found.[1]

There have been many highly publicized cases of plagiarism in modern times. For example, a popular American novel, "Wild Oats," contained "no fewer than 53 'chunks' plundered almost verbatim" from a British novel, "The Rachel Papers!"[2]

Documentation. Crediting a source of information is accomplished by documentation, the recording of footnotes and the listing of sources in the bibliography of the report. Footnotes cite references or further evidence. All material quoted, as well as paraphrased material, must be footnoted. The placement of footnotes vary. Some of the common formats used for documentation follow:

1. *Footnote–Bibliography Format.* This format is preferred by many because of its convenience. Footnotes appear at the bottoms of pages on which the reference is cited. The reader need not thumb through the report to locate sources of information. Having the footnote on the same page as the information cited is convenient for researchers, especially when microfilming is employed or when pages are photocopied. A bibliography, an alphabetical listing of sources of information, is included in the report. (*Note.* Since this format, footnotes appearing at the bottoms of pages, is the most popular, it is the one depicted in the model report illustrated in this textbook.)

2. *Endnotes–Bibliography Format.* Using this format, reference citations are numbered consecutively in the text. All of the footnotes are listed consecutively on a separate "endnotes" page, in the same order that citations appear in the text. This reference page appears at the end of the body of the report. Although this format facilitates typing, it is inconvenient for the reader, who must turn to the endnotes page to check sources of information. A bibliography is included in the report.

[1]John Greenway, "The Honest Man's Guide to Plagiarism," *National Review,* XXXI, no. 51 (December 21, 1979), 1624.

[2]Elizabeth Peer, Lea Donosky, and George Hackett, "Why Writers Plagiarize," *Newsweek,* XCVI, no. 18 (November 3, 1980), p. 62.

3. *Citation–Bibliography Format.* Using this format, citations (author's surname, publication date, page number) are made within the textual portion of the report. Example:

To achieve parallel structure, notice the parts of speech used in headings. (Jennings, 1981, p. 265)

The bibliography entry provides additional information about the reference:

Jennings, Lucy Mae, *Secretarial and General Office Procedures.* Englewood Cliffs, N.J.: Prentice-Hall, Inc., 1981.

4. *Footnotes Only.* This format eliminates the bibliography and is not commonly used for business reports.

Figure 3–6 presents the footnote guidelines for Prentice-Hall, Inc.

FIGURE 3–6. Prentice-Hall footnote guide
Reproduced with permission from *Prentice-Hall Author's Guide* (Englewood Cliffs, N.J.: Prentice-Hall, Inc., 1978), pp. 26–29.

FOOTNOTES

The main purpose of footnoting is to provide complete data in consistent form. There are many systems; the one we recommend for clarity and completeness is illustrated by the following rules and examples:

1 Follow this order of items in a reference to a book: (a) name of author (or translator, editor, compiler) as it appears on the title page, with first name first; (b) chapter title, if needed; (c) title of book and subtitle, if any; (d) edition, if other than the first; (e) city of publication; (f) name of publisher, exactly as it appears on the title page of the book; (g) date of publication; (h) chapter or page of book referred to. (Omit "vol." and "p." or "pp." when both are given; see footnote 5 in the following examples.)

For a book with no author given:

[1]*A Manual of Style,* 12th ed. (Chicago: The University of Chicago Press, 1969), pp. 80–84.

For a book with one author:

[2]Paul D. Brandes, *The Rhetoric of Revolt* (Englewood Cliffs, N.J.: Prentice-Hall, Inc., 1971), pp. 114–15.

For a book with two or three authors:

[3]Lynn Quitman Troyka and Jerrold Nudelman, *Steps in Composition* (Englewood Cliffs, N.J.: Prentice-Hall, Inc., 1970), pp. 50–51.

FIGURE 3–6 (continued)

For a book with more than three authors:

[4]Julian W. Smith and others, *Outdoor Education,* 2nd ed. (Englewood Cliffs, N.J.: Prentice-Hall, Inc., 1972), pp. 104–7.

For an edited book or one revised by a person other than the original author:

[5]David Burner, Robert D. Marcus, and Jorj Tilson, eds., *America Through the Looking Glass: A Historical Reader in Popular Culture* (Englewood Cliffs, N.J.: Prentice-Hall, Inc., 1974), I, 40–42.

[6]Paul Ivey and Walter Horvath, *Successful Salesmanship,* 4th ed., rev. by Wayland A. Tonning (Englewood Cliffs, N.J.: Prentice-Hall, Inc., 1961), pp. 201–7.

For a translated book:

[7]Thomas Mann, *Death in Venice,* rev. ed., trans. Kenneth Burke (New York: Alfred A. Knopf, Inc., 1965), p. 26.

or

[8]T. E. Shaw, trans., *The Odyssey of Homer* (New York: Oxford University Press, 1956), p. 62.

For a book in a series:

[9]William David McElroy, *Cell Physiology and Biochemistry,* 3rd ed., Foundations of Modern Biology Series (Englewood Cliffs, N.J.: Prentice-Hall, Inc., 1971), p. 38.

2 Follow this order of items in a reference to a periodical: (a) author's name, if any, as for a book; (b) title of article; (c) title of periodical (spelled out in full, unless periodical is a legal, technical, or scientific journal; see footnotes 17 and 19); (d) volume number, if any; (e) issue number, if any; (f) date of publication; (g) page number. (Omit "vol." and "p." or "pp." when both are given.)

[10]David Herbert Donald, "Between Science and Art," *The American Historical Review,* 77, no. 4 (April 1972), 445–52.

[11]Hilton Kramer, "Thirty Years of the New York School," *New York Times Magazine,* October 12, 1969, pp. 28–31.

3 Follow this order of items in a reference to a newspaper: (a) name of paper, followed by city of publication, if that is not included in the name; (b) date; (c) section number if the issue contains sections numbered separately; (d) page number; (e) column number, if needed.

[12]*New York Times,* May 10, 1970, sec. 2, p. 11.

[13]*Christian Science Monitor* (Boston), September 26, 1971, p. 8, col. 3.

4 Put chapter and article titles and titles of unpublished works in quotes (see footnote 17 for an exception to this rule); underscore for italics book and periodical titles and titles of separate volumes in a multivolume work.

For a chapter of a collective work:

[14]Richard L. Park, "India's Foreign Policy," in *Foreign Policy in World Politics,* 4th ed., ed. Roy C. Macridis (Englewood Cliffs, N.J.: Prentice-Hall, Inc., 1972), pp. 368–70.

For an unpublished work:

[15]Louise U. Sorenson, "An Analysis of Defense Spending" (unpublished Master's thesis, ——— University, 1973), p. 11.

For an article in an encyclopedia:

[16]"Descriptive Geometry," *Encyclopedia Britannica* (1972), 7, 292–95.

For an article in a legal journal:

[17]Cox, *Labor Law Preemption Revisited,* 85 HARV. L. REV. 1337 (1972).

For an article in a loose-leaf supplemented service:

[18]"P-H Survey: Employee Testing and Selection Procedures—Where Are They Headed?" *Personnel Management: Policies and Practices,* April 22, 1975 (Englewood Cliffs, N.J.: Prentice-Hall, Inc.).

For an article in a technical or scientific journal:

[19]N. Sissenwine, M. Dubin, and H. Wexler, "U.S. Standard Atmosphere, 1962," *Jour. Geophys. Res.,* 67 (1962), 3627–30.

For a volume in a multivolume work:

[20]Raymond E. Brown, Joseph A. Fitzmyer, and Roland E. Murphy, eds., *The Jerome Biblical Commentary, Volume II: The New Testament and Topical Articles* (Englewood Cliffs, N.J.: Prentice-Hall, Inc., 1968).

5 Use vol., pt., chap., sec., no., bk., p. or pp. in this form when needed. For numbers with these elements, follow the style (roman or arabic) used in the book or periodical you are citing.

6 In citing consecutive page numbers (or dates), omit hundreds from the second number unless the first number ends in two zeros; in that case repeat the full form. If the next to last figure in the first number is zero, do not repeat it in the second number.

pp. 11–12	1811–12
pp. 111–12	1800–1804 (not 1800–04)
pp. 200–204 (not 200–4)	1898–1904
pp. 204–5 (not 204–05)	1904–5 (not 1904–05)

7 Give the publisher's name in its current form, using "Co." or "Company," "Inc." or "Incorporated," "Ltd." or "Limited," "&" or "and," as the publisher's imprint reads. If a book is published by a subsidiary of a publisher, give both names—the subsidiary second.

8 Use "n.d." when, after careful search, the date of publication cannot be found; similarly, "n.p." when the place of publication cannot be determined. When more than one page is referred to, show inclusive pages—"pp. 10–11"; "pp. 10–25." Do not use "pp. 10f." or "pp. 10ff."

9 A full reference should be given the first time in each chapter a book or periodical is cited. Further reference in the chapter to the same source should be shortened as follows: *for a book,* last name of author (if no confusion with an-

FIGURE 3–6 (continued)

other author of the same last name would result); short title, and page number; *for a periodical,* last name of author, short title of article, and page number. (A long title should be shortened in the second and subsequent references; for example, Ernest Baker, *Political Thought in England from Herbert Spencer to the Present Day,* to Baker, *Political Thought.*)

10 Do not use "op. cit." (in the work cited) or "loc. cit." (in the place cited)—instead, use the short-title form described above. Repeating author and title will save the reader the trouble of searching back through the notes to identify a particular reference. "Ibid." (in the same place) may be used for a reference to the same work cited in the immediately preceding footnote.

11 Give the full name of the author in the first reference in each chapter, even when the author's full name appears in the text. This is a convenience to the reader, especially if the work is cited in shortened form in subsequent references.

PRIMARY RESEARCH

When information is unavailable from secondary sources, the investigator must gather information firsthand; this is called primary research. Four common methods of primary research are:

1. Questionnaires (surveys)
2. Interviews (interrogation)
3. Experimentation
4. Observation

Questionnaires. A questionnaire consists of a set of questions formulated to gather information that can be statistically evaluated. Usually, a questionnaire is mailed and is accompanied by a cover letter which explains the purpose of the questionnaire and encourages a response. Figure 3–7 shows an example of a typical cover letter.

Care should be taken in the preparation of questionnaires, for the findings should be valid—measure what they purport to measure—and reliable. The following are suggestions for preparing a questionnaire:

1. *Avoid a long, involved questionnaire.* If the questionnaire is too imposing, the respondent may be reluctant to complete it.

2. *Avoid prejudicial questions that structure the response.* For example, if you ask, "Do you prefer Campbell's Soup" you are leading the respondent to a response. A more objective phrasing would be, "What brand of soup do you prefer?"

THE JOSE CAMARO CORPORATION

211 Wedgewood Drive

Macon, Georgia 31201

November 21, 1982

Mrs. Jennifer T. Paige
27 Glenwood Road
Mobile, AL 36606

Dear Mrs. Paige:

The Jose Camaro Corporation is conducting a survey to
determine whether its electric corn poppers are being
properly advertised in Mobile.

Your completion of the enclosed questionnaire would be
very much appreciated. It should take about five minutes
of your time to check the items listed. The results of
this survey will help to improve the sales of corn
poppers by determining the effectiveness of advertising
programs.

Upon receipt of the questionnaire, a ballpoint pen will
be sent to you as a gift.

Your responses to the checklist items will be kept
confidential.

Please respond by December 21.

Sincerely yours,

Karen T. Hightower

Karen T. Hightower, Manager
Sales and Promotion Department

Enclosure

FIGURE 3–7. A typical cover letter mailed with a questionnaire

3. *Questions should be placed in logical sequence.* A disjointed, illogical listing of questions is confusing and will discourage the respondent. Related questions should be categorized or grouped.

4. *Start with an easy question.* The first question can be a "throwaway" question that will not be tabulated. Its purpose is to induce the respondent to continue.

5. *Try to keep all questions simple.* If you must include complex questions, go from the simple to the complex. Avoid questions that will tax the memory. Example: "What were you doing on this day four years ago?"

6. *Avoid skip-and-jump responses.* These responses confuse the respondent. Example: "If you responded 'yes' to question 10, skip questions 11–16 and complete 17–19. If you responded 'no' to question 10, complete questions 11–16 and skip 17–19."

7. *Structure the questions so that they can be tabulated easily.* Questions that require long, involved written responses make statistical tabulation very difficult, if not impossible. Example: "Tell what you like and dislike about word processing."

8. *Test the questionnaire before using it.* A pilot study will reveal defects in the questionnaire before an expensive, mass mailing takes place. For example, if two thousand questionnaires are to be ultimately mailed, the pilot study could consist of one percent or twenty questionnaires mailed. The author once conducted a study on the exploration function of schools—how they help students to explore their personal and vocational interests. He sent out a pilot study and was startled at the replies to the question, "Does your school pay attention to the exploration function and how?" Teachers responded, "Yes, they have a unit on explorers—Marco Polo, Christopher Columbus, and so on." Since this was the pilot study for a national study, it saved the writer considerable time, effort, and money to spot this glaring error in interpretation or meaning. Subsequently, for the major mailing he started the questionnaire with his definition of the term "exploration function."

9. *Responses should be easy to record.* Provide specific instructions for completing the survey instrument. A simple check mark ($\checkmark$), circling an item   3 , or writing a letter or numeral (C) will encourage the completion of a questionnaire. Examples:

	Yes	No
Does your company have a person who manages communications?	($\checkmark$)	( )

How many vice presidents does your company have?

1   2   ③   4   5   6 or more

Indicate the highest level of education completed:

A Elementary School
B Junior High School
C High School
D Junior College
E College (Four Years)
F Graduate School   C

10. *Number questions.* Numbering questions facilitates tabulation and makes reference to a specific item easy.

11. *The questionnaire should be attractive and uncluttered.* If the questionnaire is a mass of printed material with little blank space, it may appear too difficult and time consuming to complete.

12. *Generally, avoid prying, personal questions that do not elicit truthful responses.* People may not respond truthfully if questions are asked that will place them in a demeaning position. Example: "Do you bathe daily?" (Some people will respond "yes," even if they do not!)

13. *Use concrete, clear terms.* Certain terms are nebulous in meaning and should be avoided. For example, the question, "Do you eat out frequently?," is an imprecise question. "Frequently" is a relative term—some people think eating out daily is frequently; others think biweekly is frequently; others think weekly is frequently. "Many" is another word subject to individual interpretation. Use concrete words when possible.

14. *State a deadline for returning the questionnaire.* You will have a great deal of difficulty tabulating data if responses trickle in over an extended period of time. Stating a deadline may activate the respondent to complete the questionnaire, if not the respondent may procrastinate. To expedite returns, be sure to enclose a stamped, addressed return envelope.

Sampling. If the group being surveyed is small, the entire group (also called the "universe") can be surveyed. At times, especially when dealing with large groups, it is difficult and/or uneconomical to gather information from the entire universe. For example, if you wanted to know how many people in the United States have seen a commercial on television, it would be prohibitively expensive and time consuming to attempt to question everyone in the population. A *sample*, perhaps of two thousand people, would suffice. The sample selected should have the characteristics of the entire population. This is called "representativeness." The sample is often referred to as a *representative sample*, for the sample reflects the whole. Sample reliability (consistency) and validity (truthfulness) is very essential. There are many techniques of sampling:

1. *Random sampling.* This is a chance sampling, for each person in the universe has the same likelihood of being selected. *Example:* A blindfolded person draws 100 names from a bowl containing slips of paper with the names of every student in the college.

2. *Quota sampling.* This technique consists of selecting proportionately the makeup of the sample. For example, if you were to survey the student population of your college, you would select a proportionate number of freshmen, sophomores, juniors, seniors, and graduate students.

3. *Area sampling.* This technique draws its sample from various divisions of an area. For example, if you were taking a sample of the population of New England, you might select a proportionate number of people geographically from Maine, Vermont, New Hampshire, Massachusetts, Connecticut, and Rhode Island.

4. *Stratified random sampling.* This sampling technique consists of separating the universe into subgroups and taking a random selection from the subgroups. For example, you could separate the student population of your college into subgroups as follows: freshmen 40 percent, sophomores 30 percent, juniors 15 percent, seniors 15 percent. Next, you would take a random sample of each subgroup. The size of this sample is relative to the subgroup's proportion of the whole; therefore, the random sample of the freshman subgroup would consist of 40 percent, sophomores 30 percent, juniors 15 percent, and seniors 15 percent.

5. *Systematic sampling.* When this technique of sampling is employed, selections are taken at constant intervals from the universe. For example, selecting every fifth person listed in a telephone directory.

Interviews. Conferring with people face-to-face is an effective means of obtaining information. The interview should be planned in advance. The interviewer should prepare questions, maintain objectivity, and record responses accurately. *Personal interviews* provide first-hand interactions. Body language can be observed. Personal interviewing can be very expensive, especially if long-distance travel costs are involved.

Telephone interviews. Although asking quesions by telephone may be less expensive than personal, face-to-face interviews, there are some disadvantages. Generally, the interview must be brief and the interviewee may terminate the interview abruptly by hanging up.

In a *structured interview*, predetermined questions are asked; an interview form will help ensure that all questions are asked. In some situations, the potential respondent receives a copy of the questions before the interview. Also, there is a uniform pattern of questions for all respondents. An interview form aids in tabulation, which is an advantage. In an *unstructured interview*, the discussion tends to be spontaneous, depending on the interaction of the individuals.

Be sure to document the interview: names of interviewer and interviewee, place, date, time, subject, and so on.

Experimentation. Most people associate experimental research with scientists; however, the experimental method of research can be used in the business world. Experimentation is used to test a hypothesis (a tentative proposition), an assumption, or a theory. The following is an example of a hypothesis:

> The installation of a word processing system will result in substantial savings at the Miles Corporation.

Experimental research can be undertaken to prove or disprove a hypothesis.

Matched Groups: Experimental and Control. In an experimental study, the researcher measures one variable while other variables remain constant. In statistics, a variable is any magnitude exhibiting a number of different values. Two identically *matched groups*, an experimental group and a control group, are used. In the experimental group, a variable is introduced. The investigator, by comparison with the control group, determines if the variable results in a significant, measurable change.

For example, let us assume that a company is interested in determining if a proposed word processing system will result in substantial savings.

> *Hypothesis: A word processing system will result in substantial savings.*

Researchers could test the hypothesis by comparing two, identically matched office groups—the only variable between the two offices is that one office has a word processing system, the other does not. (See Figure 3–8.)

After a specified time, the cost of processing words in both offices is calculated. If Office A had substantial savings, it would prove the hypothesis—

that a word processing system will result in substantial savings. If, on the other hand, there were no significant savings, the hypothesis would be disproved.

It should be noted that in some instances disproving a hypothesis can provide important information.

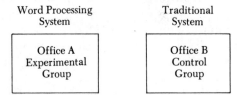

FIGURE 3–8.   Word processing versus traditional system

Observation. This method of research entails watching certain actions or activities and recording these observations. For example, assume that you want to determine the number of people, potential customers, who will pass a store you wish to rent. You can stand in front of the store and count the number of people who walk by or the number of cars that pass by. If the findings are to be valid, it is critical that the observer be an objective and accurate recorder of the activity or situation.

Summary

An effective report writer must have specialized training in the techniques of report writing. It is important that business reports follow a prescribed format and be well written. Reports provide a continuous flow of information vital for management decision making.

Creating an effective written report involves five steps:

1. Planning
2. Investigating
3. Outlining
4. Writing
5. Presentation

During the planning stage, the writer must:

1. State the problem;
2. Determine the purpose of the report;

3. List the factors;

4. Specify the delimitations; and

5. Plan an orderly presentation.

Generally, research findings are classified as either *secondary* or *primary*.

Secondary research entails the review of research others have conducted; that is, sources other than the researcher. Secondary research materials are often found in libraries. Information contained in a library is classified by either the Dewey Decimal System or the Library of Congress method. The researcher should collect data and information from the library in an organized fashion. The researcher should give credit to the original source of information, otherwise plagiarism, literary theft, will take place. Crediting a source of information is accomplished by documentation, the recording of footnotes and the listing of sources in the bibliography.

When information is unavailable from secondary sources, the investigator must gather information firsthand; this is called primary research.

Four common methods of primary research are:

1. Questionnaires (surveys)

2. Interviews (interrogation)

3. Experimentation

4. Observation

A questionnaire consists of a set of questions formulated to gather information that can be statistically evaluated. Personal interviews, conferring with people face-to-face, is another effective means of obtaining information. Telephone interviews are less effective. Experimentation is used to test a hypothesis, an assumption, or a theory. Observation entails watching certain actions or activities and recording these observations.

Discussion

1. Explain how reports are used by executives in the decision-making process.

2. Why should a business report be planned?

3. Why does secondary research generally precede primary research?

Study questions

1. How would you define the term "report"?
2. List some of the diverse communications classified as reports.
3. Explain the movement of reports within a business organization.
4. List the five steps in creating a written report.

[handwritten: 5 Steps / Planning / Investigate / Outline / Writing / Presentation]

5. Assume that you are writing a report on a new car for the company president. List six factors you would review: (Example: 1. Cost)
6. What are some of the delimitations to achieving the objectives of a report?
7. What is the direct order of arrangement?
8. What is the indirect order of arrangement?
9. What is the preliminary outline? *[handwritten: – working outline, guides research]*
10. List the four main sections of the body of a report.
11. Generally, there are two basic sources of report findings. What are they?
12. List the two basic classification systems used by libraries.
13. What is plagiarism?
14. List four basic methods of gathering information firsthand (primary research).
15. List thirteen suggestions for preparing a questionnaire.
16. List the five sampling techniques discussed in the textbook.
17. Conferring with people face-to-face in order to obtain information is called?
18. What method of research is used to test a hypothesis, a tentative proposition, an assumption, a theory?
19. What method of research entails watching certain actions or activities?

Activity

1. Assume that you have been asked to write a report on moving the corporate headquarters of a business from New York City to Danbury, Connecticut. Draw up a working, tentative outline for the report. Under the findings section, list the factors (such as taxes).

2. Stand in front of the Administration Building of your college (or the Student Center or Library) and conduct observational research. Select one item of clothing (shoes, sweaters, shirts, blouses, etc.) and record your observations. Draw up a sheet to record your observations. For example, if you select shirts, list the kinds of shirts worn, color, style, and so on. Observe one hundred students.

ACHIEVEMENT OF LEARNING GOALS

Check the appropriate boxes to determine whether you have or have not achieved the learning goals of this chapter.

I Can:

	YES	NO
1. Comprehend the role of reports in the decision-making process.	☐	☐
2. Plan an effective business report.	☐	☐
3. Investigate a problem by using secondary and/or primary research.	☐	☐

If any of your responses were "no," it is suggested that you review pertinent chapter parts.

Report Organization

1. Outline the content of a report.
2. Write an objective, concise, accurate, clear, well-organized report.
3. Classify a report by subject matter, function, format, length, formality, or time.
4. Construct memorandum reports, letter reports, manuscript reports, and form reports.
5. Prepare a proposal.

Outlining the report (step 3)

The next step in the creative process is to outline the content of the report (see Figure 4–1.

FIGURE 4–1. Outline Divisions:

I.
  A.
    1.
      a.
      b.
        (1)
        (2)
          (a)
          (b)
    2.
  B.
II.
III.
IV.
V.

HEADINGS AND SUBHEADINGS

The headings and subheadings contained in the outline become the captions in the report.

    I. Summary
   II. Introduction
       A. Definition
       B. Statement of Problem
       C. Sources of Information
       D. Scope
  III. Comparative Analyses of Plans
       A. Price
       B. Seating Capacity
       C. Range
       D. Maintenance
       E. Safety
       F. Luxury
       G. Operational Expenses
  IV. Conclusions
   V. Recommendations

As a Heading Guide. The outline serves as a guide for writing centered or side headings. The Roman numeral items are center headings and the capital letter items are side headings. Also, the outline is the basis for the *table of contents*, an outline with page numbering.

First and Last. It is interesting to note that the outline is the first and final parts of the report that are written, the outline is written when the report is begun, and the table of contents is written last, since it must include the page numbers.

Parallelism. The outline should have good parallel construction; that is, captions should be of equal value—roman numerals, for example—and similar grammatical construction. Good parallelism dictates a consistent, logical balance among related parts.

Writing the report (step 4)

THE FIRST DRAFT

Using the outline as a guide, the first draft of the report is written in rough form. Since the mind races ahead of the hand, experienced authors jot down their ideas rapidly. If there is a question about grammar or spelling, the author simply circles the portion in question. Later, the circled portions are verified for accuracy.

A Second Reading. It is a good idea to read the first draft again after several days and edit the copy. You will be amazed at the errors you will find after this cooling-off period. Pay close attention to punctuation, spelling, word choice, grammar, and format. Many experienced writers read the text aloud; if it can be articulated smoothly, the chances are good that the report is comprehensible. The text is then rewritten (final draft), incorporating the changes—for some writers, this rewriting is considered a second rough draft which is then revised and written again as the final draft.

WRITING STYLE AND CONTENT

Objectivity. Writing with objectivity means using facts not feelings, and omitting personal prejudices and biases. Some companies permit the use of first-person pronouns (I and we) in informal memo and letter reports; however, first-person pronouns generally are not used when writing formal reports. Well-written, formal reports are objective; they are similar in some respects to scientific reports. Subjective terms such as "I," "my," and "you" are omitted. The writer observes and/or records factual information.

Subjective	Objective
I believe word processing. . .	The facts indicate that word processing. . .
My feeling is that electronic mail. . .	Research findings reveal that electronic mail. . .
We surveyed offices in. . .	Offices were surveyed in. . .

Pure Objectivity. Some philosophers contend that complete objectivity is impossible, for we cannot escape from ourselves. We are the receptors and interpreters of stimuli; therefore, we are consciously or subconsciously subjective. However, it is imperative that we attempt to be as objective as possible. Try to avoid any biases or prejudices. A good report writer strives for the truth, an objective interpretation of factual information. Approach a problem with an open mind, without preconceived notions and emotional involvement. Also, it is safer to state "the facts indicate," rather than "I think," especially if a wrong decision has been made based on the study. This absolves the writer of personal responsibility for an erroneous opinion.

Conciseness. It is essential that business reports be concise. Verbose expression is a luxury few can afford in the business world. Conciseness usually increases clarity. Enumerations aid clarity, for they usually consist of brief, succinct statements.

Accuracy. Since reports are used as the basis for decision making, errors can be costly. A report should measure what it purports to measure. It should be statistically valid (truthful) and reliable (consistent); a careless error in tabulating data can invalidate a study costing thousands of dollars.

Language Usage. Clarity and ease of reading are general characteristics of effective business reports. Ponderous language may impede communication. Plain language is generally preferred. It is important to identify the experience background and educational level of the typical reader of the report, for the language and content are relative to the readership. The use of *jargon,* words peculiar to a profession, will depend on whether the report is written for internal or external readership; the complexity of graphic aids is also relative to readership.

When a report is prepared for wide readership, such as a corporate annual report, the adjustment problem is more complex. Some writers anticipating diversified readership keep the report proper rather simple and place complex, supporting information in the appendix. Technical language is avoided when there is general readership.

Organization. A logical presentation is understandable and meaningful. The outline provides major headings and subheadings for the body of the report. Major headings are center headings; minor headings are side headings.

FIGURE 4–2.   A common format for three levels of headings

First-Degree Heading	Introduction
Second-Degree Heading	STATEMENT OF THE PROBLEM
Third-Degree Heading	Definition.
Second-Degree Heading	PURPOSE OF REPORT
Second-Degree Heading	DELIMITATIONS

Classifying reports

Since there is a seemingly endless variety of reports, it is convenient to classify them by the following:

- *Subject Matter*
- *Function*
     Information reports
     Analytical reports
     Interpretive reports

- *Format*
  Memorandum reports
  Letter reports
  Manuscript reports
  Form reports
  Computer printouts
- *Length*
  Short reports
  Long reports
- *Formality*
  Informal reports
  Formal reports
- *Time*
  Periodic reports
  Special reports
  Progress reports

Some reports fall into several categories; for example, a memorandum report, besides being classified by format, is usually an information report, an informal report, and a short report.

CLASSIFICATION BY SUBJECT

An obvious way to classify reports is by subject area, such as transportation, finance, sales, advertising, promotion, and so on. Major areas can be divided into subareas for report writing purposes:

Records Management
- Filing systems
- Storage
- Retrieval
- Control
- Micrographics
- Disposition of records
- Records inventory
- Protecting records

CLASSIFICATION BY FUNCTION

There are three basic classifications of reports by function:

1. *Informational reports* present information only, without interpretation of any kind.

2. *Analytical reports* present information plus analyses. Analytical reports usually contain conclusion and recommendation sections. They are structured to provide solutions to problems. Many research reports are analytical in nature.

3. *Interpretive reports* provide information and interpret details. They do not contain conclusions and recommendations.

CLASSIFICATION BY FORMAT

It is common practice to classify reports by format, such as memorandum reports, letter reports, manuscript reports, printed form reports, and computer printouts.

Memorandum Reports. These reports are the most common internal written reports. Most memo forms contain the following guide words:

- To
- From
- Subject
- Date
- Telephone
- File number
- Department

The memorandum format is generally used for brief, informal reports. Memo reports can be handwritten or typed. Typewriting a memo report increases its formality. (See Figure 4–3.)

Letter Reports. Letter reports are more formal than memo reports. Letter reports are used mainly for external communication; however, they may also be used within a company. Internally, the letter report form is generally preferred over the memo report for high-echelon reports. Letter reports are typed on letterhead stationery. The format for a letter report is similar to that used for a regular letter. (See Figure 4–4.)

Manuscript Reports. A manuscript report contains written passages in a traditional format, including captions, footnotes, and illustrations. The manuscript report usually contains the following essential parts:

- Preliminary
  Title page
  Table of contents
  Summary

Interdepartment Message			

To:	NAME
	  April Mancini
		TITLE
		  Manager
			DATE
			May 8, 19--

	AGENCY	ADDRESS	
Fr:	NAME David Wiley	TITLE	TELEPHONE X7240
	AGENCY	ADDRESS	

Subject: Microfilm Installation, Pasadena Office

At the end of one year, the new microfilm system has proved of value:

1. File space has been reclaimed. (Saving: $2,000 in one year)
2. Efficiency has improved.
3. Response time is now less than two minutes. (Previously two hours)
4. File availability is now unlimited.
5. Worker morale has improved. (Less turnover of personnel)
6. Information is now better organized.

                                            D. W.

FIGURE 4-3. Memorandum report

- Body
    Introduction
    Findings or text
    Conclusions
    Recommendations
- Addenda
    Appendices
    Bibliography

Form Reports. When short reports are repetitious in nature, pre-printed forms can be used. The use of forms saves the writer time, ensures uniformity, and facilitates the tabulation of data. (See Figure 4-5.)

Computer Printouts. In the modern office, reports can take the form of computer printouts.

CLASSIFICATION BY LENGTH

Special business reports are also classified by length:

1. Short reports
2. Long reports

MONTOYA and PAISANO
6087 Monte Vista Boulevard
Albuquerque, NM 87106–4410

July 7, 19--

Mr. Joseph Coronado
Manuel Industries
8632 Mesa Trail
El Paso, TX 79902-4361

Dear Mr. Coronado

SUBJECT: FURNITURE SUGGESTIONS

An analysis of your floor plan indicates that
your needs will best be met by The Series 29
furniture. The following units are suggested:

```
 5  Acrylic see-through panels
 8  Lateral files
 3  Movable walls
14  Bookcases
 2  Tables
 8  Storage cabinets
 2  Tackboards
 3  Display shelves
 8  Acoustical panels
 1  Credenza
20  Desks
35  Chairs
```

The enclosed catalog provides descriptive information about this furniture (size, construction,
price, etc.). Also enclosed is a floor plan
illustrating our suggested placement of this
office furniture.

Please call collect at (505) 236-8211 if you
have any questions.

Sincerely yours

Thomas Montoya

Thomas Montoya, President
csk
2 Enclosures

FIGURE 4–4. Letter report

Edward & Albert
ASSOCIATES
200 Washington Street
Rutland, Vermont 05701-3216

Monthly Sales Report

Name ___Scott R. Adams_____   Date _April 17, 19--_

Location _Miami, Florida_____

Sales of Stationery:

	Quantity	Price
Bond Paper	20 Reams	$100
Onion Skin Paper	10 Reams	40
Carbon Paper	_____	____
Pads	200____	150
TOTAL		$290

Scott R. Adams
Signature

Mail this completed form to:

Ms. Nancy R. Curtis, Manager
Edward & Albert Associates
200 Washington Street
Rutland, Vermont 05701-3216

FIGURE 4-5. Preprinted form report

Effective business writing is clear, concise, and to the point. The length of a report is determined by completeness. The report is terminated when its purposes have been achieved. Often, an executive will state whether a brief or extensive study is desired.

Generally a report of ten or less pages is considered a short report; a report of eleven or more pages is considered a long report.

The following are usually classified as short reports: short manuscript reports, memo reports, letter reports, printed form reports, and computer printouts. Generally, short reports do not entail extensive research, for they convey easily procurable information.

Some reports are too long for the memo letter report format, yet not formal or complex enough to be major formal reports. In such instances, the short manuscript report format is used. The report is typed on plain 8½ by 11 inch paper.

Short Report. A short report is not as structured as a long formal report; it does not contain as many component parts. For example, a short report may consist of only the following component parts:

- Title page
- Table of contents
- Text
- Bibliography

Very abbreviated short reports consist of a title page and textual portion.

The following reports are usually classified as short reports—some may also be classified under other categories as well; for example, the annual report is a short, periodic report.

- Annual reports
- Credit reports
- Inquiry reports
- Inspection reports
- Letter reports
- Justification reports
- Memorandum reports
- Periodic reports
- Progress reports
- Proposals
- Recommendation reports

Long Report. A long, formal report is highly structured and may include some or all of the following parts:

Cover.	Protects the report; enhances appearance; provides identification—title, author, date.
Title fly.	Contains report title.
Title page.	Complete report identification—title; subtitle; author's name, title and address; recipient's name, title, and address; completion date.
Copyright page.	Included only if report is registered with the Copyright Office.
Letter of authorization.	Copy of letter or memorandum from originator authorizing report.
Letter of acceptance.	Copy of letter by writer accepting responsibility to write report.
Letter of transmittal.	Letter or memorandum from author to reader —identifies report problem, objectives, delimitations, need for report, research methods employed, scope, acknowledgments, overview of report, follow-up studies needed, and friendly close (offer to discuss report).
Table of contents.	Outline of report containing major divisions and subdivisions. Lists corresponding page references. (Note: This is the last part of the report prepared.)
List of tables.	Lists report tables in consecutive order and page numbering.
List of figures.	List of illustrations other than tables in consecutive order and page numbering.
Summary.	Digest and preview of main ideas or principal findings of report.
Preface.	Tells general character, use, scope, and objectives of report.
Introduction.	Includes: definition of terms, statement of problem, purpose, scope, sources of information, definitions, research methods and procedures employed, delimitations, questions, historical background, hypothesis, or-

ganizational plan. (Note: If a letter of authorization is not included, the introduction may cite the authorization for the study.)

Findings or text.   Contains: review of related literature, presentation of research findings, illustrations, analyses, interpretations, sources of information.

Conclusions.   Analysis of findings—answers to problems.

Recommendations.   Resulting from analyses—suggested actions.

Endnotes.   A numeric listing of footnotes. This section is included only if footnotes are not cited at the bottom of pages.

Appendix or appendices.   Includes ancillary materials too detailed or complex for report body such as memos, letters, maps, questionnaires, tables, figures, compilations, lists, photographs, exhibits, forms, computer printouts and blueprints.

Bibliography.   Alphabetic listing of reference sources consulted or used—books, periodicals, interviews, newspapers, speeches, journals, guides, directories, etc. Sources may be grouped under separate headings, such as reference works, books, periodicals, etc.

Index.   Alphabetic listing of key topics and respective page numbers.

CLASSIFICATION BY FORMALITY

Reports cover a wide range of formality. Generally, the continuum is as shown in Figure 4–6. Informal reports are usually written in a casual style; formal reports in a more deliberate style. However, both informal and formal reports should be well written. Informal reports generally convey routine information and remain within the company. Reports meant for internal readership tend to be less formal than those written for external readership; however, there are many exceptions.

CLASSIFICATION BY TIME

There are three basic time classifications of reports:

1. Periodic reports
2. Special reports
3. Progress reports

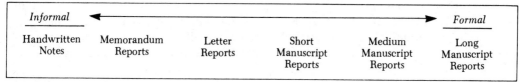

Informal					Formal
Handwritten Notes	Memorandum Reports	Letter Reports	Short Manuscript Reports	Medium Manuscript Reports	Long Manuscript Reports

FIGURE 4–6. The report continuum

Periodic Reports. Certain reports, such as reports by salespeople, reports to stockholders, and financial statements occur with scheduled regularity: weekly, bimonthly, monthly, quarterly, semiannually, yearly. These periodic reports provide routine data about the operation of a business. Computer-generated printouts are often used as the format of periodic reports.

Special Reports. Special or non-routine reports are written only when the need for them arises. They are thought of as one-shot activities; for example, a study of the need for a new parking garage.

 Progress Reports. Progress reports are written sequentially while an activity is being undertaken. The time frame for an activity may be as shown in Figure 4–7. A progress report can be written as each major activity on the construction schedule is completed.

FIGURE 4–7. Sample time frame

Progress Report and Month	Construction Schedule
No. 1 April:	Land acquisition
No. 2 May:	Prepare the lot for building, remove trees, fill in swamp
No. 3 June:	Dig foundation and pour concrete foundation
No. 4 July-August:	Steel framing
No. 5 September:	Roof, exterior construction
No. 6 October-November:	Interior construction
No. 7 December:	Final completion report, including total costs, etc.

Proposals

WHAT ARE THEY?

A proposal is a specialized report which delineates a problem, proposes a plan of action or research to be undertaken, and offers solutions. In effect, a proposal seeks authorization, acceptance, or support for the research or ideas it details.

In some circumstances, a proposal is written to activate research, obtain funding, promote the sales of goods and services, convince, plan changes, or persuade. Proposals are submitted internally (within an organization) or externally (to other organizations, businesses, and governmental agencies).

WHAT THEY INCLUDE

Research proposals contain a variety of component parts. Some of the statements found in a typical proposal are:

- An introductory statement, including the title and nature of the proposal.
- The problem, including background information.
- The objectives or purposes.
- The scope and limitations of the problem.
- The methods of solving the problem.
- The research and procedures to be followed.
- Cost estimates, expenditures to be budgeted or funded.
- Needed facilities and equipment.
- Time schedules.
- Legal details, if applicable.
- Personnel involvement.
- A request for permission to proceed or to provide solutions to the problem.

Proposals range in formality and length as do regular reports. A proposal can be in memorandum, letter, or report form. The proposal in Figure 4–8 is in letter–report form.

Summary

In Chapter 3, the first two steps of effective report writing (planning and investigating) were discussed. This chapter concerns the remaining steps (outlining, writing, and presentation).

Outlining the content of the report is the third step in the creative process. The headings and subheadings contained in the outline become the captions in the report.

The outline serves as a guide for the writing of the first, rough-draft copy of the report. The first draft is usually written rapidly in order to jot down

FIGURE 4–8. A sample proposal

Dear Mr. Bukowski:

Title   SUBJECT: PROPOSAL FOR A PARKING GARAGE

Nature of the Proposal   This proposal for a new parking garage is presented to you for consideration.

Statement of the   For the past three years, we have had inadequate
Problem, Including   parking space at our administrative office building in
Background Information   Oklahoma City. A preliminary study by Mr. Forrest T. Morgan, Office Manager, indicates that an additional 439 parking spaces will be needed when the addition to the building is completed in April 19--. Thirty-nine of the present parking spaces will be lost on the construction site. (A copy of Mr. Morgan's study is attached.)

Objectives or   Specifically, the purpose of this proposal is to pro-
Purposes   vide a solution to this problem, inadequate parking space.

Scope and   The investigation will be limited to resolving the
Limitations   parking problem at the administrative office building in Oklahoma City.

Methods of Solving   A study will be undertaken to determine the cost of
the Problem, Research   building a one thousand-space parking garage on the
and Procedures to be   adjoining (north) lot of the administrative office
Followed   building. Architects will be contacted for suggestions for the construction of the proposed parking garage.

Cost Estimates   The initial study and fees for architects will require
Needed Facilities and   an expenditure of $20,000. No special facilities or equip-
Equipment   ment will be needed. The feasibility study will be com-
Time Schedule   pleted by November 21, 19--.

Legal Details   Our legal department will be consulted.

Personnel   The study will be undertaken by Ms. Alison Rubin,
Involvement   Administrative Assistant to Mr. Morgan. Ms. Rubin will receive secretarial assistance from Mr. Calvin S. Grant and Mr. Juan Carlos.

Request for Permission   May I have your authorization to proceed with this
to Proceed   investigation? If you need any additional information concerning this proposal, please do not hesitate to contact me.

                                            Respectfully submitted,

                                            Steven Scott Neilson
                                            Steven Scott Neilsen
                                            Vice President

mm
Enclosure

main ideas on paper. Later, the manuscript is verified for accuracy (grammar, spelling, etc.). Ultimately, a final draft is created. When writing a business report, special consideration must be given to:

- Objectivity
- Conciseness
- Accuracy
- Language
- Organization

There is a seemingly endless variety of reports. It is generally convenient to classify them by:

- Function
- Format
- Length
- Formality
- Time

Discussion

1. The outline of the report "appears" in or determines the structure of two distinct parts of the report. Name the two parts and discuss their functions.
2. Why is objectivity so important in business writing?
3. What determines the format (note form, memo form, letter form, manuscript form) of reports?

Study questions

1. What is meant by objectivity in report writing?
2. What is jargon? bad diction
3. List six convenient classifications of reports.
4. List five common formats for reports. Function, format length. Formality, Time
5. Differentiate between an informational report and an analytical report.
6. List the component parts of a long report. Example: Cover, Flyleaf.
7. Reports are classified by degrees of formality. List the continuum of report formality.
8. What is a progress report?

Activities

1. Compose a memo report

   To: Carol Goldstein, Manager
   From: (Your Name)
   Subject: Advertising Plans for Champion Tennis Racquets
   Date: (Today's)

   Tell Carol about your advertising plans for promoting the sales of Champion Tennis Racquets. These are some facts about the tennis racquets:

   - Price: $69.95
   - Nylon Strung
   - Steel Frame
   - Weight: 2 Pounds
   - Leather Grip
   - Cover Included

   List the various media to be used (ratio, TV, newspapers, magazines, etc.).

2. Compose a letter report to Ms. Sharon Wilson, President; H. B. Anderson Company; 101 Starling Drive; Salt Lake City, UT 84121–4387. Tell Ms. Wilson about the earnings of your company and its activities. Ms. Wilson is interested in purchasing your company.

ACHIEVEMENT OF LEARNING GOALS

Check the appropriate boxes to determine whether you have or have not achieved the learning goals of this chapter.

I Can:

	YES	NO
1. Write an objective, concise, accurate, clear, well-organized report.	☐	☐
2. Classify a report by subject matter, function, format, length, formality, or time.	☐	☐
3. Construct memorandum reports, letter reports, manuscript reports, and form reports.	☐	☐
4. Prepare a proposal.	☐	☐

If any of your responses were "no," it is suggested that you review pertinent chapter parts.

Illustrations in Reports

LEARNING GOALS

1. Understand the need for illustrations in reports.
2. Differentiate between tables and figures.
3. Know the format of basic diagrammatic representations.
4. Determine which graphic aids are best suited for specific illustrative purposes.

Illustrations are visual aids that enhance the expression of ideas, clarify, and provide information. Tables, figures, and computer printouts are used to present graphically supportive statistical and factual data in an interesting manner. Generally, they are considered to be an essential accompaniment of a business report. Reading a mass of numerical data on a page can make understanding difficult and deaden interest. Visual presentations, such as diagrams, graphs, photographs, maps, tables, cartoons, and so on, aid comprehension, elucidate relationships, stimulate interest, and promote understanding.

A visual aid usually appears near the material in the text it supports; however, illustrations may be presented in the appendix when ancillary supplementary information is desirable. To be effective, illustrations should be both accurate and attractive. Some companies have graphic artists who are responsible for the rendering of visual aids.

Tables

A *table* is an orderly arrangement of related facts, data, information, and so on in rows and columns. Some computer printouts are in tabular form and can be classified as tables. Usually, tables are numbered consecutively. Typists call the process of arranging columns in typewritten form "tabulations." (See Table 5–1.)

TABLE 5–1. Projected sales of communicating word processors

	1990	1995	2000
Boston	35	50	65
Chicago	20	35	50
Denver	15	30	45
New York	40	55	70
Salt Lake City	10	25	40
San Diego	18	33	48
San Francisco	40	55	70
Seattle	16	31	46
TOTALS	194	314	434

Source: Primary

Figures

A *figure* is a catch-all term denoting all illustrations other than tables. It includes such diverse graphic aids as maps, graphs, diagrams, photographs, drawings, charts, and certain computer printouts. Usually, all figures are numbered (Example: "Figure 5") in a report.

Dependent illustrations have textual material supporting or introducing them; *independent illustrations* require no supportive explanations or discussions and are meaningful without text reference. Independent illustrations, of necessity, require a title and are numbered consecutively. Generally, the use of illustrations with supporting text is preferred, since an independent illustration may not be fully understood.

BAR GRAPHS

A *graph* is a diagrammatic representation (bars, lines, curves, etc.) of statistical relationships and variables. Bar graphs contain bars (vertical or horizontal) to compare quantitative data. Most bar graphs contain bars or heavy lines of varying lengths to illustrate comparisons (Figures 5–1 and 5–2). However, in a subdivided bar graph, the bars are the same length; each bar represents 100 percent, the entire universe. The bar is divided into shaded or colored segments representing various percentages of the whole. (See Figure 5–3.)

Duo-directional Bar Graphs. These graphs show deviations, plus or minus, from zero.

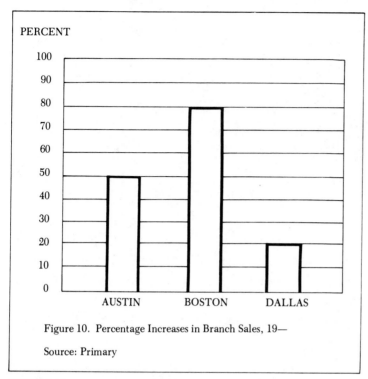

Figure 10. Percentage Increases in Branch Sales, 19—

Source: Primary

FIGURE 5–1. Vertical bar graph

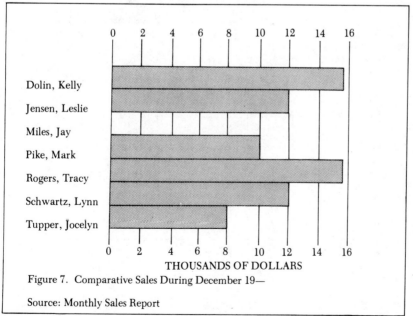

Figure 7. Comparative Sales During December 19—

Source: Monthly Sales Report

FIGURE 5–2. Horizontal bar graph

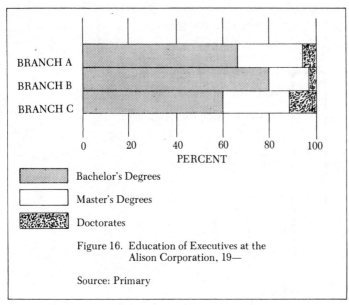

Figure 16. Education of Executives at the
Alison Corporation, 19—

Source: Primary

FIGURE 5–3. Subdivided bar graph

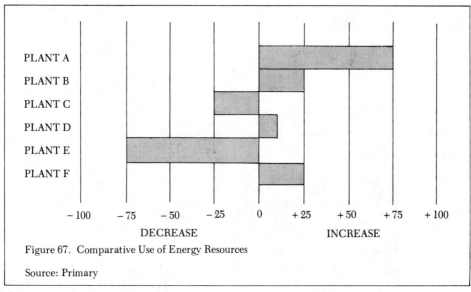

Figure 67. Comparative Use of Energy Resources

Source: Primary

FIGURE 5–4. Duodirectional bar graph

PIE GRAPHS

Pie graphs, also called circle graphs, are commonly used to represent area. The entire area of the circle represents the universe, the whole 100 percent.

Each segment of the circle—slice of the pie—represents a percentage or part of the whole. The largest slice of the pie starts at noon; the slices then decrease in size in a clockwise direction.

A protractor is used to draw the pie graph. Each slice of the pie needs to be transposed from percent to degrees. Since a circle contains 360 degrees, multiply the total number of degrees by the percentage you wish to illustrate to determine the degrees of the slice.

> *Example:*
>
> 360 Degrees in a circle
> × .15 Percentage to illustrate
> ――――
> 54.00 Degrees

See Figure 5–5a for an illustration of a pie graph. A slice of the pie can be separated for emphasis (Figure 5–5b).

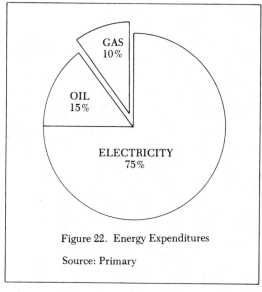

Figure 22. Energy Expenditures

Source: Primary

FIGURE 5–5a.   Pie graph with separated slice

LINE GRAPHS

These graphs, often drawn on graph paper, are used to plot variables on a time grid. The vertical axis is an arithmetic scale (units, dollars, pounds, etc.); the horizontal axis is used to plot time (days, months, years). (See Figure 5–6.)

A multiple-line graph consists of more than one series plotted on a grid. Each line must be distinguished from another (especially if lines intersect);

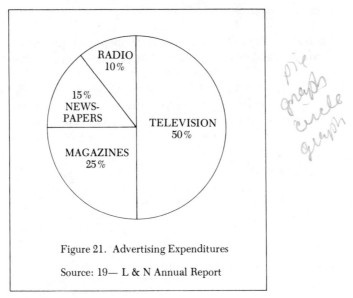

Figure 21. Advertising Expenditures

Source: 19— L & N Annual Report

FIGURE 5–5b. Pie graph

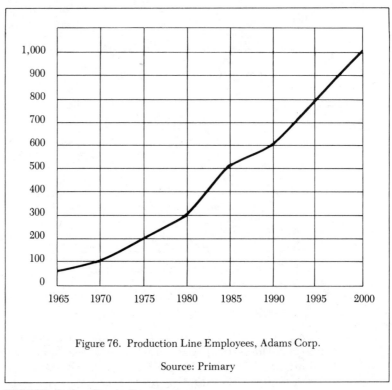

Figure 76. Production Line Employees, Adams Corp.

Source: Primary

FIGURE 5–6. Single-line graph

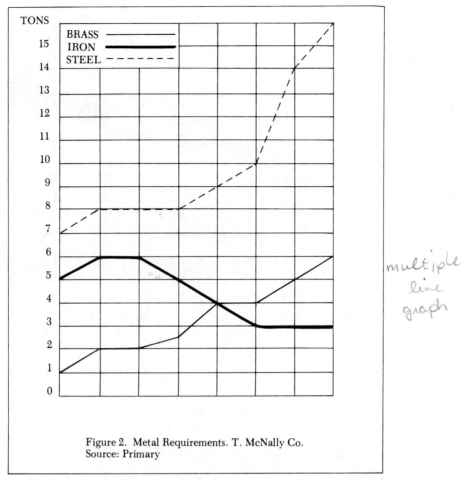

Figure 2. Metal Requirements. T. McNally Co.
Source: Primary

FIGURE 5–7.   Multiple-line graph

therefore, different forms of lines are drawn (solid, dots, dashes, dots and dashes). A legend explains what each line represents. Colored lines can also be used to distinguish one from the other. (See Figure 5–7.)

BAND GRAPHS

Band graphs, also called "belt graphs," show contrasts among a series of components over a period of time. The band graph depicted is divided into three bands or strata. (See Figure 5–8.)

PICTOGRAMS

This popular form of bar graph uses a series of pictures or symbols instead of bars to make numeric comparisons of data. Each symbol depicted represents a

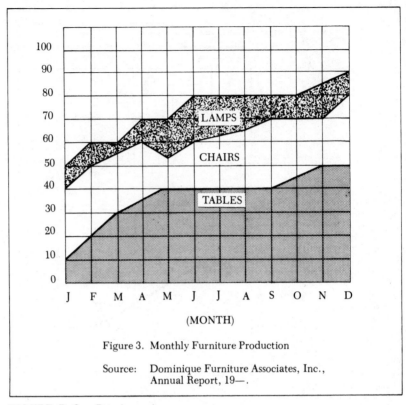

Figure 3. Monthly Furniture Production

Source: Dominique Furniture Associates, Inc.,
          Annual Report, 19—.

FIGURE 5–8. Band graph

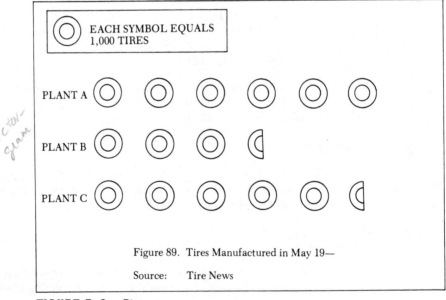

Figure 89. Tires Manufactured in May 19—

Source: Tire News

FIGURE 5–9. Pictogram

number of units. This simple form of linear diagram is very effective, for it is easy to understand and enlivens graphic presentations. (See Figure 5–9.)

MAPS

Maps are very useful for depicting spatial relationships. They are used primarily in the business world to show location (salespeople, offices, and so on) and statistical information. Various graphic techniques are used when constructing maps as visual aids. Pictorial devices (color, cross-hatching, dots, etc.) are used to represent quantitative relationships. (See Figure 5–10.)

RATIO GRAPHS

These graphs reveal visually the relationship in size, quantity or amount when comparing similar things. (See Figure 5–11.)

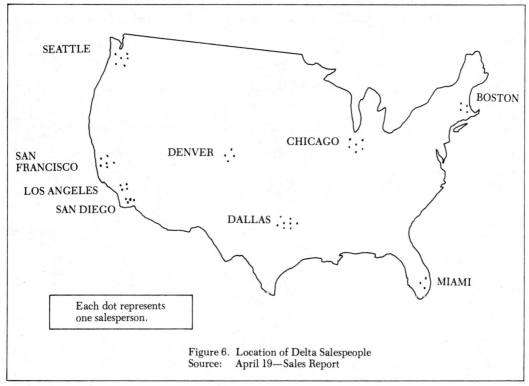

Figure 6. Location of Delta Salespeople
Source: April 19—Sales Report

FIGURE 5–10. Map   Maps

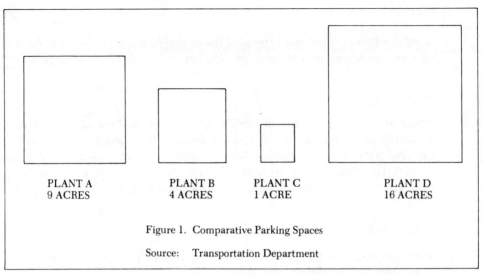

PLANT A
9 ACRES

PLANT B
4 ACRES

PLANT C
1 ACRE

PLANT D
16 ACRES

Figure 1. Comparative Parking Spaces

Source: Transportation Department

FIGURE 5–11. Ratio graph

CARTOONS

Cartoons are an effective medium for expressing emotions and conveying ideas. They should be in good taste and well executed to be effective. (See Figure 5–12.)

I don't think Harry ever fully recovered from his oral presentation before the board of directors!

FIGURE 5–12. Cartoon

Charts used in a presentation (Courtesy of CIGNA Corp.)

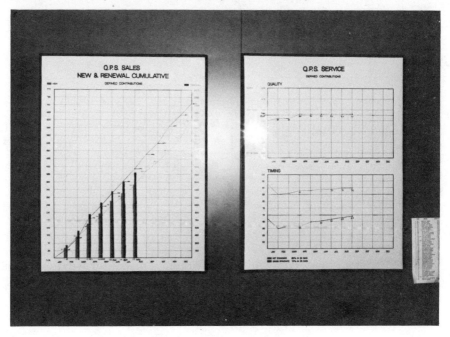

ORGANIZATION DIAGRAMS

These are very effective for illustrating the chain of command of an organization. (See Figure 5–13.)

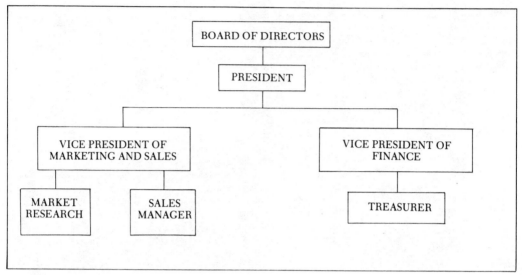

FIGURE 5–13. Organization diagram

FLOW CHARTS

These charts depict the operational sequences that take place. (See Figure 5–14.)

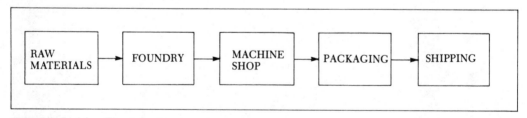

FIGURE 5–14. Flow chart

PICTURES

It is common to use pictures for illustrative purposes. The term "picture" encompasses drawings, photographs, and paintings. These visual representations enhance reports, especially when in color. (See Figure 5–15.)

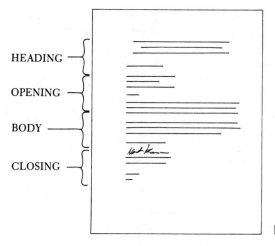

HEADING

OPENING

BODY

CLOSING

FIGURE 5–15. Picture as an illustration

Summary

Illustrations are generally considered to be an essential accompaniment of business reports. Illustrations are visual aids that enhance the expression of ideas, clarify, and provide information. Visual presentations, such as diagrams, graphs, photographs, maps, tables, and cartoons, are commonly used.

A visual aid usually appears near the material in the text it supports; however, illustrations may be presented in the appendix when ancillary supplementary information is desirable. Illustrations should be both accurate and attractive.

A *table* is an orderly arrangement of related facts, data, information, and so on in rows and columns. A *figure* is a catch-all term denoting all illustrations other than tables. It includes such diverse graphic aids as maps, graphs, diagrams, photographs, drawings, charts, and certain computer printouts.

A *graph* is a diagrammatic representation (bars, lines, curves, etc.) of statistical relationships and variables. Pie graphs are commonly used representations of area. Line graphs are used to plot variables on a time grid. Band graphs show contrasts among a series of components over a period of time. Pictograms use a series of pictures or symbols instead of bars to make numeric comparisons of data. Maps depict spatial relationships. Ratio graphs reveal the relationship in size, quantity or amount when comparing similar things. Cartoons are effective for expressing emotions and conveying ideas. Organization diagrams illustrate chains of command. Flow charts depict operational sequences. Pictures (drawings, photographs, paintings) enhance reports.

Discussion

1. Differentiate between tables and figures.
2. Tell how graphic determinations are made.

[handwritten: figures - all illis-trations other than tables]

[handwritten: Tables - related facts and info put in rows or colums]

Study questions

1. What are the purposes of illustrations in reports? *[handwritten: visual aid]*
2. When are illustrations placed in the appendix of a report? *[handwritten: when sup-lemental info. is desired]*
3. Define the following terms:
   Table *[handwritten: - related facts, info put in colums]*
   Tabulation *[handwritten: - process of arranging tables in typewriten form]*
   Figures *[handwritten: - all illistrations other than tables]*
   Dependent illustrations *[handwritten: - require textual material to support them]*
   Independent illustrations *[handwritten: - require no textual supportive material. they are fully understood (sometimes) and require titles]*

Activity

From various sources (magazines, newspapers, annual reports, and so on), collect samples of as many of the following visual aids as you can:

- Table
- Vertical bar graph
- Horizontal bar graph
- Multiple bar graph
- Subdivided bar graph
- Duo-directional bar graph
- Pie graph
- Single-line graph
- Multiple-line graph
- Band graph
- Pictogram
- Map
- Ratio graph

- Cartoon
- Organization diagram
- Flow chart
- Pictures
    Drawing
    Photograph
    Painting

ACHIEVEMENT OF LEARNING GOALS

Check the appropriate boxes to determine whether you have or have not achieved the learning goals of this chapter.

I Can:

		YES	NO
1.	Understand the need for illustrations in reports.	☑	☐
2.	Differentiate between tables and figures.	☑	☐
3.	Explain the format of basic diagrammatic representations.	☑	☐
4.	Determine which graphic aids are best suited for specific illustrative purposes.	☑	☐

If any of your responses were "no," it is suggested that you review pertinent chapter parts.

Presenting the Report
(Step 5)

1. Prepare a report for effective presentation.
2. Know the proper format for formal business reports.
3. Understand the function and format of an abstract and a log.

The first two steps in the report-writing process, planning and investigating, were covered in Chapter 3. The next two steps, outlining and writing, appear in Chapters 4 and 5. This chapter discusses the fifth and last step in this process, presentation of the report.

Appearance

CONSERVATIVE FORMAT

covers colors are black!

Test question

The report should be attractive in appearance and correct in format. Generally, a conservative cover is preferred. Black is a popular cover color for formal reports. Dark brown, dark blue, and gray also present a dignified image. Some sales reports have brightly colored covers. Avoid the temptation to embellish the report with loud colors, gaudy illustrations, decorations, and so on. It should be noted that some reports are color coded. For example, all reports pertaining to advertising may have green covers, sales reports blue, and so on.

Paper. Quality white bond paper, 8½ by 11 inches, is preferred for manuscript reports. Most reports are typed doubled spaced; however, some brief reports are single spaced. Use a dark ribbon and make corrections neatly.

page #s on report

Pagination. Lowercase Roman numerals (i, ii, iii, iv, v, etc.) are typed at the bottom of prefatory pages. The page number does not appear on the title page, the first page of the text, or on the first page of a major section. Arabic numerals are used when typing page numbers on other pages. The common procedure is to go down four lines from the top edge of the paper, type the page number at the right margin, and triple space down to type the text.

The method of reproduction of reports depends on the number of copies needed. If a few copies are required, carbon copies or photocopies will suffice. If many copies are needed, stenciling or mimeographing can be used. If there is a large distribution and good quality copies are required, offset printing or standard printing may be preferred.

Margins. The typing on page one of the report and each major section (start of a chapter, for example) begins on line 13; this ensures a two-inch top margin. Subsequent pages have top margins of one inch. Side margins on pages are one inch; bottom margins are an inch or an inch and a half. If the report is bound on the side, an extra half inch is allowed; therefore the left margin is one and a half inches.

Formal report illustrated

Figure 6–1 is an illustration of an analytical, formal business report in its entirety. This report can serve as a model for business reports or college term papers.

Presentation

The mode of presentation is usually relative to the formality of the report. A memo report, form report, or letter report may be simply handed to the recipient or mailed.

A consequential report requires a formal presentation. An appointment can be made to present the written report with the writer available for oral comments. In some instances, a formal oral presentation is in order. This presentation can be made before a group of interested people (see Chapter 14, Oral Presentations, for information about speaking before a group).

FIGURE 6-1. An analytical, formal business report

A STUDY OF REMOTE DATA ENTRY

VOICE RECOGNITION

Presented to

Mr. Kenneth J. DeSanti, President
Electronic Technology Corporation
1899 Los Grandes Way
Los Angeles, California 90027

by

Pamela R. Bates, Manager
Research and Development Department

April 15, 19

FIGURE 6–1. *(cont.)*

ELECTRONIC TECHNOLOGY CORPORATION

1899 Los Grandes Way

Los Angeles, California 90027

April 15, 19--

Mr. Kenneth J. DeSanti, President
Electronic Technology Corporation
1899 Los Grandes Way
Los Angeles, California 90027

Dear Mr. Desanti:

This is the study of voice recognition systems that you assigned
on March 15, 19--.

Since technology in remote data entry is relatively new, the
findings are primarily from current articles on the subject. An
encyclopedia and books were used for background information on
computers.

Studying voice recognition has proved to be both interesting and
informative. This new communication mode is emerging from the
research and development stage. Practical applications in the
field have just begun. The future of voice recognition seems to
be very promising, indeed.

If you have any questions concerning this study, please do not
hesitate to contact me.

Respectfully submitted,

Pamela Bates

Pamela Bates, Manager
Research and Development Department

ii

FIGURE 6–1. *(cont.)*

TABLE OF CONTENTS

iii

FIGURE 6-1. *(cont.)*

line 7   one inch
—Triple space

Summary

A newly implemented mode of computer data entry is voice recognition. Voice recognition entails the input of computer data by direct speech, telephone, or radio. Some newly developed computers have voice data entry and audio response capabilities--you can talk to these computers and they speak back.

Seventy-five percent of the executives of the Electronic Technology Corporation have not learned keyboarding or touch typewriting and are reluctant to interact with computers. Voice recognition would encourage our executives to use computers, especially when their hands and eyes are performing other tasks.

Voice recognition can be employed for data entry or communications. There are two major voice recognition systems, dependent and independent.

Presently, there are some problems:

1. The operator cannot speak in a conversational pattern.

2. The rate of entry needs speeding up.

3. The cost is relatively high.

New technological advances and increased sales should resolve these problems in the immediate future.

The advantages are:

1. Keyboarding is not required.

2. It is more natural and convenient to input data by speech.

3. Keyboarding errors are eliminated.

4. Direct entry by voice, radio, or telephone can take place.

Future expectations are very promising. Present applications of voice recognition systems have proved to be successful.

iv  *use three in foot report*

FIGURE 6–1. (*cont.*)

A STUDY OF REMOTE DATA ENTRY: VOICE RECOGNITION

Introduction

A newly implemented mode of computer entry is voice recognition.

Voice communications with computers are being used today for various

applications in the business world. Some newly developed computers

have voice data entry and audio response capabilities. Robert Huber

states:

> With little real awareness on the part of most manufactur-
> ing personnel, voice communication with computers has been
> extracted from laboratory cocoons, tried, modified, and refined
> in a variety of industrial applications and environments, and
> now put to work for pay. As one user puts it: 'This still
> gets some people bug-eyed, the idea of talking to machines.
> And I meet a lot of skeptics. But it is paying its way in
> our plant. It is for real.'[1]

PURPOSE OF THE REPORT

Specifically, it is the purpose of this study to determine whether

automatic speech recognition computers should be purchased by the

Electronic Technology Corporation.

STATEMENT OF THE PROBLEM

Seventy-five percent of the executives at the Electronic Technology

Corporation have not learned touch typewriting or key punching and are

reluctant to interface with a computer. Using speech recognition, a

----

[1] Robert F. Huber, "Tell It to Your Machine," *Production*, 85, no. 6
(June 1980), 105.

FIGURE 6-1. *(cont.)*

person does not have to be an expert to operate a computer--the computer is <u>told</u> (commanded) what tasks to perform.

When the hands and eyes of a computer operator are being used (not available for keyboarding or keypunching), talking to a voice terminal can be invaluable.

There are certain performances or operations that would be speeded up if automatic speech reognition were used at the Electronic Technology Corporation--communications, inspections, quality control, and inventorying.

DEFINITION

In the laboratory, experimental computers have been able to talk to people (output) for some time; however, people speaking to computers (input) is a complicated and relatively new process. Voice data entry terminal systems programmed to recognize voice input are now available.[2] Voice recognition entails the input of computer data by the human voice. In a voice recognition system, a person can speak directly to a computer or remotely by radio or telephone. Voice recognition devices "convert audio signals to digital impulses for use by the computer."[3]

SOURCES OF INFORMATION

Information for this study was obtained from library sources (articles, encyclopedias, books). Since voice recognition is just emerging from the experimental laboratory, current magazine articles were the primary source of information. A survey of executives at the Electronic Technology Corporation

---

[2]V. Thomas Dock and Edward Essick, <u>Principles of Business Data Processing with Basic</u> (Chicago: Science Research Associates, Inc., 1978), p. 213.

[3]Donald D. Spencer, <u>Data Processing: An Introduction</u> (Columbus, Ohio: Charles E. Merrill Publishing Company, 1978), p. 176.

FIGURE 6–1. (*cont.*)

was conducted to determine the opinions of executives concerning computer data entry (see Appendix B).

Findings

Keypunching and keyboarding have been the major forms of entering computer data in the past. Voice recognition is a transition from finger to speech input. Input/output equipment has consisted of the following: keyboard devices, optical devices, magnetic tape units and cassettes, printers, and microfilm techniques.[4]

> Since the inception of electronic data processing--in fact, since the beginnings of the U. S. industrial revolution--data entry technologies have revolved around the keyboard for automated data processing. ...
> Today, there is a new mode of data entry on the horizon that will have as fundamental an impact on that field as the keyboard has had on EDP. The new mode is voice recognition ...[5]

The voice recognition process can be diagrammed as follows:

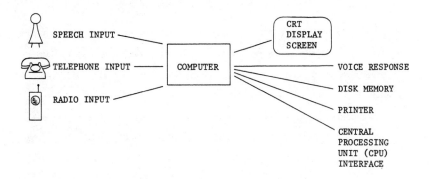

---

[4]L. C. Hobbs, "Computer," <u>Collier's Encyclopedia</u> (1980), 7, 125–126.

[5]"Remote Data Entry Recognizes a Strong New Voice," <u>Data Communications</u>, 8, no. 8 (August 1979), 15.

FIGURE 6-1. *(cont.)*

COMMUNICATIONS

Since their inception in the early 1950's, computers were used primarily for record keeping and accounting purposes. Electronic data processing revolutionized the handling of financial records. "Yet the current and future outlook is different. Today computers are used on-line as a communicating tool."[6] The modern corresponding secretary in a word processing center spends most of the time keyboarding. Lucy Jennings contends that "the secretary must be able to use the computer on-line as a communications tool with the same ease and efficiency with which the secretary uses the telephone."[7]

Advanced word processing systems will consist of an executive speaking to a voice recognition computer. The computer will display on a CRT screen the message for editing; and, at the press of a button, the message will be printed.

DATA ENTRY

The keyboard has played a major role in computer data entry in the past. Today, there is an exciting, new way to enter data, remote data entry by voice recognition. Both a voice recognition device and a keyboard terminal perform the same function.

An operator can speak (dictate) on a telephone to a voice recognition computer and see the words displayed on a video screen. The message can be edited and printed. A programmer can converse with a computer. (See

---

[6]Lucy Mae Jennings, Secretarial and Administrative Procedures (Englewood Cliffs, N.J.: Prentice-Hall, Inc., 1978), p. 650.
[7]Ibid.

FIGURE 6–1. (*cont.*)

5

Appendix A for an actual conversation between a programmer and a computer.)

There are two major voice recognition systems, speaker dependent and speaker independent.

<u>Speaker Dependent System</u>. The machine is programmed to recognize the voice of one or more operators. Therefore, it can respond to a larger vocabulary than a speaker independent system.

<u>Speaker Independent System.</u> The machine is programmed to recognize the voices of casual operators, such as the general public.

VOICE RECOGNITION PROBLEMS

There are problems with voice recognition systems that have to be resolved:[8]

1. The operator cannot speak in a conversational pattern. There must be short pauses before and after words.

2. The speed of entry is good, but needs improvement. Presently, in some instances, standard keyboarding is faster.

3. The cost is high. A Threshold basic system is priced at $67,000.

Researchers are working to resolve the problem of not being able to speak conversationally. One company, Threshold, claims that it has developed a continuous speech recognition process. Presently, research is being conducted on increasing the speed of voice entry. It is expected that costs will decrease as production increases.

ADVANTAGES OF VOICE RECOGNITION SYSTEMS

There are obvious advantages to a voice recognition system:

---

[8] Huber, "Tell It to Your Machine," p. 104.

FIGURE 6–1. (*cont.*)

6

1. Keyboarding ability is not required.

2. It is easier and more natural to speak to input data than use fingers (keypunching and keyboarding).

3. There is a probability for typographical errors to occur when keyboarding. This is eliminated by direct communication by voice to a computer. Also, immediate correction is possible.

4. Direct entry to computers by voice, radio or telephone can take place.

FUTURE EXPECTATIONS

Growth in the use of voice recognition systems should be spectacular in the next decade. A diversity of applications should evolve. It is predicted that "by 1988, the sales of speech recognition products will be in the $1½ billion range. ... proponents envision whole plant networks in which workers can communicate ..."[9]

The executives of two voice equipment manufacturing companies are so optimistic about voice input and voice response, they have developed units that connect to home computers. Sales of these units have been brisk.[10] It is interesting to note that voice response will also become increasingly popular in the future. Since 1964, voice response has been available.[11] For example, your automobile and microwave oven will talk back to you. Your car will be programmed to inform you when you are driving too rapidly or when your gas supply is getting low. Your microwave oven will instruct you in proper settings.

---

[9]Huber, "Tell It to Your Machine," p. 105.

[10]"Computer Talk: It's Here and Now Technology," Infosystems, 26, no. 8 (August 1979), 68.

[11]Elias M. Awad, Introduction to Computers in Business (Englewood Cliffs, Englewood Cliffs, N.J.: Prentice-Hall, Inc., 1977), p. 244.

FIGURE 6-1. (*cont.*)

Audio response will play an important role in future communications. Telephones will have voice recognition capabilities and audio response. Presently, some banks provide account information by telephone using voice recognition/audio response; brokerage firms quote stock prices using voice recognition/audio response.

An exciting development is a hand-held calculator with voice recognition capabilities and communication capabilities. Speaking of sophisticated, new calculators, Paula Lippin states:

> ... there is one device that utilizes the technologies of voice recognition and voice synthesization (the voice triggers digital signals [recognition] that key into a memory bank, and the machine responds by talking [synthesization] to the operator.) Another offers communication capabilities, literally turning the calculator into a 'portable office.'[12]

Conclusions

1. Audio response and voice recognition are feasible and available. The technology is suitable for practical applications in business and industry.

2. Voice recognition systems are promising for the future and have a tremendous growth potential.

3. There will be a wider range of applications in the future.

4. Newer developments suggest:

    a. Speech dependent systems will be replaced by independent systems.

    b. Continuous speech will be used for data entry in the future as equipment becomes more refined.

---

[12]Paul Lippin, Managing Editor, "The High-end Trends in Calculators," Administrative Management, LXI, no. 11 (November 1980), 53.

FIGURE 6-1. (*cont.*)

8

5. The price of voice recognition systems will decrease as the market expands.

6. Voice recognition data entry is particularly valuable when hands-off operations are desirable. Also, it is invaluable when the eyes are being used for other tasks.

7. Accuracy is improved by voice input. Also, immediate correction can be made.

8. Executives at the Electronic Technology Corporation are receptive to implementing voice recognition and would benefit by such systems.

9. The convenience of voice recognition in communications, inspecting, quality control, and inventorying would offset the added cost of implementation.

Recommendations

In light of the conclusions, one voice recognition unit should be purchased for the home office of the Electronic Technology Corporation on a trial basis. After one year, if this unit proves economically justifiable and worthwhile, it is recommended that five additional units be purchased for the branch offices of the company.

FIGURE 6–1. (*cont.*)

9

BIBLIOGRAPHY

Awad, Elias M., <u>Introduction to Computers in Business</u> (Englewood Cliffs, N.J.: Prentice-Hall, Inc., 1977.

"Computer," <u>Collier's Encyclopedia</u> (1980), 7, 113-132.

"Computer Talk: It's Here and Now Technology," <u>Infosystems</u>, 26, no. 8 (August 1979), 68.

Dock, V. Thomas and Edward Essick, <u>Principles of Business Data Processing with Basic</u>. Chicago: Science Research Associates, Inc., 1978.

Huber, Robert F., "Tell It to Your Machine," <u>Production</u>, 85, no. 6 (June 1980), 104-105.

Jennings, Lucy Mae, <u>Secretarial and Administrative Procedures</u>. Englewood Cliffs, N.J.: Prentice-Hall, Inc., 1978.

"Remote Data Entry Recognizes a Strong New Voice," <u>Data Communications</u>, 8, no. 8 (August 1979), 15.

Spencer, Donald D., <u>Data Processing: An Introduction</u>. Columbus, Ohio: Charles E. Merrill Publishing Company, 1978.

FIGURE 6-1. (*cont.*)

APPENDIX A

A computer can be programmed by voice commands. The following is a

transcript of an actual conversation between a programmer and a computer:

Machine: COMMAND =

Programmer: "Turn"

Machine: OPTION =

Programmer: "One"

Machine: Z =

Programmer: "Zero"

Machine: LEFT/RIGHT?

Programmer: "Left"

Machine: STOCK DIAM =

Programmer: "Three"

Machine: PART DIAM =

Programmer: "Two"

Machine: LENGTH OF CUT =

Programmer: "Three"[13]

---

[13]Huber, "Tell It to Your Machine," p. 102.

FIGURE 6-1. *(cont.)*

APPENDIX B

Survey of Executives

ELECTRONIC TECHNOLOGY CORPORATION
1899 Los Grandes Way
Los Angeles, California 90027

Respondent's Name _____ Address _____

Voice recognition entails the input of computer data by direct speech, tele-phone, or radio. Please place a check (✓) in the space provided.

1. Have you learned keyboarding (touch typewriting)? Yes __25%__ No __75%__

2. Do you feel comfortable entering computer data by
   keyboarding? Yes __18%__ No __82%__

3. Do you feel comfortable entering computer data by
   keypunching? Yes __18%__ No __82%__

4. Would you prefer speaking to a computer than
   "fingering" commands? Yes __98%__ No __2%__

5. Would you benefit performing functioning tasks
   by speaking to a computer while your hands are
   busy? Yes __96%__ No __4%__

6. Would you benefit performing functioning tasks
   by speaking to a computer while your eyes are
   busy? Yes __96%__ No __4%__

7. Would the convenience of computer voice recognition justify the additional cost? Yes __98%__ No __2%__

8. Please list company activities that would benefit
   most from voice recognition.

   a. Inventorying   __76%__

   b. Communication   __98%__

   c. Inspection   __87%__

   d. Quality control   __79%__

   e. Miscellaneous   __2%__

Please return this checklist to: Pamela R. Bates
Research and Development Department
Electronic Technology Corporation
1899 Los Grandes Way
Los Angeles, California 90027

Abstract

[handwritten: contains all the essentials and ideas of your report]

[handwritten: is a mini report that is usually no more than one page in length.]

[handwritten: Test question]

It may cost a considerable sum of money to reproduce and distribute a long, formal report in its entirety, especially if many copies are required. An abstract, which is a digest or abridgment of the report, can be written after the report is completed. The abstract contains the essential thoughts of the report: statement of the problem, research methods employed, findings, conclusions, and recommendations. Usually, the abstract is short, no longer than one page. It is a mini-report, containing all the essential information and ideas.

In addition to saving printing costs, a condensation saves time, for the reader need not read the entire report in detail. A very wide dissemination of the report becomes possible. *[handwritten: Saves costs and time]*

Logging the report

The completed report should be entered in a report log, if one is kept. It is necessary to inventory reports to determine if they are effective, relevant, and necessary. Some of the pertinent facts about reports that can be logged are:

- Title
- Author
- Recipient(s)
- Date

- Purpose
- Frequency of issuance
- Disposition
- Retention period

- Cost
- Value of findings
- Number of copies

Summary

There are five steps in creating an effective report:

1. planning,
2. investigating,
3. outlining,
4. writing, and
5. presentation.

This chapter concerns the final step, presentation.

The report should be attractive in appearance and correct in format. A conservatively colored cover creates a dignified image.

Quality white bond paper is preferred for manuscript reports. Most reports are typed double spaced. Page one of the report has a two-inch top margin; subsequent pages have one-inch top margins. Side margins are one inch; bottom margins are an inch or an inch and a half. If the report is bound on the side, an extra half inch is allowed for the left margin.

Lowercase Roman numerals are typed at the bottom of prefatory pages; Arabic numerals are used when typing page numbers on other pages.

The method of reproduction of reports depends on the number of copies needed. If a few copies are required, carbon copies or photocopies will suffice. If many copies are needed, stenciling or mimeographing is commonly used. Offset printing or printing is preferred when there is a large distribution and good quality copies are required.

The mode of presentation is usually relative to the formality of the report. A memo report, form, report, or letter report may be simply handed to the recipient or mailed; however, a consequential report requires a formal presentation.

An abstract containing the essential thoughts of the report can be written after the report has been completed. An abstract permits a very wide dissemination of a report at minimal cost.

The completed report should be entered in a report log. Pertinent facts about the report are records recorded in the log.

Discussion

1. Why is the format of a report so important? *Appearence is important*
2. Why should special attention be given to the mode of presentation of a report?

Study Questions

1. What color cover should be used? *Black*
2. What is the size of a typical sheet of typewriting paper used for manuscript reports? *8½ – 11"*
3. How are the prefatory pages numbered? *lower case roman numeral*
4. What margins should be used? *2" from top on first page 1" everywhere else on other pages*
5. What is an abstract of a report? *mini report, no longer then one page that essentials*
6. Explain the purpose of the report log. *Pertinent facts are recorded in log*

Activities

1. Write a report in manuscript form consisting of the following parts:

   - Title Page
   - Letter of Transmittal
   - Table of Contents
   - Summary
   - Introduction

   - Findings or Text
   - Conclusions (Optional)
   - Recommendations (Optional)
   - Appendix (Optional)

   Your instructor will designate the length of the report. Use secondary (library) and / or primary sources to obtain information. If possible, include a table or graphic illustration in the body of the report.

It is suggested that only one student write a report on a topic. The topics selected can also be the topic for an oral presentation (see Activity at the end of Chapter 14, Oral Presentations).

The following is a suggested list of topics in the field of communications:

- Theory of Human Communication
- Language and Culture in Communication
- Communication Networks—Satellite Communications
- Written Media in Business—Company Magazines, Manuals, Handbooks, Newsletters, and so on
- Interviewing
- Conferences
- Speeches
- Tape Recorders
- Videophone (Telephone-TV)
- Controlling Written Communications—Editorial Approaches, News Releases, and so on
- Live Dictation of Business Messages
- Machine Dictation of Business Messages
- Listening as a Communication Skill
- Editing Typewriters/Communicating Typewriters
- Microfilming Systems
- Word Processing
- Electronic Mail
- Employment Applications
- Plagiarism
- Computers and Communication Systems
- Telegraphic Communications
- Interoffice and Intraoffice Memoranda
- Telephone Communications
- Duplicating Communications
- Photocopying Communications
- Facsimile
- Nonverbal Communications (Body Language, and so on)
- Television Communications
- Radio Communications (Two-way, and so on)

- Audiovisual Aids Used in Communications (Overhead Projector, Movies, Slides, Posters, Filmstrips, and so on)
- Business Letters (Format, Style, and so on)
- Graphic Illustrations
- Postal Services (New Regulations, Optical Character Readers, ZIP, and so on)
- Library Resources for Business Writing
- Electronic Conferencing Systems
- The Automated Office

Three essentials of a good report that should be observed are:

- *Correct format*—refer to the model report in this chapter for an acceptable format.
- *Appropriate content*—research the topic well, using secondary and/or primary research.
- *Prescribed business writing*—objectivity, clarity, correctness, comprehensiveness, and so on.

If your instructor does not designate otherwise, include:

- A minumum of three footnotes
- A minimum of five items in the bibliography

The report must be presented in typewritten form. Since the instructor may keep the original submitted, it is suggested that a copy (carbon copy, photocopy) of the report be made. Your instructor will designate the due date.

2. After completing the report in the first activity, write a brief abstract, no longer than one page in length. The abstract should contain all the essential ideas of the report.

ACHIEVEMENT OF LEARNING GOALS

Check the appropriate boxes to determine whether you have or have not achieved the learning goals of this chapter.

I Can:

	YES	NO
1. Prepare a report for effective presentation.	☑	☐
2. Describe the proper format for formal business reports.	☑	☐
3. Understand the function and format of an abstract and a log.	☑	☐

7

Memorandums

LEARNING GOALS

1. Understand the uses of memorandums in the business world.
2. Know the format of a memorandum.
3. Write effective memorandums.

The interoffice memorandum, commonly called the "memo," is used for internal written communication. Generally, it is considered to be incorrect business procedure to use the memo form for external communications; the business letter is used primarily for this purpose. It should be noted, however, that on some occasions, business letters are sent within an organization. For example, a very important message from a manager to the president may be sent as a letter to give it special emphasis and formality.

Memos may be transmitted to different departments within a business office or to distant branches or divisions of the same company. Since the memo stays within a business, it is a more informal medium of communication than the business letter; *it has no salutation or complimentary close*. As a testimony to their informality, some memo forms state that a handwritten reply at the bottom of the form is acceptable.

Because of its ease of use, the memo form is the major means of written communication within a business. It is designed for fast, efficient, economical communication. Memos are used when it is important to have a written record of communications. Oral communication (face-to-face, telephone, and so on) can be used for less important communications. Copies of memos are usually filed; therefore, it is important that they be well written.

Test question

memorandums are used only for internal uses in the business

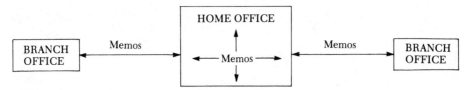

FIGURE 7-1. Flow of memorandums

Memo format

Memos can be typed on plain sheets of paper; however, in most offices memo forms are used. The forms may be in single sheets, pads or packets. Packets contain carbon paper and colored sheets for duplicate copies. Colored sheets facilitate filing.

There is an endless variety of memo styles, for most businesses design their own forms. Many companies have correspondence style manuals or stylebooks that illustrate acceptable form. Brief messages are placed on forms 8½ by 5½ inches (half sheet); longer messages are placed on forms 8½ by 11 inches (full sheet). Figures 7-2 and 7-3 show generally acceptable memo formats.

FIGURE 7-2. Memo typed on a half-sheet of plain paper

```
TO:      Tracey Witkowsky                              May 2, 19--
         Adjustment Department

FROM:    James Thayer
         Finance Department

SUBJECT: New Directive Concerning Adjustments


This is to inform you that, starting on May 15, 19--, no
cash will be refunded to customers for returns made
after two weeks (fourteen days) from the purchase date.

                              J. T.


nk
cc  John Villeux
```

```
┌──────────────────────────────────────────────────────────────────────┐
│                     REED AND SCOTT CORPORATION                         │
│                              MEMO                                      │
│                                                                        │
│  TO  Candice Chase, Personnel        DATE  January 8, 19—              │
│                                                                        │
│  FR  Jayne Calabrese, President                                        │
│                                                                        │
│  RE  New Employees                                                     │
│                                                                        │
│                                                                        │
│      The following people were employed January 1, 19--:              │
│                                                                        │
│                Patricia Christy, Advertising                           │
│                Angelina DeMeo, Sales                                   │
│                Stephen Goldstein, Accounting                           │
│                Karen Hunter, Word Processing                           │
│                Jean Kendall, Accounting                                │
│                David Hilliard, Advertising                             │
│                                                                        │
│                          J. C.                                         │
│                                                                        │
│      ja                                                                │
│                                                                        │
└──────────────────────────────────────────────────────────────────────┘
```

FIGURE 7–3. Printed memo form

Since memos stay within a company, expensive bond paper is not necessary. To save time and thus to expedite the memo-writing process, multiple-copy memo forms and packets are commonly used in the business office. Also convenient to use are preassembled sets of memo forms containing carbon tissues (snap-out forms) or carbonless forms using NCR (No Carbon Required) paper. NCR paper contains a dye that forms images under pressure from a pen or typewriter.

Writing style

Because memos are informal, conversational language is used. Personal titles (Mr., Mrs., Miss, Ms., Dr.) are usually omitted after the guide words TO and FROM.

Generally, memos are initialled by the author; however, important memos are signed. The initials appear at the bottom of the message or next to the senders typed name on the "FROM" line.

FROM: Nathan Tyler *nt*

In some offices, informal reports as well as routine correspondence are typed in memo style.

FIGURE 7-4. Informal note *very brief*

FROM THE DESK OF
REBECCA LYNN

April 2, 19--

Karen,

Please add an item to the agenda for the April 9 meeting--

"8. A report of current TV advertising by Eric Ostrander."

See you at the meeting!

Becky

FIGURE 7-5. Special attachment form

Data Automation, Inc.

TO: *Tom Edwards*

FROM: *Judy Walsh*

DATE: *May 5*

☑ TYPE ON PLAIN PAPER

☐ PHOTOCOPY

☐ TYPE ON LETTERHEAD
      STATIONARY

3 Carbon Copies
1 Enclosure

INTEROFFICE ENVELOPES

Some offices save considerable sums of money by using special interoffice envelopes. The envelopes illustrated in Figures 7-6 and 7-7 can be used many times, rather than once!

The name of the recipient is crossed out and the same envelope is used again. The interoffice memorandum envelope is usually colored to distinguish it from regular business letters. This facilitates sorting and handling of envelopes in the mail room.

FIGURE 7-6. Interdepartmental reusable envelope, letter size

INTERDEPARTMENT MAIL
Reusable Envelope

INSTRUCTIONS
1. CROSS OFF all previous addresses and names.
2. ENTER NEW address and name as indicated.
3. SPELL OUT name of agency. Don't use initials.
4. DON'T OVERLOAD. Use large Interdepartment Envelope.
5. DON'T SEAL, unless confidential. Tuck flap in.
6. IF CONFIDENTIAL, write your name and address in space provided on flap, and seal with tape.

NAME
Give return address ONLY if envelope is to be sealed.

Do NOT seal this envelope unless confidential material is enclosed

KREVOLIN   NATHAN
BUSINESS EDUCATION   176   SS

AGENCY		
UNIT &/OR ADDRESS		
NAME		Att.

AGENCY		
UNIT &/OR ADDRESS		
NAME		Att.

AGENCY		
UNIT &/OR ADDRESS		
NAME		Att.

AGENCY		
UNIT &/OR ADDRESS		
NAME		Att.

AGENCY		
UNIT &/OR ADDRESS		
NAME		Att.

AGENCY		
UNIT &/OR ADDRESS		
NAME		Att.

FIGURE 7–7. Interdepartmental reusable envelope, 9 by 12

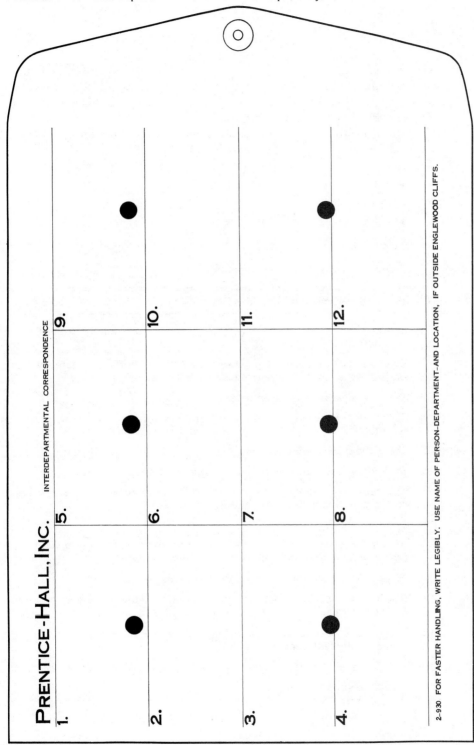

Summary

The interoffice memorandum or memo is used for internal written communications. Since the memo stays within a business, it is a more informal medium of communication than the business letter. The memo is designed for fast, efficient, economical communication.

In most offices memo forms are used. There is an endless variety of memo styles; however, most memos contain four guide words:

- To:
- From:
- Subject:
- Date:

FIGURE 7–8. Memo writing guides

---

1. Follow the format, printed or typewritten, approved by your place of employment.

2. Complete all the essential parts of the memorandum form: date, to, from, subject, department, telephone extension, and so on.

3. Keep the message simple and clear.

4. Generally, depending on the recipient, an informal style of writing is acceptable.

5. Check the message for accuracy.

6. File a copy of the memorandum for future reference.

7. To expedite communications, it is permissible in some offices to reply in handwriting directly on the memorandum received.

8. Enumerate listings.

9. The tone of the memo is generally informal. When writing to a superior, a greater degree of formality may be desirable.

10. Outline form is acceptable for some memo messages.

11. If the message is routine, sign or type your initials. If the message is important, sign your name.

12. Plain paper is used for continuing pages when a memo is more than one page in length. Staple the sheets together.

13. Omit personal titles for most informal communications (Mr., Mrs., Miss, Ms., Dr.).

In addition to memos, informal notes and specially printed forms are also used to expedite interoffice communication.

Because of the informal tone of memos, conversational language is used. Personal titles are usually omitted after the guide words TO and FROM. Most memos are initialled by the author; however, important memos are signed.

In some offices, informal reports as well as routine correspondence are typed in memo style. Special interoffice envelopes are used for the distribution of memos.

To speed up communications, it is permissible in some offices to reply in handwriting directly on the memo received. The outline form is acceptable for some memo messages.

Discussion

1. Explain the purposes of memorandums in business organizations. *fast, efficient, economical uses*
2. Why is there an infinite variety of memo styles and forms in use?

Study questions

1. Differentiate between a memorandum and a letter. *memorandums are more informal and briefer*
2. What are the essential guide words that appear on memo forms? *To, from date, subject*
3. Describe the style of writing used when composing memorandums. *informal style of writing Conversational language is used*

Activities

1. Write a memo to Jason Foster in the Supply Department. List supplies you need (pencils, bond paper, pads, etc.).

2. Write a memo to Susan Wycoski in the Advertising Department. Explain your ideas for Christmas advertising of perfume. Cite the media to be used (radio, TV, newspapers, etc.) and the advantages of each.

3. Write a memo to Mitch Rosenberg in the Accounting Department. Explain that he is to write a section of the corporate annual report. Give details on the topics he is to write about.

4. Write a memo to Clay Reed who works in the Traffic Department. Tell him about a meeting on parking problems on April 25. List some of the parking problems to be discussed at the meeting.

5. Write a memo to Thomas Pringle who works in the Design Department. Inform him that a more compact food processor is needed.

Customers have been complaining that there is not enough counter space for the bulky food processor being manufactured.

ACHIEVEMENT OF LEARNING GOALS

Check the appropriate boxes to determine whether you have or have not achieved the learning goals of this chapter.

I Can:

	YES	NO
1. Understand the uses of memorandums in the business world.	☑	☐
2. Explain the format of a memorandum.	☑	☐
3. Write effective memorandums.	☑	☐

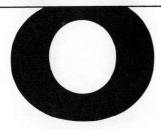

Business Letters

1. Understand the uses of business letters.
2. Know the stationery used for business correspondence.
3. State the component parts of a business letter.
4. Comprehend the basic punctuation patterns used in business letters.
5. Recognize the four basic letter styles.
6. Write a letter in the Administrative Management Society (AMS) style.
7. Formulate correct letter placement.
8. Ascertain the executive's roll in the letter writing process.
9. Implement new Postal Service regulations applying to business letters.

The business letter is the major form of external written communication in the business world. It provides a tangible record of communications, permits the writer to carefully formulate thoughts, and facilitates communications over long distances.

Emphasis in the past has been placed on the content of business letters; however, in light of soaring costs (estimates range from $6 to $13 to produce a one-page medium length letter), it is equally imperative that business administrators also pay close attention to the process of managing these communications. Word processing techniques, described in Chapter 21, expedite the efficient and rapid handling of business letters. This chapter, however, concerns the format or general make-up of business letters. The executive should know what constitutes an effective, acceptable business letter.

Appearance

A REFLECTION OF THE AUTHOR

A business letter is an extension of the author. (*Note.* The author is also called the "dictator," "principal," "word originator," or "writer." The business letter represents the absent communicator, for the letter is the total substance of the writer before the reader. Therefore, the letter should create a positive impression by portraying a perfect image. The business letter should be thought of as a qualitative instrument of expression.

THE AUTHOR'S RESPONSIBILITY

The business executive cannot slough off responsibility and blame the secretary for errors in format, spelling, grammar, and so on. The principal—the person who signs the letter—is intentionally or unintentionally being evaluated by the quality and appearance of the letter. Even in situations where routine correspondence may go out under the signature of a competent secretary, the content and quality of the communication is still the ultimate responsibility of the administrator. Model letters or letter guides should be made available for secretaries delegated letter-writing tasks. The executive should constantly monitor these model letters or guides to be sure they are current and valid.

Stationery — letter head stationary

To create a distinctive visual impression, most business letters are typed on attractive, high-quality *letterhead stationery*. The letterhead usually includes the company name, address, and telephone number. It may, however, contain additional information, such as company products or services, a slogan, cable address, teletypewriter code, the company logo, and so on. The use of color, fine printing (engraving in some instances), stylized letters and artwork, and pictures create a distinctive, prestigious image of the company.

A DISTINCTIVE LETTERHEAD

The letterhead is usually printed, embossed, lithographed, or engraved at the top of the paper; however, it may appear elsewhere (either side or bottom) to create a distinctive impression. (See Figure 8–1.)

Executive Letterhead. An important officer of a company may have executive letterhead stationery that includes the name, title, and telephone extension, as well as the company name and address. Executive letterhead stationery is usually of better quality than the kind used for general communications. (See Figure 8–2.)

If a letter is more than one page in length, succeeding pages do not have an imprinted letterhead. These plain sheets of paper match identically the size and quality of the first page (letterhead).

The company name and address are preprinted on an envelope of matching quality. This is the *return address.* (See Figure 8–3.)

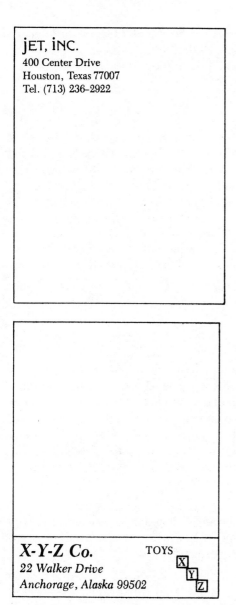

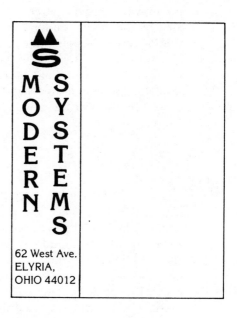

jET, iNC.
400 Center Drive
Houston, Texas 77007
Tel. (713) 236–2922

M O D E R N   S Y S T E M S
62 West Ave.
ELYRIA,
OHIO 44012

X-Y-Z Co.   TOYS
22 Walker Drive   X
Anchorage, Alaska 99502   Y Z

FIGURE 8–1. Sample business letterheads

PAPER STYLES   *Bond paper*

To further enhance the image of the company, *bond paper* is preferred. Bond paper is a heavier weight (16, 20 or 24 pounds) and better quality (usually 25 percent cotton fiber content) than less expensive paper. Top executives may

Test question

FIGURE 8-2. Executive letterhead stationery

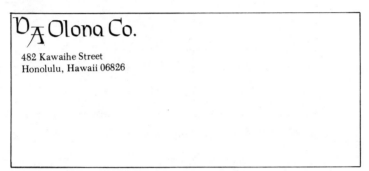

FIGURE 8-3. Envelope with imprinted return address

use paper that is entirely composed of cotton fibers. When held up to a light, a watermark can be seen on quality bond paper. The watermark consists of an emblem or words.

Special smooth finishes on some bond papers permit easy erasing with a soft pencil eraser. A distinct disadvantage of these *"easy-erase" papers* is that they smudge easily.

Copy Making. Onionskin paper, a thin, tissue-like paper, is used when making carbon copies. This lightweight stationery makes it possible to insert carbon paper or carbon packs (Figure 8-4) into the typewriter and ensures more legible copies. Also, the lighter paper saves storage space and mailing costs. Carbon paper is coated with carbon on one side. The impact of the typewriter keys or element transfers the image of the keys struck to the onionskin paper.

When responding to a letter, a copy of the reply can be typed on the back of the original letter received. This procedure saves space, paper, and time, and ensures that the reply stays with the original.

To facilitate the distribution of carbon copies, different colored sheets of onionskin paper may be used by a company. Also, the word "COPY" may be printed on onionskin paper.

Carbonless paper packs may be used by a company; however, they are relatively expensive. In some companies, photocopies are made instead of

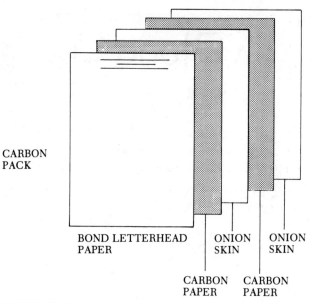

CARBON
PACK

BOND LETTERHEAD   ONION   ONION
PAPER   SKIN   SKIN

CARBON   CARBON
PAPER   PAPER

FIGURE 8-4. Carbon pack

WORD
EXPEDITORS, INC.
20 Mountain Circle
Akron, Ohio 44306

FIGURE 8-5. Large or legal envelope

carbon copies. Some manufacturers of copying machines contend it is less expensive to make photocopies than to type carbon copies. (Please refer to Chapter 23 on Reprographics.) Multiple carbon copies may require a great deal of handling, especially if many carbon copies are made. Correcting errors can be a long, tedious task. Correcting paper, correcting typewriter ribbons, correction fluid and erasers are commonly used to eliminate typing "goofs." Using photocopying equipment, only a corrected original copy is necessary.

ENVELOPES   *two Standard sizes*   *Legal, Commercial*

Envelopes are usually in two standard sizes, large or legal (9½ by 4⅛ inches) and small or commercial (6½ by 3⅝ inches). (See Figures 8–5 and 8–6.)

COMMUNICATIONS, INC.
Las Palmas Street
San Juan, Puerto Rico 00921

FIGURE 8–6.   Small or commercial envelope

One sheet of paper can be mailed in either a large or small envelope. However, if two or more sheets are to be mailed in one envelope, use the large envelope only.

Large or small envelopes can be *window envelopes*, that is, have a clear, transparent opening for the address of the correspondent (the inside address on the letter) to be read. (See Figure 8–7.)

Window envelopes save time, since it is unnecessary to type the correspondent's address on the envelope. Also, they prevent errors, such as placing the letter in the wrong envelope.

TYPE

Matching Type and Paper.   Most frequently, white paper and black type are used; however, some companies prefer lightly tinted paper with matching colored type. For example, light beige paper may be used with brown type or

FIGURE 8-7. Window envelope

pale green paper with dark green type. Typewriter ribbons can be purchased in a variety of colors, such as blue, brown, green, and red.

Visual Style. A high-echelon executive can create a distinctive visual image by:

- Using an electric typewriter. The even impact of keys gives uniform shading to typewritten letters.
- Typing on one side of the paper only.
- Using a Mylar ribbon. This ribbon is used only once; however, the impressions are sharp, as though they came off a printing press. (*Note.* A Mylar ribbon is coated on one side. Care should be taken in discarding a one-time use Mylar ribbon. If confidential information were typed, a discarded film ribbon can be easily read!)
- Using an executive typewriter with proportional spacing and justifying capabilities. (*Note.* Editing typewriters perform this function.)
- Using a typewriter with interchangeable elements if varied type styles are needed.

STATIONERY SIZES   8½ - 11" - half of this is Baronial

Most stationery for typewriting correspondence in the business world is 8½ by 11 inches. This is called *standard stationery* (also known as "regular" or "business stationery"). Other stationery sizes in use are:

Baronial	5½ by 8½ inches = half of stationery
Executive	7¼ by 10½ inches
Monarch	7½ by 10 inches

138

Baronial 5½/8½   Government (8 by 10½)
Executive 7½/10   Legal (8½ by 13 or 14)
Monarch 7¼/10½

| Government | 8 by 10½ inches |
| Legal | 8½ by 13 or 14 inches — *must know this* |

See Figure 8–8 for proportionate sizes.

Test question

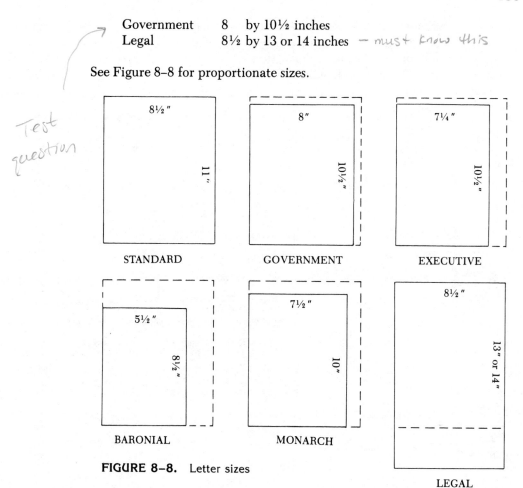

FIGURE 8–8. Letter sizes

Standard stationery is widely used in the business world. Baronial stationery, half the size of standard stationery, is generally used for brief messages; monarch and executive stationery are used by top echelon officers of a company. As the title implies, government stationery is used by governmental agencies. Legal stationery, in the main, is used for legal documents.

Letter parts

PROPER LAYOUT

The layout of a business letter is important, for it contributes to proper appearance. Often, the style used is dictated by the correspondence manual of a company.[1] If company policy does not dictate letter style, it is at the discretion of the executive; therefore, it is essential that the executive be familiar with the component parts of a letter, acceptable punctuation patterns, and basic styles.

Letterhead	**J. PORTER & SONS**
Date	21 Commerce Street
File Number	May 4, 19-- Lansing, Michigan 48906
Inside Address	File X239
	Electronic Communications, Inc.
	1500 Grande Vista Avenue
Attention Line	Los Angeles, California 90032
Salutation	Attention of Mr. Roberto Valenti
Subject Line	Gentlemen:
Body (Message)	SUBJECT: ADJUSTMENT
	The Alpha RX372 desk top printing calculator sent to us on April 24 is defective. The roll paper does not feed automatically as advertised.
	Specifically, make the following adjustment: Send to us a new Alpha RX327 desk top printing calculator.
	Please send directions for returning the defective calculator.
Complimentary Closing	An immediate adjustment would be very much appreciated.
Company Name	Yours truly,
Signature	JONATHAN PORTER & SONS
Typed Name Identification	*Forrest L. Porter*
	Forrest L. Porter
Reference Initials	Managing Director
Enclosure Notation	alk
Carbon Copy Notation	Enclosure
Postscript	cc Ms. Jennifer Springer
	Enclosed is a copy of the order form.
Initials (a postscript should be initialed)	F.L.P.

FIGURE 8–9.   Parts of a business letter

[1]Many companies have detailed correspondence manuals that guide the writer in letter style, envelope usage, paper size, layout, and so on.

A typical business letter consists of many component parts. (See Figure 8 – 9 .)

Punctuation patterns   *He went over this in class*

Business letters are punctuated as follows:

1. *Standard Punctuation*. When standard punctuation is used, a colon is typed after the salutation and a comma follows the complimentary closing. Standard punctuation is widely used in the business world.
2. *Open Punctuation*. Open punctuation is preferred by some executives, since it speeds up the typing of business letters. In open punctuation, no marks of punctuation appear after the salutation and complimentary closing.
3. *Closed Punctuation*. Closed punctuation is rarely used in the United Sates; however, it does appear in letters from some foreign correspondents. In closed punctuation, each line of the letter, except the message, ends in a mark of punctuation.

Styles of letters

There are three basic letter styles: *Extreme Block   Block   Semi Block*

1. *Extreme Block*. This is a very popular style in the business world, for it is easy to type and helps avoid placement errors. All lines begin at the left margin. Open punctuation is generally used when typing extreme blocked style. This style is also called "full block style."
2. *Semiblock*. The semiblocked letter is set up in the conventional style; it is the style taught to you by your English teachers. The date is typed at the center point or justified (made even) with the right margin. Paragraphs in the body of the letter are indented. The closing section of the letter (complimentary closing, writer's name and identification) start at the center point. Standard punctuation is generally used when typing semiblocked letters.
3. *Block*. The blocked letter is similar to the semiblocked style with one major exception: paragraphs are blocked, not indented. The blocked letter is usually typed with standard punctuation.

AMS LETTER FORMAT

The Administrative Management Society (AMS) has suggested a simplified letter format:

STANDARD

use either Standard or Open

OPEN

CLOSED

FIGURE 8–10. Punctuation forms

1. Full block style
2. Open punctuation
3. No salutation
4. Enumerated paragraphs
5. No complimentary close

A subject line replaces the salutation. Although easy to type, a letter without a salutation and complimentary close tends to be cold and unfriendly. Most executives prefer more cordiality in their correspondence.

FIGURE 8–11. Extreme block or full block style

easy to type

Everything on left hand side

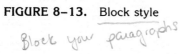

FIGURE 8–13. Block style

Block your paragraphs

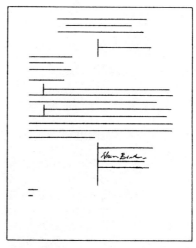

FIGURE 8–12. Semiblock style

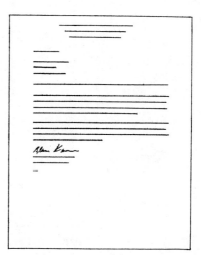

FIGURE 8–14. AMS Simplified style

American Management Society very informal

143

FIGURE 8–15. Formal or official style

The formal or official letter style is used when writing to prominent individuals, such as a senator, college president, or governor. The inside address is typed below the signature section of the letter. No reference symbols are typed on the letter.

LETTER PLACEMENT

A letter should be framed on the paper with equal margins on the sides and on the top and bottom.

Test question maybe?

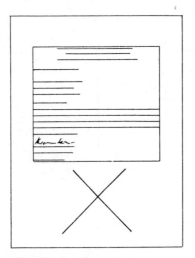

FIGURE 8–16a. Bad placement

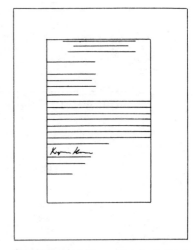

FIGURE 8–16b. Good placement

144

The competent secretary knows specifically the correct placement of a letter. Side margins are relative to the length of the message—a short letter should have wide margins; conversely, a long letter should have narrow margins. (See Table 8–1.)

TABLE 8–1. Margin guide for letters

		Pica	Elite
Short	up to 99 words	22–67	25–80
Average	100–200 words	17–72	20–85
Long	201 + words	12–77	15–90

The date is usually typed about 2½ inches from the top edge of the paper (on line 15); the inside address is usually typed a bit more than a half inch below (five lines below the date). Usually, the message of a short, average, or long letter is single spaced; however, a very brief message can be double spaced. The executive should be able to scan a letter for acceptable appearance.

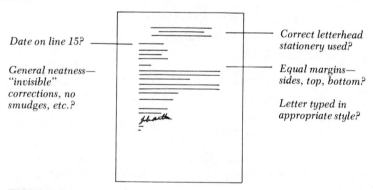

FIGURE 8–17

Subsequent pages of a letter (Page 2, etc.) should have the same margins that a long letter has. The page should have a brief heading consisting of the following:

- The name of the correspondent
- The page number
- The date

The format is usually as shown in Figure 8–18. Another acceptable heading is shown in Figure 8–19.

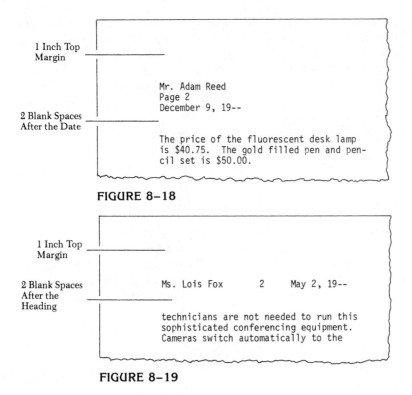

1 Inch Top
Margin

2 Blank Spaces
After the Date

```
Mr. Adam Reed
Page 2
December 9, 19--

The price of the fluorescent desk lamp
is $40.75.  The gold filled pen and pen-
cil set is $50.00.
```

FIGURE 8–18

1 Inch Top
Margin

2 Blank Spaces
After the
Heading

```
Ms. Lois Fox        2      May 2, 19--

technicians are not needed to run this
sophisticated conferencing equipment.
Cameras switch automatically to the
```

FIGURE 8–19

The executive's role

<u>DISPATCHER OF IDEAS</u>

In the letter writing process, the executive is a dispatcher of ideas. Five terms are used to identify the person who formulates the message:

Test question

- Author
- Dictator — *old fashion term*
- Principal — *term most widely used*
- Word originator
- Writer — *old fashion term*

The terms "author," "principal," and "word originator" are used primarily in offices with word processing systems. The terms "dictator" and "writer" are used in traditional office systems.

Communications Cycle. The communicator is involved in five steps:

146

Step 1. The message is *formulated* mentally.

Step 2. The message is *dictated* to a person or to a machine.

Step 3. The message is *translated* into written form, usually type-written.

Step 4. The message is *verified* for accuracy, the appearance is judged, and, if acceptable, signed.

Step 5. The message is *transmitted* to the recipient.

If the communicator has been effective, the message will be clear and understandable, and feedback will result.

The process is diagrammed in Figure 8–20.

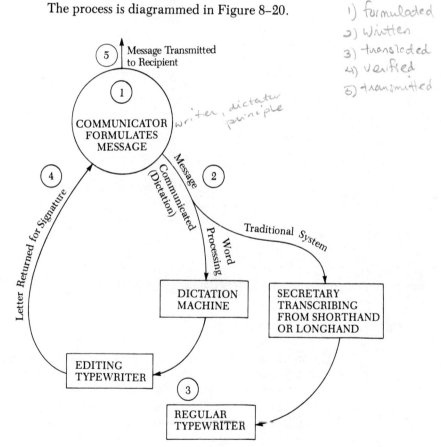

FIGURE 8–20. Five-step communications cycle

Cycle Modifications. There are modifications of the communications cycle. For example, the communicator in a traditional system may record the message on a dictation machine and have a secretary in a typing center transcribe the message, or the message can be dictated directly to a typist—no secretary taking dictation or dictation machine is involved.

It is predicted that by the end of the decade, voice operated terminals will be in general use. The principal will speak to a computerized dictation machine which will convert the sounds to typewritten messages. The letter writing process of the future is diagrammed in Figure 8–21.

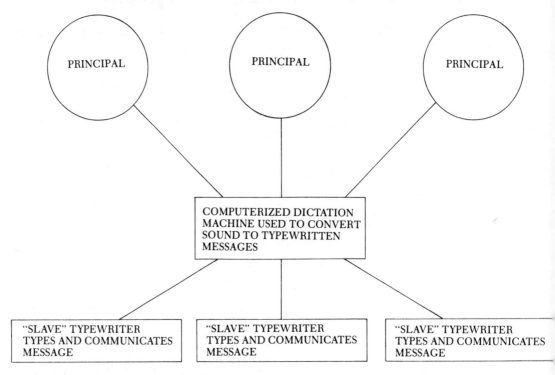

FIGURE 8–21. Letter writing for the future

The model report in Chapter 6 gives a detailed statement of voice communications with computers, voice entry and response.

The letter should be proofread carefully by the secretary or a proofreader before it is submitted for signature. The alert executive will check the letter carefully for the following before signing:

Accuracy

Completeness

Spelling, grammar, punctuation, and so on

Content

Format

Appearance

Placement

Style

The signature should be in ink or ball point pen. If a secretary has the authority to sign an executive's name, it should be initialed as follows:

Jose M. Ramos
l.c.k.

If the document fails to meet the criteria for acceptance, it should be returned for retyping.

New Postal Service regulations

Since business letter format is structured to some extent by the United States Postal Service, it is necessary to examine some of the new postal regulations.

OCR AND BAR CODE REQUIREMENTS

The Postal Service has purchased *Optical Character Recognition* (OCR) equipment and bar code readers to expedite the sorting of mail. OCRs "read" envelope addresses from the bottom upward, right to left. The OCRs are so "smart," that they know if the ZIP Code and address are correct. For example, ZIP Code numbers in Wisconsin begin with 5. If a letter addressed to Madison, Wisconsin has a ZIP Code beginning with 9, the OCR would have the envelope sorted by a person!

ZIP CODE

When you use ZIP Code, your mail is processed by high-speed sorting equipment. If ZIP Code is not used, your letter is manually sorted and may be delayed.

The letterhead on stationery (letter and envelope) should contain the ZIP Code number. Also, the inside address of the letter should contain the ZIP Code of the addressee.

Nine-Digit ZIP Code. To further improve sorting efficiency, the Postal Service has expanded some ZIP Codes from five to nine digits. This will further automate the handling of mail and lower costs of processing mail. The Postal Service is using the term "ZIP plus four" to emphasize the new nine-digit code.

In addition to ZIP Code numbers, optical character recognition equipment can "read" addresses; therefore, the Postal Service suggests specific two-letter state name abbreviations (Table 8–2).

TABLE 8–2. Two-letter state name abbreviations

Alabama	AL	Montana	MT
Alaska	AK	Nebraska	NE
Arizona	AZ	Nevada	NV
Arkansas	AR	New Hampshire	NH
American Samoa	AS	New Jersey	NJ
California	CA	New Mexico	NM
Canal Zone	CZ	New York	NY
Colorado	CO	North Carolina	NC
Connecticut	CT	North Dakota	ND
Delaware	DE	Ohio	OH
District of Columbia	DC	Oklahoma	OK
Florida	FL	Oregon	OR
Georgia	GA	Pennsylvania	PA
Guam	GU	Puerto Rico	PR
Hawaii	HI	Rhode Island	RI
Idaho	ID	South Carolina	SC
Illinois	IL	South Dakota	SD
Indiana	IN	Tennessee	TN
Iowa	IA	Trust Territories	TT
Kansas	KS	Texas	TX
Kentucky	KY	Utah	UT
Louisiana	LA	Vermont	VT
Maine	ME	Virginia	VA
Maryland	MD	Virgin Islands	VI
Massachusetts	MA	Washington	WA
Michigan	MI	West Virginia	WV
Minnesota	MN	Wisconsin	WI
Mississippi	MS	Wyoming	WY
Missouri	MO		

Source: United States Postal Service, Mailers Guide, Pub. 19, January 1978, p. 39.

PROHIBITIONS

The United States Postal Service has established the following minimal physical dimensions for all mail.

Length	5 inches
Height	3½ inches
Thickness	.007 inch
Aspect Ratio	Must be rectangular

ENVELOPES

The envelope contains the address of the correspondent, the person to whom the letter is going. The sender's address is usually preprinted or typed in the upper left corner.

Since Optical Character Recognition equipment "reads" the address of the person to whom the letter is going, the address must follow a prescribed format and be in the "read zone." The following procedures are suggested by the Postal Service:

1. The correspondent's address should be in the lower left portion of the envelope. The read zone is 2½-inches high, 8 inches long. It starts 1 inch from the left margin and ½ inch from the bottom of the envelope.

2. The address should be typed in block style (even at the left), single spaced, and in all capital letters. Punctuation is not needed.

3. Leave one space between the state and ZIP Code number.

4. On-arrival directions, such as "Personal" and "Confidential," are typed below the return address; postal services, such as "Special Delivery" and "Registered" are typed under the stamp. As stated previously, the OCR scans lines from the bottom of the envelope upward. If special directions were placed in the lower left corner (which is part of the OCR read zone), the OCR would reject the envelope and it would have to be sorted by hand. This delay could be costly if the correspondence requires rapid delivery. Figure 8–22 illustrates proper placement.

FIGURE 8–22. Addressed envelope

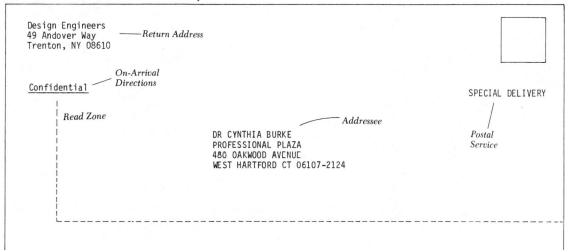

Summary

The business letter is the major form of external written communication in the business world. It provides a tangible record of communications.

In light of soaring costs ($6 to $13 to produce a one-page medium length letter), word processing techniques have been implemented to expedite the efficient and rapid handling of business letters.

A business letter is an "extension" of the author who is intentionally or unintentionally being evaluated by the quality and appearance of the letter.

To create a distinctive visual impression, most business letters are typed on attractive, high-quality letterhead stationery. Onionskin paper is used when making carbon copies.

Envelopes are usually in two standard sizes, large (or legal) and small (or commercial).

There are six basic stationery sizes: standard, baronial, executive, monarch, government, and legal. Most business stationery is standard (8½ by 11 inches).

A business letter may contain some or all of the following parts:

- Letterhead
- Date
- File number
- Inside address
- Attention line
- Salutation
- Subject line
- Body or message
- Complimentary closing
- Company name
- Signature
- Typed name
- Identification
- Reference initials
- Enclosure notation
- Carbon copy notation
- Postscript

The punctuation patterns of letters vary. Standard and open punctuation patterns are commonly used; closed punctuation is rare.

There are four basic letter styles: extreme block, semiblock, block, and indented. The Administrative Management Society has suggested a simplified letter format that incorporates full block style. This letter eliminates the salutation and complimentary close. Also, open punctuation is used.

The formal or official letter style is used when writing to prominent individuals. The inside address is typed below the signature section of the letter.

Ideally, a letter should be framed on the paper with equal side and top and bottom margins.

There are five terms used to identify the person who formulates the message: author, dictator, principal, word originator, and writer.

The communicator is involved in five steps: message formulation, message dictation, translation into written form, message verification, and message transmission.

Since business letter format is structured to some extent by rulings of the United States Postal Service, the competent communicator must be cognizant of new postal regulations pertaining to ZIP Coding, two-letter state abbreviations, physical dimensions of mail, envelopes, and the like.

Discussion

1. Why is the appearance and quality of business letters so important?
2. Who is responsible ultimately for the quality of a letter (format, spelling, grammar, etc.)? Is it the secretary or the principal? *principal*

Study questions

1. What is the major form of external written communication in the business world? *Business letter*
2. What is the major reason for writing letters in the business world? *Tangible form of commun.*
3. How much does it cost to produce a business letter? *6 - 13 dollars*
4. What is letterhead stationery? *Includes name, address, tele #.*
5. What is bond paper? *Quality paper cotton paper*
6. When is onionskin paper used? *When making carbon copies!*
7. Why are carbonless paper packs not used frequently? *Expensive, tedious to correct*
8. Why are window envelopes used? *faster, efficient use of time*
9. List the names of six stationery sizes. *Standard, Binomial, Government, Monarch Legal, and Executive* *← Standard Executive Monarch Binomial Govert Legal*
10. List seventeen parts of a business letter.
11. List the three punctuation patterns. *Open, Closed, Standard*
12. What are the four basic letter styles? *Extreme block, semiblock, and block and indented*
13. How does the AMS simplified letter differ from most letters? *full-block style*

14. Glancing at a letter, how can good placement be judged? *If it is framed*
15. List the five terms used to identify the person who formulates the business letter. *Author, dictator, writer, principle, and originator*
16. Why should ZIP Code be used? *Expedite mail delivery*

Activity

1. Obtain a real business letter. Identify in writing (directly in the margin of the letter) the component parts (letterhead, date, inside address, and the like). If you cannot locate a business letter, compose your own (similar to the one illustrated in this chapter) and identify the component parts in the side margin.

ACHIEVEMENT OF LEARNING GOALS

Check the appropriate boxes to determine whether you have or have not achieved the learning goals of this chapter.

I Can:

	YES	NO
1. Understand the uses of business letters.	☐	☐
2. Judge the stationery to be used for business correspondence.	☐	☐
3. State the component parts of a business letter.	☐	☐
4. Comprehend the basic punctuation patterns used in business letters.	☐	☐
5. Recognize the four basic letter styles.	☐	☐
6. Write a letter in the Administrative Management (AMS) style.	☐	☐
7. Formulate correct letter placement.	☐	☐
8. Ascertain the executive's roll in the letter writing process.	☐	☐
9. Implement new postal service regulations applying to business letters.	☐	☐

If any of your responses were "no," it is suggested that you review pertinent chapter parts.

Composing
Business Letters

LEARNING GOALS

1. To compose effective business letters.
2. To understand basic methods of responding to correspondence.

General guidelines

The business letter is used primarily to transmit ideas, thoughts, and information outside the company; however, some business letters stay within the organization. The letters that remain within the business are usually formal letters to individuals at higher echelons, for example, a letter from a department manager to the president. In some situations, letters to individuals at lower echelons are sent. A letter of commendation is a good example. It should be noted that most internal correspondence uses the memorandum format.

Certain techniques or procedures will assist in the creative process. The following steps in composing business letters are suggested:

1. *Visualization*—Try to visualize the recipient of the letter. The letter should be geared to the personality, educational level, viewpoint, and temperament of the reader.

2. *Formulation*—Formulate your thoughts. Determine what function the letter will fulfill: Is it to inquire, to inform, to persuade? What action do you want the recipient of the letter to take?

3. *Gathering Pertinent Information*—If the letter is technical or involved, it may entail a study of previous correspondence, research,

and the gathering of enclosures. Jot down pertinent information or ideas to be conveyed.

4. _Design or Planning_—Outline the basic message to be conveyed. Determine an appropriate sequence of ideas. The organization of a business letter is determined by the kind of message being conveyed. For example, a letter refusing a request may start with an explanation, then proceed to an implied refusal, and terminate with a cordial closing. An effective organizational plan or outline may be mental or written, whatever best suits the author. Some executives prefer to write brief notes on a sheet of paper or in the margins of letters that are being answered.

The composition of business letters is a highly specialized form of writing. Expertise in basic English skills (grammar, vocabulary, mechanics, spelling, sentence structure) is important if communication is to be precise and effective. Here are some basic rules for writing business letters:

1. The tone of the letter should be conversational, natural, pleasant, and positive.
2. Psychology should be used to ensure that the reader will react to the correspondence in the manner expected.
3. Use the "you" attitude rather than the "I," "we," or "my" attitude.
4. Be courteous and considerate.
5. Business letters should be attractive, free from errors, and correct in content and format.
6. Write clearly, concisely, and positively. Whenever possible, use concrete words. Try to avoid rambling, incoherent, negative passages.

Due to the large volume of correspondence received in the modern business office, three basic methods of response have evolved:

1. Form letters ← _preprinted in advance_
2. Guide letters ←
3. Individual letters _

3 basic responses have evolved.

Form letters

ROUTINE CORRESPONDENCE

Form letters are printed in volume and are commonly used for the expeditious handling of routine correspondence, such as letters of acknowledgment, collection letters, credit letters, and order letters. For example, an insurance

```
Your purchase of stock has been registered in CNG books and we welcome
your participation in our future.  Please note the enclosed postage-paid
questionnaire postcard asking how you became interested in CNG stock and
the name of the broker who sold it to you.  This information will help
us to maintain effective communication programs which will benefit both
CNG and its stockholders.

We will keep you fully informed about our operations.  In addition to
the annual report, you will receive quarterly reports and usually a
special letter to stockholders included with the dividend payment.

Dividends are paid in March, June, September and December.  The announced
dividend increase to be paid in December 1981 of 55 cents per share, an
increase of 10 cents quarterly per share, makes this the 22nd consecutive
year of increased dividend payments.  We have paid dividends without
interruption for 130 years, longer than any other utility listed on the
New York Stock Exchange.  Our common stock ticker symbol is "CNG", and
it is listed in the Exchange transactions in newspapers as "CnnNG".

CNG, founded in 1848, serves 122,000 gas customers in the Hartford-New
Britain area and in Greenwich.  Also, we provide a central steam and
chilled water climate control service and distribute propane.

Our supply position has been traditionally good.  We emphasize modern
management techniques and innovation, work aggressively to obtain
adequate rates of return and participate fully in national programs for
the advancement of the gas industry.

We welcome your comments at any time or a visit by you to CNG.

Sincerely,
```

FIGURE 9–1. Form letter regarding purchase of stock
(Courtesy of Connecticut Natural Gas Corporation)

company may receive numerous requests each week about premium payments. A standard reply letter can answer this anticipated question. Thousands of copies of a letter can be printed in advance, or a printed letter with checkoff items can be used. Some form letters have blank spaces for the insertion of additional information.

Editing Typewriters. When it is necessary to give the impression of a specially typewritten letter, not a mass-produced letter, editing typewriters can be used. The message is stored in the memory of the typewriter (or on disk), and it is typed by pressing a button. (See Chapter 21 for more information about editing typewriters.) Editing typewriters type at speeds ranging from 15 characters per second to over 600 words a minute. Since support personnel are capable of handling form letters, the executive is "emancipated" from a routine task.

Guide letters

PARAGRAPH SELECTION

A guide letter contains paragraphs that are prepared and numbered in advance. Paragraphs are combined to facilitate responding to standard inquiries. The typist merely types the paragraphs numbered in the sequence indicated by the principal. The principal might say, "Please send 13, 18, 23, 54, and 67 to Mr. Jones." Editing typewriters facilitate the typing of guide letters

CONNECTICUT NATURAL GAS CORPORATION • P.O. BOX 1500 • HARTFORD, CONN. 06101 • (203) 525-0111

In response to your inquiry regarding the purchased gas adjustment (PGA) on your gas bill, we hope you will find this additional information helpful

The PGA is the difference between the cost of gas represented in the most recent rates we are allowed to bill you and the costs of gas we must pay. Each month we make a calculation to determine this difference which may vary from month to month. This calculation is submitted to the Public Utilities Control Authority for approval before it is applied to your bill.

The PGA helps us maintain our ability to pay for the energy we provide to customers by enabling us to recover, on a timely basis, the increased cost of gas which our suppliers are charging us. The PGA does not provide any extra profit; we charge only the exact amount of increased cost of gas to us which is not included in our base rates.

The PGA is necessary because our suppliers' price changes are put into effect rapidly by approval of the Federal Energy Regulatory Commission. Our regulated rates, on the other hand, are arrived at after time-consuming hearings at which careful consideration is given to our overall costs in providing the services you need. Increases in the cost of wages, plant and equipment, taxes, postage, gasoline for trucks, and all other business expenses are not included in any way in the purchased gas adjustment.

The PGA will continue to be necessary as long as the current price instability in natural gas and energy sources, which is the result of the lack of a national energy policy, continues to exist.

<u>What's In It for Our Customers</u>?

First, it makes it possible for us to continue to supply you with energy; second, it makes it possible for us to adjust your bill downward immediately if gas costs go down, as well as upward if gas costs go up. For your protection, each adjustment must be documented in terms of actual costs and approved by the State Public Utilities Control Authority.

If you have further questions, please feel free to call us at our office in your area.

                                        Customer Relations Dept.

FIGURE 9-2. Form letter (Courtesy of Connecticut Natural Gas Corporation)

since paragraphs prerecorded on disks can be printed at high speeds. In some offices, the secretary is empowered to formulate the response by selecting the paragraph numbers.

In some instances, an entire "model" letter may serve as a guide letter. The secretary merely copies the guide that is usually located in a correspondence manual. It is very important that guide letters be revised frequently, so that they are current.

Individual letters

There is a seemingly infinite variety of individual business letters; however, the vast majority fall into broad classifications. These common business letters are discussed in this chapter and the next.

ADJUSTMENT LETTER

Most businesses today try to keep their customers satisfied and, therefore, have fair, liberal adjustment policies. It is usually easier to retain a customer than to attract a new one. Adjustment letters fall into three broad classifications:

1. letters requesting an adjustment,
2. letters granting an adjustment, and
3. letters refusing an adjustment.

Requesting an Adjustment. This letter usually consists of three component parts:

1. the request for an adjustment,
2. providing details, and
3. an optimistic statement.

Figure 9–3, for example, is a letter requesting adjustment. The first three paragraphs conform to the guidelines for this type of letter.

Granting an Adjustment. The message of a letter granting an adjustment follows this pattern:

1. The adjustment is granted and explanations are given.
2. Details are presented when needed.
3. The closing is cordial.

Refusing an Adjustment. An effective letter refusing an adjustment is difficult to write because the recipient of the letter will probably be upset by the

```
Gentlemen:

Please repair or replace without charge the
35mm Atlas camera, model X-253, purchased
from your company on April 21, 19--.

The programmed automatic exposure, electric
eye and self timer are defective.

Since the camera is still under warranty
against defective material or workmanship
for one year from the date of original
purchase, please repair or replace it as
soon as possible.  I wish to take pictures
at my son's graduation from college on May
21.  I mailed in the warranty card to your
company, so it should be in your files.  This
is a fair adjustment request.

Your immediate attention to this matter
would be very much appreciated.

                        Sincerely yours,

                        Richard Hanson
```

FIGURE 9–3. Letter requesting adjustment

refusal. The customer must be convinced that the course of action is reasonable, fair and, in some instances, necessary. The plan of a letter refusing an adjustment follows:

1. Start with an inoffensive, "neutral" opening statement.
2. Reinforce this statement.

```
Dear Dr. Jackson:

Good News!  Your Bristol ladies' 6-function
LOD watch has been repaired without charge
and is being returned by first class mail to
you.

The defective backlight mechanism has been
replaced and the watch is now functioning
perfectly.

We are confident that your Bristol LOD watch
will give you many years of satisfactory
service.

                    Yours truly,

                    Sam Collins
```

FIGURE 9-4.   Letter granting adjustment

3. State the reason for the refusal.
4. State the refusal.
5. Convince the customer that your response is reasonable.
6. End cordially.

See Figure 9-5 for an example of a letter refusing an adjustment.

April 19, 19--

Fred Bering
112 Northvale Avenue
Bloomington, Illinois 47565

Dear Mr. Bering:

This will confirm that we tested your meter on
April 7, 19-- and found it to be operating perfect-
ly. I would also like to take this opportunity
to reaffirm your conversation with Mrs. Davis.

The two-month period ended February 19, 19-- was
18.7% colder than the same period last year. Normally, increases in consumption track increases
in degree days; however, your gas usage was only
10.5% higher than this period last year. In addition, your rate of gas use, as measured by the
number of cubic feet used for each degree day,
has declined 7.7% over last year. Both of these
facts tell us that your home is being operated
efficiently.

I know you were surprised to receive a bill for
316 CCF in February, but you have to keep in mind
that the prior four months were estimated, and
any gas used but not billed during that period
would automatically be included in the February
reading.

Thank you for bringing your questions to our
attention.

Sincerely,

Charles H. Cassidy

Charles H. Cassidy
Vice President
Customer Relations

CHC:cd

FIGURE 9-5a. Refusing an adjustment
(Courtesy of Connecticut Natural Gas Company)

Dear Mrs. Brown:

Thank you for your letter about the Lady Jane
comforter that you purchased from our company.

The "Storm Queen" with its fiberfill quilting
is a very popular sales item. We have sold
over two hundred of these energy-saving
blankets.

State law dictates very specifically that
bedding items are not returnable; therefore,
we cannot make the adjustment you desire.

It would be illegal for us to accept this
merchandise. There is a statement to this
effect posted in the bedding department.
This law was instituted to protect consumers,
such as yourself, from health hazards. You
can be confident that all merchandise sold
in our bedding department is factory fresh
and clean.

Since the color of the comforter does not go
well in your master bedroom, perhaps you can
use the comforter in another room. The enclosed
flyer indicates that a new line of "Storm King"
comforters will go on sale December 1. Perhaps
you can purchase a more suitable comforter at
a reduced price at that time.

Cordially yours,

Sam Collins

FIGURE 9–5b. Letter refusing an adjustment

COLLECTION LETTER

Maintaining Customer Goodwill. Good collection letters are difficult to write
and require a great deal of thought and skill. Ideally, debts should be collected
without creating animosity or ill will. The goodwill of the customer is of para-

Test question

– more than half retail is done on credit basis

Credit managers – look for: ability to pay and willingness to pay

164

FIGURE 9–6. Collection forms (Courtesy of Sage–Allen)

SA–69

WE THANK YOU FOR YOUR RECENT PAYMENT. HOWEVER, IN
VIEW OF THE CONDITION OF YOUR ACCOUNT, IT IS NOT
SUFFICIENT AND WE MUST ASK FOR AN ADDITIONAL PAYMENT.

IF THIS IS NOT POSSIBLE, THEN PLEASE COME IN TO OUR
CREDIT OFFICE OR TELEPHONE US AS TO YOUR PLANS.

SAGE-ALLEN
Department of Accounts
278-2570 Ext. 482

Amount Paid $.................

PROTECT YOUR CREDIT — IT IS YOUR MOST VALUABLE ASSET!

PLEASE DETACH AND MAIL WITH YOUR REMITTANCE IN THE ENCLOSED SELF ADDRESSED ENVELOPE

Date

TO PRESERVE

YOUR GOOD CREDIT RECORD

FOR THE FUTURE

P A Y

THIS SMALL BALANCE IMMEDIATELY

$...................

SAGE-ALLEN & COMPANY Inc.
Collection Department
278-2570, Ext. 480

SA 64

 stringency - severness (Test question)

FIGURE 9–6. (cont.)

Amount Paid $..............

PROTECT YOUR CREDIT — IT IS YOUR MOST VALUABLE ASSET!

PLEASE DETACH AND MAIL WITH YOUR REMITTANCE IN THE ENCLOSED SELF ADDRESSED ENVELOPE

DATE

SOMETIME AGO YOU PROMISED TO PAY YOUR LONG OVERDUE ACCOUNT. HOWEVER, WE STILL SHOW A BALANCE OF $_____. PLEASE CONTACT US IMMEDIATELY.

SAGE-ALLEN & CO., INC.
COLLECTION DEPARTMENT
278-2570 Ext. 480

SA-323

Date   Balance $..............

PROTECT YOUR CREDIT — IT IS YOUR MOST VALUABLE ASSET!

PLEASE DETACH AND MAIL WITH YOUR REMITTANCE IN THE ENCLOSED SELF ADDRESSED ENVELOPE

SECOND REQUEST

IT WILL ONLY TAKE MINUTES TO SEND US YOUR PAST DUE PAYMENT OF $..............

UPON RECEIPT OF PAYMENT WE WILL REMOVE YOUR ACCOUNT FROM OUR COLLECTION FILES.

SAGE-ALLEN & COMPANY Inc.
Collection Department
278-2570, Ext. 480

SA 62

FIGURE 9-6. (cont.)

Amount Paid $ ....

PROTECT YOUR CREDIT — IT IS YOUR MOST VALUABLE ASSET!

PLEASE DETACH AND MAIL WITH YOUR REMITTANCE IN THE ENCLOSED SELF ADDRESSED ENVELOPE

DATE _____

ACCOUNT NUMBER _____   BALANCE _____

UNLESS WE HEAR FROM YOU REGARDING YOUR PAST DUE BALANCE
BY ( ) WE SHALL BE OBLIGED TO CONSIDER DRASTIC
ACTION.

SAGE-ALLEN & CO., INC.
COLLECTION DEPARTMENT
278-2570 Ext. 480

SA-322

Amount Paid $ ....

PROTECT YOUR CREDIT — IT IS YOUR MOST VALUABLE ASSET!

PLEASE DETACH AND MAIL WITH YOUR REMITTANCE IN THE ENCLOSED SELF ADDRESSED ENVELOPE

FINAL NOTICE

Date _____

Unless we hear from you within 10 days, you leave us
no alternative but to forward your outstanding balance
to an attorney or collection agency for proper action.

SEND FULL REMITTANCE TODAY

Balance _____
Due _____

SAGE-ALLEN & COMPANY, Inc.
Collection Department
000-0000, Ext. 000

SA-65

167

900 MAIN STREET, HARTFORD, CONNECTICUT 06103
PHONE 278-2570

Dear Mr. Anson:

Your Sage-Allen charge account has now reached a balance that exceeds your credit limit.

This is to inform you that the credit limit on your account is $1,200.

At this time we must <u>temporarily</u> suspend your charge privileges until your balance is reduced to within your credit limitations.

If you wish to discuss the matter further, please call us at 278-0000 Ext. 000.

Very truly yours,

SAGE-ALLEN & CO., INC.

Credit Office

BKR:mw

SA-350

FIGURE 9-7. Collection letters (Courtesy of Sage-Allen)

mount consideration when writing collection letters. The tone of the message is very important. An effective collection letter will result in the payment of money due and will retain the goodwill of the customer.

Degree of Severity. An important consideration is the degree of severity employed. Usually, a simple reminder is first sent to a delinquent customer.

Strengency

900 MAIN STREET, HARTFORD, CONNECTICUT 06103
PHONE 278-2570

In reviewing your account, we find in the last _____

months, there has been only _____ payments made

totaling $_____.

Please contact us as soon as possible to make payment

arrangements. If we do not hear from you within 10

days, you leave us no alternatives but to take further

collection action.

                              SAGE-ALLEN & CO., INC.

                              COLLECTION DEPARTMENT
                              278-0000 Ext. 000

SA-114

This may be a duplicate invoice in another color or a duplicate invoice with "reminder" or "past due" stamped on it. Next, a series of collection letters is sent out. Ultimately, a collection agency may be employed or legal action taken. Hopefully, drastic action will be averted by tactfully worded collection letters. Various appeals, such as fair play, reputation, cooperativeness, and so on, are made. A typical series of collection forms, letters, and telegrams is shown in Figures 9–6, 9–7, 9–8, and 9–9.

900 MAIN STREET, HARTFORD, CONNECTICUT 06103
PHONE 278-2570

Dear Mr. Anson:

   If you prefer dealing with us rather
than our agent in your local area, contact
us at once and arrange for payment on your
account.

   Or, you may make payment in full by
enclosing a check, or money order, and
mail immediately.

                    Very truly yours,

                    SAGE-ALLEN & CO., INC.

                    Collection Division
                    Credit Department

BKR/lv

FIGURE 9-7. (cont.)

CREDIT LETTER

More than half of the business that is transacted is on a credit basis; that is, payment is deferred to a later date by the purchaser. Although numerous credit letters are written in the business world, the broad majority concern:

1. Inviting credit
2. Refusing credit
3. Granting credit

900 MAIN STREET, HARTFORD, CONNECTICUT 06103
PHONE 278-2570

Dear Mr. Anson:

SAGE-ALLEN'S OPTION PAYMENT PLAN is a privilege
granted to our customers, but requires payments
each and every month equal to 1/10th of the monthly
balance due.

Failure to pay in accordance with the above terms
has resulted in your account being in default for
a period of more than 90 days.

Effective this date, we must close your account
to any additional charges and request that you
return your credit card in the special envelope
herewith provided.

If you care to discuss this matter with the
undersigned, please call 278-0000, Ext. 000.
We shall expect your remittance within 10 days
from the above date.

Very truly yours,

SAGE-ALLEN & CO., INC.

B. K. Robinson

B. K. Anderson (Mrs.), Manager
Collection Division
Credit Department

BKA:mw
Encl.

SA-324

FIGURE 9-7. (cont.)

Forms are frequently used in credit research; for example, it is common for companies to share credit information using check-off forms.

Inviting Credit. Many businesses actively promote credit, since a large percentage of business is transacted on a credit basis.

The form for a letter inviting credit consists of:

1. a cordial statement,
2. an invitation to transact business on a credit basis, and
3. a statement motivating action.

171

FIGURE 9–8. Collection telegrams (Courtesy of Sage–Allen)

western union **Telegram**

ABLE & CO., INC.
1 MAIN ST.
HARTFORD, CT 06103

DEAR ():

WE ARE CONCERNED ABOUT THE CONDITION OF YOUR ACCOUNT AS REFLECTED BY THIS
NOTICE.

IT IS NOW URGENT TO INFORM YOU THAT UNLESS THE OVERDUE PORTION OF () IS PAID
WITHOUT DELAY, YOUR ACCOUNT WILL BE REFERRED TO OUR COLLECTION DIVISION FOR
SUCH ACTION AS MAY BE FOUND NECESSARY TO PROTECT OUR INTERESTS.

YOUR COOPERATION WILL AVOID SUCH ACTION.

S. SMITH
SAGE-ALLEN & CO., INC.

western union **Telegram**

ABLE & CO., INC.
1 MAIN ST.
HARTFORD, CT 06103

REF. NO.: 0000-0000-0

DEAR ():

BECAUSE OF YOUR FAILURE TO REMIT PAYMENT ON YOUR ACCOUNT, I HAVE BEEN GIVEN
THE AUTHORITY TO HANDLE YOUR ACCOUNT FOR PROCESSING TO OUR LEGAL REPRESENTATIVE.

SEND YOUR CHECK OR CONTACT US IMMEDIATELY. FAILURE TO HEAR FROM YOU WITHIN
10 DAYS LEAVES US NO ALTERNATIVE.

S. SMITH
SAGE-ALLEN & CO., INC.

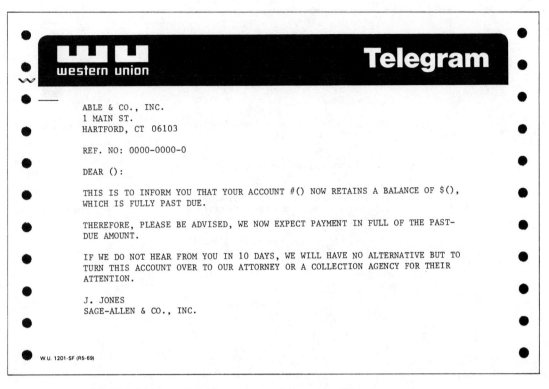

western union

Telegram

```
ABLE & CO., INC.
1 MAIN ST.
HARTFORD, CT  06103

REF. NO: 0000-0000-0

DEAR ():

THIS IS TO INFORM YOU THAT YOUR ACCOUNT #() NOW RETAINS A BALANCE OF $(),
WHICH IS FULLY PAST DUE.

THEREFORE, PLEASE BE ADVISED, WE NOW EXPECT PAYMENT IN FULL OF THE PAST-
DUE AMOUNT.

IF WE DO NOT HEAR FROM YOU IN 10 DAYS, WE WILL HAVE NO ALTERNATIVE BUT TO
TURN THIS ACCOUNT OVER TO OUR ATTORNEY OR A COLLECTION AGENCY FOR THEIR
ATTENTION.

J. JONES
SAGE-ALLEN & CO., INC.
```

W.U. 1201-SF (R5-69)

FIGURE 9–9a. Collection series: Letter 1, mild tone

```
Dear Ms. Woods:

This letter is a brief reminder that your
account is now overdue.

You have paid your bills promptly in the
past and have an excellent credit rating.

Please pay the $185 due promptly.

                    Sincerely,

                    Sam Swartz
```

Appeal to Customer's Reputation

```
Dear Ms. Woods:

The $185 balance in your account is now          Insistent Tone
three months past due.

To avoid extra charges agreed upon when          Increasing Stringency:
your charge account was issued, please           Interest Charges
pay the balance immediately.

It is only fair that this balance due be
paid, if we are to continue transacting          Appeal to Fair Play
business on a credit basis.

Your payment of the $185 balance would
be very much appreciated.

                    Yours truly,

                    Sam Swartz
```

FIGURE 9–9b. Collection series: Letter 2, more insistent tone

Refusing Credit. At times, credit must be refused. An individual may have a record of being a poor credit risk.

Credit must be refused tactfully, for a person can still be retained as a cash customer. The negative refusal, "no," should be avoided. It is implied, not stated. A suggested plan follows:

Dear Ms. Woods:

There are two major advantages to the
payment of your outstanding account:
You will avoid additional finance
charges and your credit rating will
not be tarnished.

If you are having financial problems,
perhaps you would like to discuss the
matter with our credit manager, Mr.
Rodriguez. Arrangements can be made
in special hardship cases for temporary
token payments.

We urge your cooperation in the payment
of the $185 due our company.

Yours truly,

Sam Swartz

FIGURE 9-9c. Collection series: Letter 3, more resolute tone

1. A tactful explanation of the reason for the refusal.
2. An alternative offer.
3. A cordial closing.

Increasing Stringency:

Threat of Legal Action (Note: Threat of turning account over to a collection agency is also made in the last letter of the collection series.)

Dear Ms. Woods:

We have written several letters to you suggesting prompt payment of your outstanding account. As the attached statement indicates, $185 plus interest charges are presently due.

Your account will be turned over to our legal department if payment is not made by November 24. We value your business and sincerely hope this action will not become necessary.

Please remit the amount due immediately to avoid legal complications.

Yours truly,

Sam Swartz

FIGURE 9–9d. Collection series: Letter 4, urgent tone

Granting Credit. A letter granting credit is relatively easy to write. A guide follows:

1. Grant the credit.
2. State credit terms.
3. Promote sales.
4. Close cordially.

176

FIGURE 9–10a. Letter inviting credit

Dear Dr. Shapiro:

The Wilcox Drug Company is offering credit privileges to a select group of physicians in St. Louis who have excellent credit ratings.

Because of your sterling reputation, we would like to extend to you an invitation to purchase our products on a credit basis.

The enclosed brochure lists our many fine products and customer services.

Also, enclosed is a credit application that states our liberal terms. Simply return the application form in the stamped, return envelope.

Cordially yours,

Betti Brand

FIGURE 9–10b. Letter inviting credit (Courtesy of Sage–Allen)

Sage-Allen

Dear Neighbor:

We at Sage-Allen want to say, "Hello."

For over 90 years, we have served New England families to help make their lives a little easier. It would be our utmost pleasure to serve you.

At the Sage-Allen close to your home, you will find everything you want and need. Here you will discover items from home furnishings to fashions, from cosmetics to cookware. And at Sage-Allen, quality, value and imaginative ideas go hand-in-hand with attentive service.

A Sage-Allen Charge Account makes shopping even easier. If you already have an account with us and we can be of assistance, please feel free to call our Credit Manager. If you do not have an account, please take a moment to complete the enclosed application and return it in the postfree envelope provided for your convenience.

All of us at Sage-Allen look forward to serving you.

Cordially,

Lafayette Keeney

Lafayette Keeney
Chairman and
Chief Executive Officer

	Dear Ms. LaPointe:
Tactful Explanation of Refusal	Thank you for submitting a credit application to the Jarvis Company. The application form has been carefully reviewed by our credit manager, Mr. Harold Hempel. The record indicates that your liabilities are in excess of your assets at the present time.
Alternative Offer	In light of this circumstance, it would be better for you if business transactions were conducted on a cash basis. You would not have to pay finance charges and could avail yourself of substantial discounts by paying cash for purchases.
Cordial Closing	If your ratio of assets to liabilities improves in the future, please contact Mr. Hempel. He will be pleased to reassess your application for a credit account with the Jarvis Company. In the interim, we shall be very happy to continue serving your business needs on a cash basis.

Very sincerely yours,

Michael Jarvis

FIGURE 9–11. Letter refusing credit

LETTER OF INQUIRY

A letter of inquiry is sent to obtain information. It must be carefully worded in order to persuade the reader to respond affirmatively. The inquiry must be stated precisely and correctly. If several questions are asked, they may be enumerated. Generally, the format for a letter of inquiry is as follows:

Statement Granting Credit

Credit Terms

Sales Promotion

Cordial Closing

Dear Mrs. Zimmermann:

After carefully reviewing your credit
application, we are delighted to inform
you that a charge account has been opened
in your name! Under separate cover, four
credit cards are being sent to you--one
for each member of your family.

The enclosed sheet explains in detail
credit terms. There is no finance charge
if your account is paid within thirty days.

Our annual Courtesy Days Sale for charge
customers is from January 15 through January
30. You can save 25% on many fine store
items during this sale.

We look forward to serving you.

Sincerely,

Michael Jarus

FIGURE 9-12a. Letter granting credit

1. Provide needed explanations to persuade the reader to respond favorably.
2. State the inquiry or request clearly, completely, and specifically.
3. Cite the reason for the inquiry or request. If applicable, tell how the reader will benefit from granting the action desired.

900 MAIN STREET, HARTFORD, CONNECTICUT 06103
PHONE 278-2570

Dear Customer:

We have placed your name on our list of accepted Charge
Customers. A $_____ credit limit has been placed on
your account.

If you wish to purchase merchandise on a "charge" basis,
call in person at our Credit Office or Credit Desk in
the Branch Stores, and a temporary shopping pass will be
issued for use throughout the store.

After you have established six (6) months history, please
contact our Credit Office and we will re-evaluate your
account.

                                        SAGE-ALLEN & CO., INC.

                                        Credit Division

CD:tc

FIGURE 9-12b.

4. State the action desired and a date for the reply.
5. End courteously by expressing appreciation to the reader for consideration of the inquiry or request. A stamped, addressed envelope may be enclosed to help assure a response.

ORDER LETTER

Commonly, orders are sent through the mail in letter form (Figure 9-13); however, in many instances printed order forms are used. The illustrated

The figure (a letter to order items) contains:

Gentlemen:

Ordering Statement

Please send the following items to me:

Description of Items Ordered

2 Phoenix Portable 2-Speed
Microcassette Recorders
with built-in condenser
microphone and digital
tape counter, No. 236
@ 130.50 each................. $261.00

3 Aetna Remote Control 35mm
Slide Projectors, No. 460
@ 150.00 each................. 450.00

2 Atlas Automatic Slide
Viewers, 4X Magnification,
No. 1490 @ 22.00 each........ 44.00

$755.00

Sales Tax 52.85

TOTAL $807.85

Shipping Instructions

Please ship this order by parcel post.

Method of Payment

Delivery Date

Bill my account for this purchase plus shipping charges. Delivery before May 23 will be very much appreciated.

Closing Statement

As always, it is a pleasure doing business with your company.

Sincerely yours,

Peter Slade

FIGURE 9–13. A letter to order items

order form reveals the many details that are contained in a printed order form (refer to Figure 2–3).

Order letters, of necessity, must also be clear, specific, and accurate. If not, expensive mistakes will occur. The order letter should contain the following:

1. A statement ordering the goods or services.

2. A clear description of catalog number, size, color, material, price, quantity, weight, and so on, related to the order.

3. Shipping instructions (parcel post, freight, air express, and so on).

4. Method of payment (charge, check, C.O.D., and so on).

5. Delivery date.

6. A closing statement.

SALES LETTER

Test question

Opening Is Critical. Take extreme care when writing sales letters. The opening statement of a sales letter is critical. It must capture the interest of the reader or it will be tossed into a waste basket. Usually, sales letters start with a catchy slogan, a clever statement, a quotation, an offer, a pertinent statement, and so on.

The second paragraph should sustain interest, by providing details about the product or service.

Next, persuasive evidence is presented to support claims. Very often, testimonials (by satisfied customers, experts, or prominent people), samples, free trials, statistics, and statements regarding warrantees or guarantees are used to convince the reader of the desirability of a service or product.

The final paragraph is motivational, the reader must be spurred to immediate action. Common statements are: "Act now and receive a free record." "Supply limited." "Ten percent off if you respond by April 3." "Simply check 'Yes' on the enclosed stamped card."

Briefly stated, the four component parts of sales letters are:

Test question

1. Attention
2. Details to sustain interest *tells about product*
3. Persuasive evidence *- convince you to buy*
4. Stimulate action *- make your responses easy as possible*

Summary

The business letter is used primarily to transmit ideas, thoughts, and information outside the company. There are four basic steps in composing business letters: visualization, formulation, gathering pertinent information, and design or planning.

These are some basic rules for writing business letters:

• The tone should be conversational, natural, pleasant, and positive.

Attention	Hello Shutterbug!
	GET OUT OF THE MINOR LEAGUES--JOIN THE PROFESSIONALS!
Details to Sustain Interest	The new Apex II Single Lense Reflex camera is completely automatic--it <u>focuses automatically</u>, programs the <u>correct exposure</u>, has an <u>automatic electronic flash</u>, and even <u>advances the film automatically</u>! It is "goof-proof." No more underexposed and overexposed pictures, blurred pictures out of focus, and double exposures! No more missed shots--you can shoot two frames per second!
	The Apex II has a f/1.8 lens, self timer, and built-in flash shoe. There are 22 interchangeable lenses available--zoom, telephoto, wide-angle.
Conviction	Professional photographer Mark Van Streeter uses the new Apex II! He describes it as "lightweight, compact, completely automatic, reliable, fast, and a darn good buy for $280."
Action	If you reply before May 31, you will receive a handsomely crafted, leather camera case valued at $30 without charge! Simply complete the enclosed order form, check the manner of payment, and return the form in the stamped envelope.
	Sincerely yours,
	Gary Bolen

FIGURE 9–14. Sales letter

- Psychology should be used.
- Use the "you" attitude rather than the "I," "we," or "my" attitude.
- Be courteous and considerate.
- Write clearly, concisely, and positively. Whenever possible, use concrete words.

Three basic methods of response have evolved: form letters, guide letters, and individual letters. Form letters are printed in volume. A guide letter contains paragraphs that are prepared and numbered in advance. Paragraphs are combined to facilitate responses.

There is a seemingly endless variety of individual letters. Common business letters reviewed in this chapter are: adjustment, collection, credit, inquiry, order, and sales. Adjustment letters fall into three broad classifications:

1. Letters requesting an adjustment
2. Letters granting an adjustment
3. Letters refusing an adjustment

Good collection letters are difficult to write. The tone of the message is very important. An important consideration is the degree of stringency employed. Usually, a simple reminder is sent to a customer first. Subsequent letters increase in stringency. Ultimately there is the threat that a collection agency may be employed or legal action taken.

The broad majority of credit letters concern:

1. Inviting credit
2. Refusing credit
3. Granting credit

A letter of inquiry or request is sent to secure information. It must be carefully worded in order to persuade the reader to respond affirmatively.

Commonly, orders are sent through the mail in letter form; however, in many instances printed order forms are used. Order forms, of necessity, must be clear, specific, and accurate.

Effective sales letters should be written with care. The four component parts of a sales letter are:

1. Attention
2. Details
3. Persuasive evidence
4. Stimulate action

Chapter 10 which follows contains information about career letters and personal business letters.

Discussion

1. Although business letters are used primarily for external communication, some letters stay within the organization. Explain these exceptions.
2. Explain the basic rules for writing business letters.

Study questions

1. List the four steps in letter composition.

   1) visualization 2) formulation 3) gathering 4) Planning/Designing

2. What are the three basic methods of response that have evolved due to the large volume of correspondence?

   Form letters, Guide letters, individual letters

3. Differentiate between form letters and guide letters.

   form letters are in volumes, Guide letters have paragraphs

4. What are the three broad classifications of letters found in the business world?

   Adjustment letters
   1) Requesting adjustment
   2) Granting adjustment
   3) Refusing adjustment

Activities

1. Compose a letter granting an adjustment. The motor drive on a Chef's Food Processor is defective, and a new food processor is being sent out without charge.
2. Compose a refusal to Mr. Knight, who wants to return a used, rechargeable electric shaver, Model TR 87, purchased two years ago.
3. Write a letter to Mr. Clark. Invite him to open a charge account with the Old Colony Furniture Store.
4. Write a tactful letter to Mrs. Stoloski refusing credit.
5. Compose a letter to Mr. Allen informing him that credit has been granted.
6. Compose a letter to Mr. Rapoli inquiring about a new accounting or data processing system instituted by his company. Reply date: April 14.
7. Compose an order letter in which you order a sweater. Be sure to include specific details, such as fabric, color, style, size, and so on. Delivery is by parcel post. Payment is by check.
8. Write a sales letter with a catchy opening. You are selling a lightweight, spray, steam and dry iron. The iron has nonstick coating. Its other features are a reversible cord for left- or right-handed ironing,

tap water window, yellow handle, self-cleaning, and heat-resistant cord. The price is $30, and the action incentive is a factory rebate of $10.

ACHIEVEMENT OF LEARNING GOALS

Check the appropriate boxes to determine whether you have or have not achieved the learning goals of this chapter.

I Can:

	YES	NO
1. Compose effective business letters.	☐	☐
2. Understand basic methods of responding to correspondence.	☐	☐

If any of your responses were "no," it is suggested that you review pertinent chapter parts.

10

Career Communications and Personal Letters

LEARNING GOALS   *Critical Chapter*

1. Compose effective career communications and personal business letters.
2. Recognize those situations or events requiring "goodwill" messages.

The previous chapter dealt with composing business letters. This chapter concerns career communications (employment letters) and personal business letters.

Career communications

SECURING AN INTERVIEW

People entering the business world usually write letters of application and accompanying resumes. The purpose of these communications is to secure an interview. Because of their importance, they should be well written, error free, and attractive, They are the first contact with a potential employer, and they should create a very good impression. Many college career placement offices have experts who can review your letters or application and resumes to be sure that they are perfect.

Once employed, there are other vital letters that you may write pertaining to your career or to the careers of others, such as letters of recommendation (also called reference letters) and resignation letters (termination letters).

LETTER OF APPLICATION

Solicited and Unsolicited. There are two broad classifications of application letters: solicited and unsolicited. The solicited letter is sent to a firm seeking to employ someone; the unsolicited letter is sent to a firm with the hope that there may be a vacancy. Usually, a resume, also called a data sheet, accompanies the letter of application. *The primary aim of the letter of application is to secure an interview.*

Selling Oneself. A good application letter is difficult to write, for in reality it is a sales or persuasive letter. The applicant "sells" himself or herself. The writer should not oversell nor undersell personal and professional qualifications, for the impression conveyed is vital to the effectiveness of the letter. If the writer is too lavish in personal enhancement, he or she will come across as an ego maniac. If the person is too modest and undersells qualifications, the job will be lost to another. The letter should be written with confidence and a positive tone. The four parts of this letter are:

1. A statement citing the position the writer is applying for.
2. The qualifications of the applicant.
3. References.
4. A request for an interview.

FIGURE 10–1. Letter requesting an interview (Courtesy of Aetna Life & Casualty)

November 10, 19--

10 Newton Avenue
West Springfield, MA 01089
Telephone (413) 289-6732

Good Morning!

Enclosed is a copy of my resume which I am submitting for
your review.

I am interested in joining your organization and believe
that recent and significant educational credentials (B.A.,
Graphics and Art History), coupled with creativity,
dependability, and ability to take direction will be of
interest to you and your management team.

The skills and abilities I offer include those of
Commercial Artist; but, highlight personal qualifications
as well. For example, I am well familiar with customer
and client service routines and am service-oriented. In
addition, you will find my communications skills to be
of merit.

The position in which I am most interested will require
the regular use of my commercial art skills and, based
upon my positive performance, will lead to advancement
and career opportunities.

If you require any other information or wish to arrange
a personal interview, please contact me at the above
address or phone number.

Very truly yours,

W. Smith

William Smith

Enclosure

Harrison, N.Y. 10528

July 15, 19--

Director of Creative Services
All-County Life & Casualty
1150 Framedale Avenue
Forge Village, Massachusetts 06156

Dear Mr. Craves:

I am applying for a position with your company, as I feel my experience in the graphic arts/audio visual area will be of interest to you.

I am familiar with all phases of slide photography and production, as well as techniques which make effective slide presentations. I am also well-acquainted with graphic arts, having managed and operated a graphic arts print shop with complete printing services: design and layout, Compugraphic typesetting, and offset printing. I also instructed high school students in graphic arts and photography.

The enclosed resume describes my experience in filmstrips, documentary work, and cinematography. I think you will find it interesting.

If you think, as I do, that I can make a contribution to your company, I hope you won't mind a call next week to arrange a time to see you.

Sincerely yours,

J. J. Kearney

James J. Kearney

Enclosure

FIGURE 10-1. (cont.)

FIGURE 10–1. (cont.)

Position

Qualifications

Reference

Dear Mr. Edwards:

This letter is in response to your advertisement in the New York *Times* on January 8 for a word processing specialist.

I believe that my qualifications for this position may prove to be of interest to you. I hold my Bachelor of Science degree in Secretarial Science from Central Connecticut State University in New Britain, Connecticut where I completed the Text/Word Processing option. This option consisted of specialized courses in Keyboarding, Text/Word Processing Systems, Integrated Office Systems, and Administrative Office Management.

I have had some experience in the field of word processing, for I was a correspondence secretary at the Kent Manufacturing Company in Hartford, Connecticut for two years. My duties entailed transcribing tapes on an editing CRT typewriter.

My references are cited on the enclosed resume.

May I have an interview at your convenience to discuss my qualifications? My telephone number is (203) 236-2881.

Respectfully submitted,

Warren Price

Warren Price

March 16, 19--

14 Oliver Road
Austin, Texas 78769

Manager, Creative Services
Corporate Communications
OCI Office Systems, Inc.
1100 Industrial Park
Austin, Texas 78769

Dear Mr. Bloss:

I am seeking a position in the graphic arts field as an artist experienced in layout, design, and mechanicals.

Creative Services at OCI interests me, and I would like to have an opportunity to meet with you and discuss what contribution I can make and what your department has to offer.

Enclosed is my resume. May I have an appointment?

Sincerely

Bill Bergmiller

Bill Bergmiller

RFH:mw
Enc.

___The Resume.___ The resume, a summing up of an individual's qualifications, generally accompanies the letter of application. The resume usually contains the following sections:

1. Identification of the applicant: name, address, telephone number
2. Career objective(s): vocational interests
3. Education
4. Experience
5. Activities and awards
6. Personal data
7. References

Offering Letter. If a position is offered to an applicant, a cordial letter is sent that includes the following:

1. Offering the position.
2. Providing details (salary, starting date, and the like).
3. Ending with a cordial closing.

Declining Letter. If a candidate is declined for a position, a letter of declination is sent out. The letter contains the following parts:

1. A cordial statement thanking the individual for applying for a position.
2. A positive explanation of the refusal.
3. A cordial closing.

Two very important letters.

The tone of this letter is very important, for the company wants to retain the goodwill of the applicant.

LETTER OF RECOMMENDATION

A letter of recommendation, also called a "reference letter," is written about an applicant for a position. The letter usually contains:

1. Identification of the applicant
2. Experience
3. Appraisal of qualifications (personal and professional)
4. Cordial closing

FIGURE 10-2. A resume *Know this*

```
                          RESUME


         Alison Candace Paige
         86 Judson Drive
         Newport Beach, CA 94040

         (714) 563-2721

         Career Preference.

         To be a correspondence secretary in the word processing
         center of a large company.

         Education.

         Bachelor of Science degree in Secretarial Science from Central
         Connecticut State University, New Britain, Connecticut, 1982.
         Completed the Text/Word Processing Option.  Graduated magna
         cum laude with a 3.75 cumulative credit-point average.

         Honor diploma, Hamilton High School, Newport Beach, California,
         1978.

         Experience.

         Correspondence secretary at the Kent Manufacturing Company in
         Hartford Connecticut, 1980-1982.  Part-time employee at Jones
         & Maxwell while attending college.  Performed routine typing
         and recordkeeping tasks.

         Activities and Awards.

         President of the Business Club in 1981 at Central Connecticut
         State University.  Member of the Alpha Zeta Sigma sorority and
         Iota Kappa Phi (honor society) while at Central Connecticut
         State College.  Awarded the Business Merit Award for 1982.

         Personal.

         Interests:  photography, tennis, golf, swimming, ceramics.
         Excellent health.

         References by Permission.

         Dr. Howard H. Wilson              Mr. Robert T. Kent, President
         Professor of Business Education   Kent Manufacturing Company
         Central Connecticut State Univ.   100 State Street
         New Britain, CT 06050             Hartford, CT 06111

         Dr. Michele T. DeNapoli           Ms. Valerie D. Gray
         Professor of Business Education   Principal
         Central Connecticut State College Hamilton High School
         New Britain, CT 06050             Newport Beach, CA 94041
```

FIGURE 10-3. Job offer letters (Courtesy of Aetna Life & Casualty) *Real letter*

February 13, 19--

Meridian, CT 06430

Dear

On behalf of Aetna Life & Casualty and the Creative Services Department, I would like to confirm our offer for the position of
Artist. The starting salary will be   per year, payable
bi-weekly, with review for merit increase every twelve months.

Please review the enclosed parking and employee benefits information prior to your first day. The parking lot map shows the
areas you may use; please park in the appropriate area and place
the temporary parking permit on your car's dashboard.

An orientation session will be given in the Auditorium, A floor,
151 Farmington Avenue, at 8 a.m., your first day of work. The
Security Guard at any entrance will direct you.

The booklet entitled <u>Your Second Paycheck</u> describes Aetna's benefits programs. Please read it thoroughly and bring it with you to
orientation. You will have the opportunity to enroll in most benefits plans at that time.

Be sure to have your Social Security number and license plate
number(s) available. You will need them to receive your ID card
and permanent parking sticker.

We are pleased that you have accepted this offer, and look forward
to having you start work on February 18, 19--. Please contact me
if you have any questions.

Sincerely,

Recruiting Office
(203) 273-3745

bf

cc:

enclosures

FIGURE 10–4a. Letter of recommendation

Dear Mr. Callahan:

    I am delighted to have this opportunity to recommend Adam Reed to you.

    He was a conscientious employee of our firm for twelve years. Mr. Reed worked in our Auditing Department.

    Mr. Reed is very trustworthy, industrious, and knowledgeable. He has a very pleasant personality and is highly regarded by the executives of this firm.

    If you wish additional information about Mr. Reed, please contact me.

Sincerely yours,

Sara Lasser

Identification of Applicant

Experience

Appraisal of Qualifications

Cordial Closing

December 11, 1980—

Diversified Business Division

Dear

It is my pleasure to offer you the position of Administrative Assistant, Creative Services, Corporate Communications, with a promotional increase of , bringing your annual salary to effective January 5, 19—. We would like you to join the department on that date.

I'm sure that you will enjoy the challenge and look forward to having you on the staff.

Cordially,

Bill Greer

```
                              January 7, 19--

              Mr. John Smith
              111 Park Street
              Hartford, CT

              Dear Mr. Smith:
```

Thanking *the* *Applicant*	Thank you for calling us about a position with . We appreciate your interest in our career opportunities, and we'll review your qualifications carefully.
Positive *Explanation* *of the* *Refusal*	Right now we're comparing the information you gave us about yourself with our current requirements. You'll hear from us shortly if we need more information or want to arrange an interview.
Cordial *Closing*	If you seem well matched for a position that may become available, we'll place your correspondence on file. We'll then be able to contact you as soon as something does come up to see if you're still interested.

```
              Again, thank you for sharing with us your interests and qualifications.


                              Sincerely,




                              Administrator
                              Personnel Division
```

FIGURE 10–4b. Job declination letters (Courtesy of Aetna Life & Casualty)

LETTER OF RESIGNATION

The letter of resignation is an important letter; however, it is very often dashed off with little thought. When seeking future employment, the past work experience of the applicant will invariably be investigated by the director of personnel. It is very important that your personnel file folder contains a gracious, sincere, cordial, well-written termination letter. When resigning a position, be fair; be sure to provide adequate notice.

The individual who "blows off steam" by telling people off in the letter of resignation may regret this action, for the employer may well have the last word when contacted by another employer.

The parts of a good letter of resignation follow:

1. Cordial, positive statement
2. An explanation or reason for the resignation
3. A resignation statement and the date of resignation
4. Cordial closing

FIGURE 10–5. Letter of resignation

Cordial Opening

*Reason for
Resignation*

*Resignation
Statement and
Date*

Cordial Closing

Dear Mr. Applewhite:

My association with the Marshall Company for the
past eight years has been a very pleasant one.
I have worked very diligently in the Accountant's
Office and hope my contribution to the firm was a
significant one.

I recently passed the C.P.A. examinations and
wish to start my own private accounting firm.

Therefore, please accept my resignation effective four weeks from today, April 22. I hope
this is enough time for you to find a replacement.
If not, I can resign at a mutually satisfactory
date.

My experience at the Marshall Company will
prove invaluable in the years ahead. I shall
always be indebted to the Marshall Company
for employing me "fresh" from college. My
associates and friends at your fine company
will be missed.

                    Cordially yours,

                    Mark Hill

Personal letters in the business world

At times, social propriety or etiquette dictates that letters of a personal nature be written in the business world. These goodwill letters are called personal business letters and have no specific or immediate business purpose. Their ultimate objective is to engender goodwill. It is difficult to discern the immediate value of these letters; however, if well written, they may have a beneficial, long-term effect on business.

Letters of congratulation, appreciation, condolence, and welcome are goodwill letters. These friendly letters are highly individualized or personalized; each letter is carefully thought out with the reader in mind. The executive is usually the originator of personal letters; however, in some circumstances, this duty can be delegated to a competent secretary. Although each letter is uniquely customized, there is a general pattern that can be followed to ensure effectiveness. Personal business letters should be written in a cordial tone, avoiding any "sales pitch." Timeliness is important, for it is an indication of concern.

LETTER OF CONGRATULATIONS

A letter of congratulations recognizes a special event, such as a promotion, award, graduation, or anniversary. A well-written congratulatory message is generous in praise, sincere, and brief. The parts are:

1. Specific statement of the occasion or event being noted
2. Cordial statement of commendation
3. Warm closing

LETTER OF APPRECIATION

Letters of appreciation are sent to engender goodwill. These cordial letters are effective since they are usually unexpected. A good letter of appreciation is timely, brief, friendly, and complimentary. The parts of a letter of appreciation are:

1. Statement of the reason the letter is being sent
2. Complimentary remarks
3. Cordial closing

THANK YOU.

In reviewing the payment records of our customers, we noted that you have established a record of paying your gas bills promptly. We want to thank you for this.

Your good payment record — as well as that of other customers like you — helps hold down the cost of providing gas service during these inflationary times. It reduces our collection expenses and the amount of money we must borrow to cover our expenses. This, in turn, reduces our interest costs and in the long run helps to keep rates lower than would otherwise be possible.

We congratulate you on your fine payment record, and sincerely thank you for your cooperation.

11/81

FIGURE 10–6.
Messages of appreciation
(Courtesy of Connecticut Natural Gas Corp.)

LETTER OF CONDOLENCE

Letter of condolence

Test question

Handwritten for Personal Touch. A letter of condolence, also called a "sympathy letter," is a sincere expression of sorrow when a person passes away. Social etiquette dictates that a letter of condolence be handwritten, not typed. Handwriting helps to convey an individualized, personal touch. It should be noted, however, that it is socially proper to type all other business and personal letters.

The letter should be brief. Avoid the use of specific words such as "death" and "anguish." Also, avoid religious statements. Express sympathy; provide comfort. The parts of this type of letter are:

1. Noting the passing of the individual
2. Sympathetic remarks
3. Positive closing

199

FIGURE 10–6. (cont.)

Date: December 24, 19 --

To: Second Vice President

Re: Printing Center

I'd like to express my appreciation for
the fine cooperation the Printing Center
has given us over the last week. On Monday, with very short notice, they printed
and arranged to distribute an Employee
Announcement (in three colors) dealing
with the early closing hours on December
24. Then on December 23, they printed
and distributed, within six hours, a
memo from the President to all employees--
again with very short notice. Finally,
they have been most helpful in expediting
the production of the final 19 -- edition
of Perspective.

Our primary contacts at the Printing
Center are Ben Nuveen and Nancy Brewster.
These people, and I'm sure many others,
worked very hard to help us meet our
deadlines. I wanted you to know how much
they have done and to express our thanks.

Susan Simkins
Director,
Communications

To: Sam Krevins

From: Harry Kristina

Date: September 4, 19 --

Re: Appreciation

I am writing to express my appreciation
for the most enjoyable six months I have
ever spent working and reporting to you.
I must also thank you for your support.

Not once, while personnel from within and
with-out the department paraded through
your office seeking advice and guidance,
did you raise your voice, act with arro-
gance, or treat anyone with disrespect.
You are to be congratulated! You're quite
a fellow!

For myself and the other members of the
PD section, we are sorry to see you
leave--yet happy to have had the experience of working for an individual respec-
ted by all.

Sincerely,

Harry

May 14, 19--

Dear Mrs. Schaefer:

Your after-dinner talk at the annual dinner of the Harris Corporation was excellent in every respect.

We appreciate very much your presenting this talk, especially since it required you to drive two hundred miles to our corporate headquarters.

The talk was well balanced for the occasion—it was both interesting and highly informative. There have been many favorable remarks about your quick wit, pleasant personality, and professional expertise.

Thanks for helping to make the annual dinner such a memorable one. Enclosed is an honorarium as a token of our appreciation.

Cordially,

Esther Kearney

To: Bill Smith, Vice-President, Corp. Communications

From: Karen Winston, Counsel

Date: December 31, 19--

Re: A Job Well Done

Please pass along to your staff my thanks for a job well done.

I asked them to help us last Friday with a very significant year-end project. They responded quickly and well under a tough time frame.

We are certainly fortunate to have their assistance.

FXB/msr

To: John Atkins, Director,
      Corporate Communications

From: Les Champlin, Administrator,
      Sales Promotion Programs

Date: June 23, 19--

Re: Art Services and Production--State of Tennessee
      Deferred Compensation Materials

You and your troops are to be congratulated--and thanked--
for the excellent services performed in creating and
delivering the materials needed to support enrollment
in the State of Tennessee Deferred Compensation Plan.
We received high praise for the quality of the whole
package, as well as appreciation of the fact that
all the materials arrived in Tennessee in time to meet
their needs. Furthermore, the fine result was
achieved using in-house printing services. Thanks
to the extra efforts of everyone involved, we have
some very happy clients.

As you know, the timing of our several requests and
the critical dates of arrival required unusual effort
and special attention by John Hopkins, Rosalie
Hennings, and the others who had a hand in putting
it all together. And, as usual, the project had to
engage one hand while the other was busy performing
other equally important and demanding tasks.

Please convey to everyone involved in the Tennessee
project our sincere appreciation for their jobs well
done. I know I am speaking not only for this department but also for our Marketing Directors and the
several agents and representatives in the State of
Tennessee.

Les

mkb

cc: Sue Lesser, Manager

FIGURE 10–7 (cont.)

Occasion or Event

Commendation

Warm Closing

Dear Mr. Gonzales:

Congratulations on having your biography listed in the new edition of Who's Who in the West!

Certainly, you are most deserving of this special recognition. For years, your professional contributions to the community have elevated the lives of many people in Phoenix.

I am delighted, indeed, to know such a distinguished gentleman.

Best wishes,

Mike Santinieve

December 3, 19--

Dear Mrs. Burns:

I was pleased to learn that you received an additional award for helping us improve the way we duplicate our club flyers.

Your many ideas have been valuable to the company, and we hope you'll continue to submit them.

Congratulations and best wishes for your continued success.

Sincerely,

Manuel Brooks

Manuel Brooks
Manager,
Personnel-Admin.

Dear Mrs. Hamilton and Family:

The management and staff of the Fully Company are saddened by the untimely passing of Mr. James Hamilton.

We wish to express our profound sorrow at this time.

Mr. Hamilton was a dedicated employee of our company for the past twenty years. During that time, he was held in high regard by his associates. Mr. Hamilton was kind and considerate to all who knew him.

The Fully Company is making a contribution to Alpha College, where a "Mr. James Hamilton Scholarship" will be offered to a deserving student.

Our thoughts are with you at this sad time.

Cordially yours,

Drew Sabot

Passing of Individual Noted

Sympathetic Remarks

Positive Closing

FIGURE 10–8. Letter of condolence

LETTER OF WELCOME

It may be rather difficult for a person to adjust to a new environment: school, place of employment, or community. A cordial letter of welcome can "break the ice" and help to assure a newcomer. The parts of a letter of welcome are:

1. Extending a warm welcome
2. Providing information
3. Offering assistance
4. Cordial closing

FIGURE 10–9.   Letters of welcome

	Dear Mr. Krukowski:
Welcome	Welcome to the Arrow Company!
Provide Information	We are pleased to have you join our company. The Arrow Company has been in business for over two hundred years and has a sterling reputation in the business world.
Offer Assistance	If you have any problems or concerns relating to your position, please feel free to discuss them with me. The channels of communication are always open at Arrow.
Cordial Closing	We look forward to a long, pleasant, and mutually satisfying association.
	Yours truly,
	Anne Morrow

227 MAIN STREET, NEW BRITAIN, CONN. 06050   (203) 223-3655
                                                   (203) 522-4265

Dear

WELCOME TO D&L!

As a newcomer to our company, your understanding of our
objectives and acceptance of our policies will help us
to maintain our leadership as a company and a place of
value to our community. We hope that you will always
have cause to be proud of D&L and your association with
us. We hope, too, that you will be happy with us.

We who work at D&L realize that our success depends upon
customers. That means satisfied customers who come back
like the service we give, the quality, and prices of the
goods they buy from us. It is our duty, as well as our
pleasure, to give the best possible service to the public.

It is this tradition of excellent service that we hope
you will learn and will project while working with us, no
matter what capacity you find yourself engaged in.

Once again, welcome to D&L.....Good Luck!

Sincerely,

Fred Rall

FIGURE 10-9.   (Courtesy of D&L)

206

Dear Neighbor:

We've learned of your recent move and want to extend our every best wish to you in your new home. At Sage-Allen, we fully appreciate the joy and confusion such a move can cause. By the same token, we know how much help a fine, conveniently located department store can be at such a time.

For over 90 years, Sage-Allen has been helping New England families get settled. And we hope to have the pleasure of serving you, too.

At the Sage-Allen close to your home, you're sure to find everything you want and need. Here you will find everything from home furnishings to fashions; from cosmetics to cookware. And at Sage-Allen quality, value and imaginative ideas go hand in hand with attentive service.

A Sage-Allen Charge Account makes shopping even easier. If you already have an account with us and I can be of assistance, please feel free to call upon me. If you do not have an account, please take a moment to complete the enclosed application and return it in the postfree envelope provided for your convenience.

All of us at Sage-Allen look forward to the opportunity to serve you.

Cordially,

Lafayette Keeney
Chairman and
Chief Executive Officer

FIGURE 10-9. (Courtesy of Sage-Allen)

Summary

This chapter concerns career communications (employment letters) and personal business letters. People entering the business world usually write letters of application and accompanying resumes. There are two broad classifications of application letters: solicited and unsolicited. The prime purpose of the letter of application is to secure an interview. The resume is a summing up of an individuals qualifications. The resume usually accompanies the letter of application. It identifies the applicant, states career objectives, cites education and experience, tells about activities and awards, mentions personal data, and lists references.

A letter of recommendation, commonly called a "reference letter," is written about an applicant for a position.

The letter of resignation is an important letter. It is essential that an employee's personnel file folder contains a gracious, sincere, cordial, well-written termination letter.

At times, social etiquette dictates that letters of a personal nature be written in the business world. These goodwill letters are called *personal letters* and have no specific business purpose. Letters of congratulation, appreciation, condolence, and welcome are *goodwill letters*.

Discussion

1. Explain what is meant by career communications. —employment letters
2. Explain what is meant by personal business letters.
3. Explain why a letter of termination should be gracious, sincere, cordial, and well written. Because when seeking other employment your past files may be checked. A positive termination letter will enhance future employment elsewhere.

Study questions

1. What is the difference between a solicited and an unsolicited application letter? Solicited letter sent to firm that seek employment. Unsolicited letter sent to firm with hope of vacancy
2. What is a resume? Summing up of individuals classification.
3. What is the letter called when a candidate declines a position?
4. What is another name for a letter of recommendation? reference letter
5. Should personal business letters contain a sales pitch? No
6. Should a congratulatory letter be lengthy? No, they are brief

208

Activities

1. Assume that you are applying for a position in your major. You saw an ad in your local newspaper announcing a vacancy. Compose a letter of application.
2. Compose a resume listing your qualifications.
3. Assume you are working for the Data Company. Write a negative letter of recommendation for Ms. Doreen Greene. You were not impressed by her poor performance, tardiness, and poor personality.
4. Compose a letter of resignation to the Carter Company where you have been employed for the past six years as the Director of Managerial Communications. Another company has employed you as the Vice President of Public Affairs. Write a cordial letter to Ms. Joyce Carter, President of the Carter Company. Give a month's notice.
5. Mrs. Mary Curtis has completed an outstanding research paper for your company on ways to conserve energy. Congratulate her for a job well done.
6. Write a letter to a Mr. Bruce Crane, thanking him for contributing forty engineering books to the company library.
7. Write a condolence letter to the family of Mrs. Marilyn Stowe. Mrs. Stowe passed away heroically while rescuing a child from drowning. Mrs. Stowe worked in the Credit Department of your firm for three years.
8. Judy Collins has just moved to your community. Write a letter to inform her about the available cultural activities, parks, and so on. End with a warm closing.

ACHIEVEMENT OF LEARNING GOALS

Check the appropriate boxes to determine whether you have or have not achieved the learning goals of this chapter.

I Can:

	YES	NO
1. Compose effective career communications and personal business letters.	☐	☐
2. Recognize those situations or events requiring goodwill messages.	☐	☐

If any of your responses were "no," it is suggested that you review pertinent chapter parts.

Public Relations

LEARNING GOALS

1. Understand the need for effective public relations.
2. Know the most popular communicative activities associated with public relations.

Creating and maintaining goodwill

One of the major purposes of public relations, also known as "PR" in business organizations, is to create a favorable image of a company and, thereby, create and maintain goodwill. Therefore, activities are undertaken to enhance the reputation of a company by managing external relations effectively.

Pertinent facts and ideas about a company are communicated through appropriate channels of communication, such as the press, radio, television, and films. Arthur W. Pearce lists the recipients of this information as[1]

1. The community where the business operates;
2. Present and prospective employees;
3. Customers;
4. Suppliers;
5. Stockholders;

[1]*Handbook of Business Administration* (New York: McGraw-Hill Book Co., 1970), p. 12–11.

6. The financial community; and

7. The general public.

In its broadest interpretation, a public relations program consists of a broad spectrum of activities ranging from advertising and sales promotion to employee relations. Of necessity, the discussion in this chapter is restricted to some of the most popular communicative activities associated with public relations, such as news releases, press conferences, executive speeches, media appearances, special publications, and interviews.

News releases

Businesses release news items to various media: newspapers, radio, magazines, trade publications and television. These news releases, commonly known as press releases and publicity releases, contain newsworthy information about a company: its personnel, activities (business and community), sales, financial standing, dividend declarations, products and services. At times, graphs and photographs may be submitted with the release as a means of illustrating the story. A company may invent a new synthetic fabric, donate funds to a local charitable organization, appoint a new president, or receive a government contract. All of these stories usually warrant media coverage.

The following is a typical newspaper story based upon a company press release :

Connecticut Mutual Payout

Policyholders at Connecticut Mutual Life Insurance Co. will receive a record $181 million in total policy dividends in 1981, including both normal dividend increases and an increased dividend scale, the company said Monday.

The total dividend increase will be about $23 million over 1980, with $16.5 of that arising from the increased dividend scale and the rest from normal dividend growth, the firm said.

It is the largest dividend increase in the company's history. The sixth oldest American life insurance company, Connecticut Mutual has more than 800,000 policyholders and assets of $5 billion.[2]

ADMINISTRATION OF NEWS RELEASES

PR Department. In most large business concerns, the issuance of news releases is the responsibility of the public relations department. In other companies,

[2]*The Hartford Courant,* December 24, 1980, sec. D, p. 6.

public relations firms are employed for this function. In smaller companies, this responsibility may be delegated to the director of managerial communications or to a manager familiar with publicity.

News releases are mailed, transmitted electronically, or hand-delivered to various news media. Information from the releases are printed without charge in the business/finance sections of newspapers and magazines, or in other special sections, depending on the nature of the story. Also, information is aired without charge by radio and television stations as news items. Most editors prefer to write news stories in their own style and format, so the release is likely to be modified.

Free Publicity. News releases are an excellent communicative device. They can be more effective than paid advertisements. They engender goodwill in the community, provide free publicity for the company, and generally are relatively easy to write.

Good business administration dictates that all news releases be reviewed and approved by appropriate company sources. One individual should control all news releases from the initial draft stage to the actual dissemination to the media. If news releases were distributed indiscriminately, news might be released prematurely or erroneous information might be divulged creating a credibility problem.

WRITING NEWS RELEASES

Journalistic Formula. The beginning (or lead) of a typical news release starts with the traditional 5 W's of journalism: *who, what, when, where,* and *why.* At times, if appropriate, an H is added: *how.*

Inverted Pyramid. News releases are usually written in an inverted pyramid form. The most important elements appear first. Details and less critical information follow. Because of media space limitations, parts of an article may have to be deleted. The cutting is done from the bottom upward. Each paragraph of the article should be so written that it can stand alone without losing the intended impact of the story. (See Figure 11–1.)

If we were to delete the third paragraph of the Arizona Mutual article, the message would still make sense:

Connecticut Mutual Payout

Policyholders at Connecticut Mutual Life Insurance Co. will receive a record $181 million in total policy dividends in 1981, including both normal dividend increases and an increased dividend scale, the company said Tuesday.

The total dividend increase will be about $23 million over 1980, with $16.5 of that arising from the increased dividend scale and the rest from normal dividend growth, the firm said.

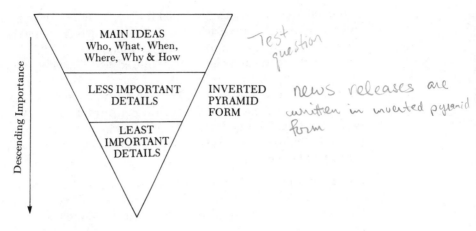

(handwritten: Test question)

(handwritten: news releases are written in inverted pyramid form)

FIGURE 11–1. How a news release is written

Even if the last two paragraphs were deleted, the article still conveys the important information.

Connecticut Mutual Payout

Policyholders at Connecticut Mutual Life Insurance Co. will receive a record $181 million in total policy dividends in 1981, including both normal dividend increases and an increased dividend scale, the company said Tuesday.

When writing a news release, jot down the five W's and H and fill in the necessary information. The 5 W's can be in any order, and the H is optional.

(handwritten: Test question 5 W's sometimes How)

Who?	New Directions Company
What?	presents a new line of clothing
When?	September 11 (Friday)
Where?	at the Harbor Hotel, San Francisco
Why?	to show spring fashions
How?	five models from the Kingsford Agency

The lead paragraph of the news release will state:

The New Directions Company will preview its new spring fashions on Friday, September 11, at the Harbor Hotel, San Francisco. Buyers and customers are invited to attend.

(handwritten: Who, what, where, when, why, sometimes How. → Journalistic formula)

214

**Be Factual.** News writing should be factual, concise, correct, and straightfor-
ward. Avoid long, subjective or editorial discourses. Only newsworthy or
topical information should be included in a news release. Superlatives or
editorial comments should not be used unless attributed to a spokesperson.

NEWS RELEASE FORMAT

Editors are deluged with unsolicited news releases and competition for space
is keen. Therefore, the releases that are newsworthy, require little editing,
and follow prescribed journalistic format and style have the greatest chances
for publication.

Some businesses have printed news release forms; others type their releases on plain bond 8½ by 11 inch paper. The format of a news release is as
follows:

1. _The information contained at the top of the news release should in-
   clude:_
   - The words "NEWS RELEASE" in capital letters;
   - The name, address, and telephone number of the sender or con-
     tact; and
   - The suggested publication or release date.

2. _The heading (headline) should be brief._ It is an index to the content of
   the article. The media editor usually writes a substitute heading. The
   heading is typed in capital letters. It should be noted that some companies prefer not to use headlines, feeling that it's more important to
   force the editor to read the lead.

3. _The body should:_
   - Include a dateline consisting of the city or point of origin and date
     (DETROIT, May 16—).
   - Answer Who, What, Where, Why, When and perhaps How in the
     lead.
   - Provide supporting details in descending order of importance.
   - End the article by centering the printer's terms: -end-, (END), ###,
     ####, -30-. If the release is more than one page in length, the word
     "MORE" is typed at the bottom of the page (right corner) and cir-
     cled—so that the word "more" will not be accidentally printed.
     The pages can be numbered 1, 2, 3, etc., or, after the first page or
     cover, Add 1, Add 2, Add 3, etc.

NEWS RELEASE

From: Anthony A. Foriccelo
        Public Relations Department
        Acme Watches
        St. Louis, MO
        (314-892-7321)

For Release: March 25, 19--

ACME TO MANUFACTURE LCD WATCHES

St. Louis, March 25--Acme Watches plans to
manufacture a ladies LCD digital watch with new
computerized machinery at its St. Louis plant
starting April 1 to capitalize on the expanding
market for electronic watches, it was announced
today.

The new chronograph watch will feature a
4-digit readout of hours, minutes, seconds, month,
day and date. Other features include a solar
rechargeable battery, backlight, and an alarm.

Acme Watches has been manufacturing watches
in St. Louis since 1945. The company employs five
hundred people and is regarded as a leading producer
of quality watches.

####

FIGURE 11-2. Typewritten news release

216

NEWS RELEASE

DUNCAN AND BROOK

732 Forrest Lane
Portland, Oregon
(503) 236-2721

RELEASE: Immediately

FROM: Susan C. Smith
          Public Relations
          Department

DATE: January 17, 19--

Portland, Jan. 17, 19--

CLARK JENSEN PROMOTED

PORTLAND, Oregon, January 17--Clark Jensen was promoted to Vice President of Advertising of Duncan and Brook on Jan. 15 in recognition of his contributions to the company in the advertising area.

Mr. Jensen served as Director of the Advertising Department since 1975. He conceived several national advertising campaigns which were exposed on radio, television and in the print media. One of his advertisements, published in the <u>Consumer's Journal</u>, won first prize in a contest sponsored by the National Advertising Council.

Prior to joining Duncan and Brook in 1974, Mr. Jensen was affiliated with several advertising firms in layout and copywriting capacities.

Mr. Jensen is a graduate of San Diego State College. He resides with his wife and two sons at Forty Flintlock Road in Portland.

####

FIGURE 11-3. News release on a printed form

To facilitate editing by the media, the body of the message should be double spaced. Generally, top and side margins are 1 inch; the bottom margin is 1½ inches. Figures 11–2, 11–3, and 11–4 are examples of different types of news releases.

Press conferences

THE PREPARATIONS

There are certain situations when special treatment should be given to important news items. A conference is called at which members of the press and other media are invited to attend. The invitation is usually by telephone or letter. Specific information about the press conference is given in the notification (topic, place, date, time). Figure 11–5 illustrates a typical letter announcing a press conference:

AT THE CONFERENCE

At the press conference, a company executive appears before the media representatives and reads a prepared, detailed announcement. The news item is read aloud, rather than presented extemporaneously, to avoid errors. Copies of the prepared speech are distributed to the members of the news media. In addition, other pertinent background information (biographical sketches, tables, figures, pictures, photographs, excerpts, etc.) is distributed. Usually the reporters and editors present are invited to ask clarifying questions after the oral presentation. The expectation is that the story will receive substantial coverage and perhaps be a major news article.

Press conferences should be held only for major news releases. If they are called indiscriminately for minor news releases, members of the press will fail to attend future press conferences.

Other public relations activities

In addition to news releases and press conferences, other communicative activities are undertaken by business organizations to ensure good public relations.

SPEECHES, APPEARANCES, SPECIAL PUBLICATIONS, INTERVIEWS

Executive Speeches. Company executives are invited to speak before various groups of people. This provides an opportunity for direct communication with other business people or the public. It is also common for business executives to talk to college groups.

News from
Xerox Corporation

For Immediate Release

XEROX OFFERS INFORMATION SYSTEM
TO SUPPORT BUSINESS PROFESSIONALS

NEW YORK, April 27 — A personal information system for business professionals that combines computing, text editing, graphics creation and communications was announced and demonstrated here today by Xerox Corporation.

The Xerox 8010 Star information system includes a two-page desktop display, a keyboard, a small processor and an unusual control device. No special skills are needed to use the equipment, the company said.

David E. .Liddle, vice president, Office Products Division, said the Star system "is specifically designed for the business professional, whose main job is to create, interpret, and manage information and distribute the results to others in a convenient form."

With the new system, these professionals can create, modify, store, and retrieve text, graphics, and records. They also can distribute documents via electronic mail to local and remote system users on Xerox Ethernet local area communications networks.

"We believe the Star system will help professional people do creative work more easily and will significantly improve their productivity in the process," Liddle said. "And since professional salaries account for the major share of office costs, even modest productivity improvements in this area could substantially increase a company's profit margins."

(More)

213657rg11 1

FIGURE 11-4. Page one of a three-page news release (Courtesy of Xerox Corporation)

```
Dear Mr. Jacobson:

A press conference will be held by the
Allison Corporation announcing the
appointment of a new president.

The conference will be in the con-
ference room of the Allison Corpor-
ation, 256 Main Street, San Francisco,
California on December 3, 19-- at 2:30 p.m.

The new president will be intro-
duced to the press and answer
questions.

Your attendance at this newsworthy
press conference would be appre-
ciated.

Sincerely yours,

Jonathan T. Hardy

Jonathan T. Hardy, Director
Public Relations Department
```

FIGURE 11–5. Letter announcing a press conference

Media Appearances. Radio, television, and films provide an opportunity for executives to communicate to large audiences. It should be noted that some businesses sponsor worthwhile programs through financial grants. This fosters goodwill and is a common practice in educational television broadcasting.

Special Publications. A company may submit articles for publication in professional trade journals. Some in-house publications, such as corporate annual reports and company magazines, are distributed externally to promote goodwill. Chapter 12 presents details about these publications.

Interviews. At times, business executives grant interviews to reporters. It is imperative that *only* authorized individuals grant interviews (usually high-echelon executives), for it takes a great deal of expertise and information to respond intelligently to probing questions by reporters.

Summary

A major purpose of public relations is to create a favorable image of a company. Facts and ideas about a company are communicated through appropriate channels of communications, such as the press, radio, television, and films.

News releases contain newsworthy information about a company. In most large business concerns, the issuance of news releases is the responsibility of the public relations department. News releases are mailed, transmitted electronically, or hand-delivered to various news media.

The beginning of a typical news release starts with the traditional 5 W's of journalism: Who, What, When, Where, and Why. If appropriate, an H is added: How.

News releases are usually written in an inverted pyramid form. Details are presented in descending order. The most important elements appear first; the least important last.

News writing should be factual, concise, correct, and straightforward. Subjective or editorial discourses should be avoided. Prescribed journalistic format and style should be followed.

Press conferences are called when special treatment should be given to important news items. A company executive reads a detailed announcement to reporters and editors. Clarifying questions are usually asked after the announcement.

Other activities for effective public relations include executive speeches, media appearances, special publications, and interviews.

Discussion

1. Explain the purpose of public relations.

Study questions

1. Why does a company engage in public relations activities? *keep good will*
2. List the most popular communicative activities associated with public relations. *Press, radio, T.U., film*
3. By what other terms are news releases known?
4. What do business news releases contain? *newsworthy info about a company*
5. In most large businesses, what department is responsible for the issuance of press releases? *Public Relations department*
6. How are news releases transmitted to various news media? *mailed, transmitted electronically, or hand delivered.*
7. What is the standard charge for printing news releases in the business/finance sections of newspapers and magazines? What is the charge by radio and television stations?
8. List the 5 W's and 1 H of a typical lead (or beginning) of a news release. *Who, what, why, where, when, How*
9. Why are news releases usually written in an inverted pyramid form? *Details are presented in order of importance*
10. Why should the body of the message of a news release be double spaced?
11. Explain the reason for calling a press conference. *When special treatments are needed for certain news item*
12. How are media representatives invited to attend a press conference? *Usually be tele, or letter.* *clarity question.*
13. How are announcements presented at a press conference?
14. What is the danger of calling press conferences indiscriminately? *Some members of press will fail to attend future press conferences.*

Activity

Compose a news release based on the following information:

Your company is manufacturing a new line of video tape recorders. Some of the features of these video tape recorders are: remote control (can record without commercials), automatic stop, 6-hour recording on a cassette, can be used with any television set, and digital timer. Make up any other details needed. Include the 5 W's + 1 H in the lead.

ACHIEVEMENT OF LEARNING GOALS

Check the appropriate boxes to determine whether you have or have not achieved the learning goals of this chapter.

I Can:

	YES	NO
1. State the need for effective public relations.	☐	☐
2. Explain the most popular communicative activities associated with public relations.	☐	☐

If any of your responses were "no," it is suggested that you review pertinent chapter parts.

12

Management–Employee Communications

LEARNING GOALS

1. Understand the need for management-employee communications.
2. Distinguish among the commonly used media for internal communication.
3. Recognize the specific purposes of company publications.

Communicating with-in the business

Employee needs

Progressive business administrators are concerned about establishing and maintaining good management–employee relations, keeping company morale high. Writing about human relations management, Gerry Morse states:

> True participative management means setting up and maintaining sufficient two-way communications. . . . Employees do want attention; they do want interest and concern; they want opportunities for self-development and self-fulfillment; they want to be heard.[1]

Some of the commonly used media for internal communications are:

- Annual reports
- Booklets and pamphlets

[1]Gerry E. Morse, "Human Relations Management: Concerns for the Future," *Management Review*, 68, no. 6 (June 1979), 48.

- Bulletin boards
- Bulletins or announcements
- Directories
- Employee letters
- Handbooks and manuals
- Magazines
- Newsletters
- Newspapers
- Pay inserts
- Posters

Some business publications designed for management–employee communications are on a formal level: they carry articles about an industry or product in a company printed magazine. Others are breezy and entertaining. They are written in a "newsy" style and list employee items for sale, engagements, information about a company picnic, and so on.

Employee-Oriented. Company employees are interested in news about the company and its activities, general information, employee benefits, company policies, and information about their jobs. To be effective, employee communications must be well written at an appropriate language level. The writer must keep the reader in mind and stimulate interest. To facilitate keeping these publications current, it is common practice to use looseleaf form binders, so that pages can be added or deleted.

Impoverished Language. At times, company publications are distributed outside the company to promote goodwill. They must, of necessity, be factual, accurate, and understandable. Edward Giblin states, "It is commonplace to find organizations where management places great emphasis, time, and energy on communications only to discover that, in spite of these sincere efforts, there is a general lack of understanding and consensus on all of the organization's goals and plans."[2] Giblin contends that management–employee communication difficulties stem from impoverished language; no one really seems to understand what is written.

Annual reports

Years ago, a separate annual report was distributed to employees. Nowadays, to avoid the expense of publishing two reports (an employees annual report

[2]Edward J. Giblin, "How to Communicate in the Tongue-tied Organization," *Management Review*, 67, no. 10 (October 1978), 69.

and a corporate annual report), many corporations distribute copies of the annual stockholder's report to employees. These annual reports usually contain financial information, summaries of company activities, new products and services, facilities, statements by executives, service to the community, employee relations, and so on.

Annual reports are usually printed on quality paper and in color. In addition to financial statements and textual material, they often contain photographs, graphics, and art. George Beisninger states, "According to *Dun's Review*, America's 15,000 publicly held companies spend more than $120 million each year to showcase and distribute a minimum of 50 million copies of their reports. This works out to about $2.50 per copy."[3]

Test question $2.50 per copy.

Booklets and pamphlets

These publications are distributed to employees. They usually contain information about safety, health, special activities, and so on. Booklets and pamphlets may be published by the company or obtained from outside sources. These publications are usually placed on racks for distribution.

Bulletin boards

Bulletin boards are effective when controlled. Cluttered bulletin boards without interesting or significant information are not usually read. An administrative secretary can be assigned the task of keeping the company bulletin boards neat, attractive, current, and informative. The administrative secretary should be the only individual authorized to place items on the bulletin board. All material for display should be presented to the secretary.

It is interesting to note that in some companies, two kinds of bulletin boards are kept: one contains light, breezy, social news; the other contains company business.

Bulletin boards should be highly visible to be effective. They should be situated in prominent positions, preferably in high-traffic areas. Very often, bulletin board announcements are typed on giant primer typewriters (each typewritten letter is about a half inch tall).

It is a good idea to date bulletin board items, so that "stale" items can be routinely removed.

[3]George L. Beisninger, "The Annual Report: Marketing the Corporation," *Management Review*, 68, no. 10 (October 1979), 64.

The clock on the bulletin board is a good attention-getting device. (Courtesy of Connecticut General Corp.)

Bulletins or announcements

It is quite common in the business world to issue written bulletins. In some circumstances, oral bulletins or announcements are made over loudspeakers. Both written and oral announcements are relatively inexpensive, fast, and efficient. Bulletins can be distributed as handout sheets or placed on bulletin boards.

Directories

In larger companies, a directory of employees is a valuable communicative tool. These directories usually list the names, titles, locations, and phone extensions of personnel.

Some directories list the home addresses and home telephone numbers of employees as well. If personnel consider this confidential information, it is not included in the directory. Some directories also contain biographical sketches and are valuable sources of information. New editing typewriters (that permit the addition and deletion of information without the retyping of the entire directory) have aided in keeping directories current at a relatively low cost.

Employee letters

It is common practice to send letters to employees for such diverse things as commendation for a job well done, for suggesting a new money-saving procedure, and to inform. Models of letters sent to employees can be found in Chapter 10. *Test question*

CONGRATULATORY LETTERS

Usually, the letters sent to an employee are of a congratulatory nature. Their purpose is to foster goodwill. Letters of commendation are most effective when individually typed and personally signed. A duplicated letter loses its effectiveness by not having a personal touch.

Handbooks and manuals *Test question*

The words "handbook" and "manual" are often used interchangeably in the business world. The terms apply to a concise, compact book used as a reference guide on a specific subject. Although there seems to be an infinite variety of manuals in use, some of the more popular manuals prepared by business organizations are:

1. *Policy manuals* that list the policy statements of a company. Various regulations and rules of the company are detailed.
2. *Procedures manuals* that detail the routines to be followed to perform a particular task, such as a correspondence manual or filing manual. Procedures manuals are also called *training manuals*.
3. *Employee manuals* that list such things as company business hours,

Employee Handbook

Welcome to Travelers. We're pleased to have you with us, and we
hope this is the beginning of a long and satisfying career for you.

Our handbook was developed for three reasons. First, to help you get
acquainted with the office during your first few weeks.

Second, to give you a source of answers to incidental questions that
might come up.

And third, to explain the things you'll naturally want to know about your
company's policies and practices--the facts behind management and
supervisory decisions.

This handbook is only one source of information, but it describes several
more important sources. It also describes several lines of communication
between you and management. Your supervisor is your most important
source of information and your best line of communication. When you
have questions, ask him or her.

At Travelers, we're committed to communication on all levels. You
have a right to know why things are the way they are, and a right to tell
us what you think of them. We believe the more you know about the
company you work for, the more satisfying your work will be.

FIGURE 12-1. The welcome from an employee handbook
(Courtesy of The Travelers Insurance Companies)

paid vacations, retirement benefits, sick leave, and insurance coverage. These manuals are particularly useful for orienting new employees. Orientation manuals usually contain such things as a statement by the company president, the company history, promotion
policies, and company benefits. Some handbooks can be purchased
by a company; for example, a secretarial handbook.

To keep handbooks current and reliable, they should be updated frequently. Many handbooks are bound in looseleaf binders to facilitate easy
change making.

Handbooks or manuals should be well organized, for they serve as reference books. They should contain a table of contents and an index. There
should be adequate center and side headings to facilitate the rapid location of
reference information.

Magazines

Company magazines are printed periodically by many business organizations
for distribution within a company and, at times, to other business enterprises.

For the purposes of this program, a qualifying alumnus shall be a regular, salaried employee of _____ and be the holder of a bachelor's degree from an eligible school. If an alumnus has received bachelors' degrees from two or more schools, only the first degree granted shall be considered.

★General Services and Facilities

The Personnel Division of the Personnel-Administration Department manages all the general services and facilities provided for employees.

See the Employee Services Directory, Section XII, for specific services and facilities and the telephone extensions to call during daytime office hours to ask about their use.

The lounge areas, the card rooms, the conference room, and the auditorium can be reserved at other than the noon hours for business meetings and other occasions; details, including any service requirements, should be given along with the request for the reservation. The Personnel Division will then coordinate all the service requirements and confirm the arrangements.

These spaces are not generally available for functions unrelated to _____ and our business. Any requests for accommodations of community groups or other organizations should be referred to the director of the Personnel Division, 1 MS.

★ Information and Services

The Information and Services Unit of the Personnel Administration Department is responsible for the release of all employee information.

• SALARY AND EMPLOYMENT VERIFICATION

All inquiries for employee salary or employment verification should be forwarded to the Information and Services Unit (X4405).

★ • RELEASE OF BACKGROUND INFORMATION

All requests for background information on employees and former employees should be transferred to the Information & Services Unit of the Personnel-Administration Department (X4405).

Without an employee's or former employee's written, specific authorization, _____ will release only general "directory information". This information consists of:

1. The fact that an individual works or has worked for _____

2. Dates of employment.

3. Title or position.

4. Office location.

Scrupulous observance of this procedure is important.

Reception of Personal Visitors

It may be necessary at times for an employee to receive a personal visitor during business hours. Generally, it is not feasible to receive the visitor in the employee's department. The Personnel Division reception room is available for that purpose. The use of the lounge areas or the Company reception room at the entrance to any _____ building is not encouraged.

Solicitation of Employees

Occasionally, solicitors enter our premises and permit employees to think that they have Company approval. Such people should be reported immediately to the Corporate Security Office (Extension 3322). The solicitation of employees or the distribution of literature on Company premises by non-employees is prohibited at all times. The solicitation of employees or the distribution of literature on Company premises by employees is prohibited except in non-work areas during non-work time. These prohibitions do not apply to our regular employee Club activities or to our customary cooperation with the United Way and similar agencies.

Parking

The company provides a specified number of parking spaces for employees. These spaces are provided at a monthly rate (to be deducted from the employee's regular pay) in inside or outside facilities. If all spaces are filled, applicants will be put on a waiting list and assigned spaces as they become available. An application for a parking space can be made with the receptionist in the Plaza Building.

Mass Transit

There are many mass transit and charter buses available from the surrounding towns. Information concerning the schedules and costs can be obtained

H.O. Edition, February, 1980

FIGURE 12–2. Sample pages from a supervisor's handbook (Courtesy of The Travelers Insurance Companies)

Customers and concerned individuals outside the business, such as members of the community, professors, and public officials, may also receive the publication.

Company magazines usually include articles that are pertinent to the activities, services and products of a business. Some of the topics of interest found in company magazines are:

- Statements concerning company policy
- New company products
- Community activities of the business
- Employee and executive activities or achievements (promotions, awards, retirements, and so on)
- General topics of interest
- Company campaigns (health, safety, and so on)
- Information about new processes and procedures
- Company goals or objectives
- Interviews
- Company problems or concerns

There is a broad range of company magazines, from relatively inconsequential publications to highly technical publications. Some companies are very serious about the quality of their in-house publications and employ an editor for this task.

Newsletters   *- Informal, casual, not well written*

Test question

Newsletters generally feature company news. Their function is to create goodwill and to inform. Newsletters are usually smaller in size than newspapers and are less formal. Often, they are duplicated on plain sheets of paper (8½ by 11 inches).

Newspapers   *More formal, printers*

The company newspaper is an important periodic source of information for employees. It is distributed more frequently than a company magazine. It often contains a statement by a company executive or the editor of the newspaper. Articles about employee and management activities, various announcements, winners of suggestion box awards, retirees, promotions, conferences or conventions, company social events (picnics, parties, banquets, etc.), and employee items for sale may be included in the company newspaper.

The newspaper usually has a more structured format than the newsletter; also, it is usually printed on a larger size of paper. All in all, it represents a more substantial effort than the company newsletter.

Pay inserts

Most employees receive their pay in envelopes. An easy and inexpensive way to communicate with them is by inserting a message in their pay envelopes. The messages are usually brief and informational. (See Figure 12–3.)

FIGURE 12–3.

Posters

Posters placed strategically throughout a business organization are an effective way to communicate ideas. They are usually designed by a graphic artist and are in color. To be effective, they must carry a limited message and be highly visible (readable) from a distance.

Summary

Progressive business administrators are interested in keeping the channels of communication open with their employees. Two-way communications are essential if morale is to be kept high.

233

Commonly used media for internal communications are varied. At times, company publications are distributed outside the company to promote goodwill.

Nowadays, many corporations distribute copies of stockholder's reports to employees. Also, booklets and pamphlets containing information about safety, health, special activities, etc., are distributed to employees. Bulletin boards are commonly used for announcements. Bulletins can be distributed as handout sheets or placed on bulletin boards.

In larger companies, directories are commonly used for listing names, titles, locations, and phone extensions of personnel. Some directories even contain biographical sketches.

Letters are sent by management to employees for such diverse things as commendation, information, etc.

The words "handbook" and "manual" are often used interchangeably in the business world. The terms apply to publications used as reference guides on a specific subject (policy manuals, procedures manuals, employee manuals).

Company magazines usually include articles that are pertinent to the activities, services and products of a business. There is a broad range of company magazines, from relatively inconsequential publications to highly technical ones.

Newsletters generally stress company news. They are less formal than company newspapers. The company newspaper is an important periodic source of information for employees. They usually contain a variety of articles ranging from winners of suggestion box awards to details about the company picnic.

Brief informational messages are often inserted into pay envelopes. This is an easy and inexpensive way to communicate with employees.

Discussion

1. Why are progressive business administrators concerned about maintaining and sustaining good management-employee relations?

Study questions

1. List the media commonly used for management–employee communications.
2. What is the range of formality of company publications?
3. Why are management–employee communications important?

4. How much does a typical annual report cost? *$ 2.50 per copy*

5. What items are usually placed on racks for distribution? *Bootletts and pamphlets*

6. What is usually placed on bulletin boards? *Company business, social news*

7. How should bulletin boards be controlled? *Through secretary*

8. What does a directory usually list? *Names, titles, locations, phone numbers*

9. When are letters usually sent to employees? *Commendation, congraduation*

10. List the three most popular kinds of manuals. *Policy manuals, Procedural manuals, and Employee*

11. List the topics usually found in company magazines. *pp. 232*

12. How does a newsletter differ from a newspaper? *newsletter are less formal*

13. What kinds of messages are inserted in pay envelopes? *Brief informational*

14. Posters should have two characteristics to be effective. Please list them. *1) carry limited message 2) be highly visable*

Activity

If possible, visit a company office and obtain samples of internal communications (company magazines, newsletters, pay inserts, etc.). If you cannot visit a company office, compose a newsletter to employees, or a pay insert.

ACHIEVEMENT OF LEARNING GOALS

Check the appropriate boxes to determine whether you have or have not achieved the learning goals of this chapter.

I Can:

	YES	NO
1. Understand the need for management–employee communications.	☐	☐
2. Distinguish among the commonly used media for internal communication.	☐	☐
3. Recognize the specific purposes of company publications.	☐	☐

If any of your responses were "no," it is suggested that you review pertinent chapter parts.

13

Electronic Mail

LEARNING GOALS

1. Comprehend what electronic mail entails.
2. Recognize the relative advantages of electronic mail.
3. Understand the various electronic mail systems and equipment currently in use.
4. Describe facsimile equipment and procedures.
5. Recognize the role facsimilie plays in electronic mail systems.

Electronic mail *Difficult chapter* [handwritten]

As the cost of conventional mail goes up, business administrators seek alternatives for transmitting written communications. Presently, the relative cost of electronic mail is more than regular mail. It is expected, however, that as technology improves, the cost of electronic mail will decrease.

Electronic mail is a communications system which entails the transmission of information or messages in electronic form. In its broadest interpretation, the telephone and telegraphic services, such as telegrams and Mailgrams, are forms of electronic mail. However, since telephone communications transmit sounds, not written messages, some businesses do not consider it to be a substitute form of mail.

He said this in class [handwritten margin note]

Electronic mail offers an enticing advantage: it speeds up time-critical communications. Electronic communications take seconds or minutes to transmit; conventional mail may take several days.

In direct business-to-business communications, the emphasis is usually on *immediacy* and *efficiency*. Business (and government and nonbusiness institutions as well) have shown a willingness to pay a premium

Electronic mail can be transmitted very quickly. [handwritten note]

for speed and certifiable delivery, with the rate of the premium depending upon the urgency of the message.[1]

An advertisement for an electronic mail systems company has a picture of a dejected mailman on the cover of a brochure. Further evidence of the decline of the U. S. Postal Service is an article in *Infosystems* entitled "Infosystems Report: Electronic Mail—The Postal Person Disappeareth."[2]

The U. S. Postal Service is struggling to retain its role as the leading deliverer of written messages. "If present trends continue, the giant U. S. Postal Service could become little more than a pygmy by the end of the next decade."[3] Although the Postal Service has a monopoly on letter mail, it does not have exclusive rights to messages transmitted by telecommunications. It is estimated that electronic communications will decrease first-class mail volume by a third by the mid-1990s.[4]

To combat the use of electronic mail by private companies, the U. S. Postal Service is offering Mailgrams (in conjunction with Western Union); electronic computer-originated mail (E-COM), an electronic-message service; and INTELPOST, a mail-via-satellite system.

Mr. Edward Radding, Vice President of Media Services for the Milton Bradley Company has stated:

> Currently we are involved with an advanced application of computer communication. We have in place across the U.S. a Retail Service Organization composed of specialized sales people. Several of these RSO people are carrying with them portable computer terminals as they make their daily sales calls in retail stores within store chains which have elected to be part of this Milton Bradley program.... Our RSO sales people also use this terminal to communicate with their management. We have a large sales force and they travel a good deal. Reaching these people at their homes can be time-consuming, inefficient, and impractical. By use of the portable computer terminal we can create two-way communication at any time. The sales person logs in and requests messages. The terminal prints out any messages management has stored for that specific sales person. Messages can also be typed into the terminal by the field sales individual to be accessed at any convenient time by the sales management group. No unanswered calls, no busy signals to waste

[1]Paul Newman, "Business Takes the Lead...Electronic Mail Is a Practical Reality," *ZIP*, 3, no. 1 (January/February 1980), 27.

[2]Frederick W. Miller, "Infosystems Report: Electronic Mail—The Postal Person Disappeareth," *Infosystems*, 25, no. 12 (December 1978), 34, 38–40.

[3]"Why Postal Service Faces Bleak Future," *U. S. News & World Report*, LXXXIX, no. 22 (December 1, 1980), 39.

[4]*Ibid.*

Computer mailbox — electronic mail

time.... We believe that our computer communications system will
continue to have a growing impact on our business in the future.[5]

Within a broad interpretation of *written* electronic mail transmission
systems, the following communications systems are included:

- Telegraphic services (telegrams and Mailgrams)
- Telex and TWX (also called Telex I and Telex II)
- Satellite services
- Computer-based message system (CBMS)
- Communicating word processors (CWP)
- Electronic computer-originated mail (E-COM)
- INTELPOST
- Datapost
- Facsimile (fax)

Figures 13–1 and 13–2 illustrate comparative communication systems.

Telegraphic services   *Samuel Morse*
                          Test Question   know this guy!!!

INTRODUCTION

The telegraph is a system for the electronic transmission of coded messages by
wire or radio waves. Samuel F. B. Morse first demonstrated his telegraph
model in 1838. It consisted of a key and electromagnet at each end of a wire.
The key sent a message in code (dots and dashes) to the electromagnet, called a
"sounder," at the other end of the wire. In 1844, Morse transmitted the biblical message, "What hath God wrought!," from Washington, D. C. to Balti-
more, Maryland.

By 1856, fledgling telegraph companies consolidated to form the Western Union Telegraph Company. In 1861, the first transcontinental telegraph
line was strung. This connected the country for the first time by rapid communications. A permanent cable was laid under the Atlantic Ocean in 1866.
By the 1970's, Western Union had one of the most modern, computerized systems in the world, serving business, government, and the public. Western
Union International, Inc., not affiliated with Western Union, provides international telecommunication services.

1861
1866

[5]In a letter to the author dated June 3, 1981.

1861 - first transcontinental telegraph line was strung
1866 - cable laid under Atlantic ocean

TRADITIONAL MAIL

TELEPHONE

TELEGRAMS

MAILGRAMS/ELECTRONIC COMPUTER-ORIENTED MAIL

TWX/TELEX/FACSIMILE/COMMUNICATING WORD PROCESSORS

FIGURE 13–1. Comparative communication systems

Telegraph service is much faster than mail; however, it is more costly. The telegraph is an excellent mode of communication for sending important messages. It should be noted that because of the cost, messages are usually brief.

There are six ways to transmit communications to the telegraph company:

240

COMPUTER-BASED MESSAGE SYSTEM

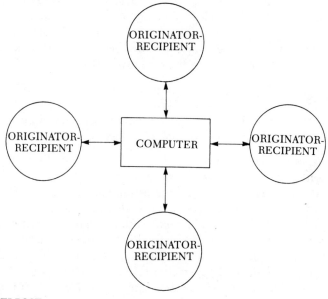

INTELPOST

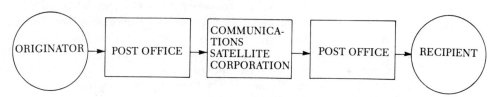

DATAPOST

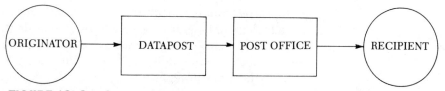

FIGURE 13–2. Comparative communication systems (concluded)

1. Telephone
2. Presenting the message in person
3. Teleprinter
4. Facsimile machine
5. Computer
6. Communicating word processors and other electronic terminals

Subscribers can communicate directly with each other by using teletype circuits (Telex and TWX). Messages are transmitted directly from person to person, without the telegraph company acting as an intermediary.

Large offices have a direct wire service to Western Union. This is called *tie line service*. Some companies have teleprinters on which a message is typed and instantly recorded in the telegraph office.

DOMESTIC SERVICES United States

There are three basic types of domestic telegraph services: telegrams (full-rate and overnight), telegraph money orders, and Mailgrams.

Telegrams. The telegram is the most widely used telegraph service. It is a rapid way to transmit a written message. A telegram is sent when speed and/or a written record are important considerations. The message is either written or typed by the sender on a telegram blank, a form provided by Western Union. Some companies make their own forms or simply type the message on a sheet of plain paper. To expedite the process, most messages are dictated over the telephone to an operator in the telegraph office. The message is then transmitted via a teletypewriter to the receiving station. The message can be delivered by teleprinter to offices having this service. It is then read over the telephone to the recipient.

For an additional fee, the message can be hand-delivered to the recipient by a Western Union messenger. The sender can request that the recipient sign a receipt, proving that the telegram was received. In some instances, the sender will mail a typewritten copy of the message to the addressee. If the telegram is phoned, a written confirmation copy can be requested by the addressee from Western Union. The written copy is mailed for a fee.

There are two types of telegrams:

1. *Full-rate telegram.* The full-rate telegram is the most expensive and fastest telegraphic service. It usually reaches its destination within two or three hours. The minimal charge is based on fifteen words. There is a charge for additional words. Full-rate telegrams can be sent anytime, day or night.

2. *Overnight telegram.* The overnight telegram is a slower and less expensive service than the full-rate telegram. It is accepted for transmission by the telegraph office until midnight for delivery the following day, usually in the morning. The minimal charge is based on one hundred words. There is a charge for additional words.

Although the use of the telegram is declining, it has a major advantage: Western Union retains a tape of telegrams transmitted which serves as proof of the content of the message.

Personal opinion telegrams, containing messages of public interest that are no more than fifteen words, can be sent to designated members of the federal and state government (President, Vice President, congressmen, Governor, Lieutenant Governor, members of a state legislature) at reduced rates.

Telegraphic Money Orders. Telegraphic money orders allow money to be sent to a distant point rapidly. The procedure is simple. The sender deposits the money to be transmitted at the telegraph office. The telegraph operator then authorizes the telegraph office at the destination to make payment. The recipient of the money must be able to provide evidence of identity and to answer a test question, such as date of birth or the name of an obscure relative. The charge is based on the sum of money being transferred, plus the cost of the telegram. *Sending money through offices all over country*

Mailgrams.. The Mailgram is a "wedding" of the services of Western Union and the U.S. Postal Service. A message is sent by telephoning (day or night), by delivering the message in person to the nearest telegraph office, or by using Telex, TWX, computer terminal, Info-Com, communicating word processor, or Western Union supplied CRT terminal.

Next, Western Union transmits the message to a printer at the post office nearest to the addressee. A Mailgram is delivered by a U. S. Postal Service letter carrier with the next mail delivery. A Mailgram may be obtained earlier by the addressee if it is addressed to a post office box.

The Mailgram is sent in a distinctive blue and white envelope which differentiates it from regular mail. The basic charge is for fifty words. There is a charge for additional increments of fifty words. A Mailgram sent by phone is about half the cost of an overnight telegram. However, business users are offered substantial discounts for higher volumes and/or term agreements of three months or longer. In volume, Mailgram messages can be priced as low as $1.00 for three hundred characters (about fifty words).

INTERNATIONAL SERVICES *World Wide Basis*

Radio communication satellites or cable are used for the following international telegraph services:

- International full-rate telegrams (radiograms or cablegrams)
- International letter telegrams (overnight telegrams)
- International Telex
- Leased channel service
- Voice/data service
- International money orders
- Database service

International Full-rate Telegrams. The international full-rate telegram is the most expensive and rapid international telegraphic service. International telegrams are also called *cablegrams* (when sent to foreign countries connected by transoceanic cable) and *radiograms* (when there is no cable connection). Radiograms can be sent to ships at sea, airplanes in flight, and trains in motion. Relay satellites are used to transmit wireless messages.

International telegrams are sent abroad by five international carriers:

1. French Telegraph Cable Company (FCH)
2. ITT World Communications (ITT)
3. RCA Global Communications (RCA)
4. TRT Telecommunications Corporation (TRT)
5. Western Union International (WUI) — Another company

Companies that send many messages abroad have a registered cable code. This is an abbreviated company name and address used to keep the word count down and thus save money. The minimal rate is for seven or fewer words. This includes the address and signature.

International Letter Telegrams. The international letter telegram is slower and less expensive than international full-rate telegrams. Service is overnight by radio or cable. The minimal rate is for twenty-two or fewer words.

International Telex. International Telex users transmit their messages directly to overseas Telex subscribers. Users have instantaneous two-way communications in writing. Messages can be transmitted overseas day or night.

Leased Channel Service. A company can lease a private communications line. This exclusive line connects a United States based firm with correspondents or branches overseas. The subscriber can use the leased line around the clock, seven days a week. There is a flat monthly charge for this service.

Voice/Data Service. Voice/Data Service allows offices on a communications network to correspond with each other using voice and data communication.

International Money Orders. International money orders are used for transmitting money abroad. This is done in conjunction with the Chase Manhattan Bank in New York City.

Database Service. Database service provides users with immediate access to their own or international computer systems. This is especially helpful for gathering, processing, and computing essential data from remote places.

SPECIAL TELEGRAPHIC EQUIPMENT AND SERVICES

Highly sophisticated equipment is used to facilitate rapid communications by Western Union.

Teleprinter. A teleprinter is used in a business office to transmit messages directly to a telegraph office or to another teleprinter terminal.

The operation of a teleprinter terminal is similar to that of a typewriter. The message is either typed or punched on tape by a secretary in the business office and then transmitted to another terminal where the message appears.

Telex and TWX (Telex I and Telex II)

Telex is also called Telex I; TWX is also called Telex II. Many large corporations, in addition to having their own internal teletypewriter systems, have Telex and/or TWX (pronounced "twix"), which are teletypewriter networks. They are operated by Western Union on an interconnected basis. Telex/TWX subscribers cannot communicate with each other. Major features of Telex and TWX communications are:

1. Teletypewriter communication can take place around the clock (twenty-four hours a day, seven days a week). Messages can be received when terminals are unattended.

2. Both sender and receiver have a permanent copy of every message.

3. Messages can be recorded on punched paper tape. This assures accuracy, for errors on the tape can be corrected prior to sending.

4. After dialing Telex-to-Telex or TWX-to-TWX, you can get an "answerback" or automatic identification. This is a safeguard against transmitting to an undesired party.

5. A telegram or international telegram and a Mailgram message can be sent by teletypewriter.

6. If the same names and addresses are used often, RediList is used. This special list for Telex and TWX subscribers saves time. One or more address lists with delivery instructions can be stored in a Western Union computer for use at any time.

Satellite services

MARITIME SATELLITE SERVICE

A specially designed maritime satellite system makes it possible for a sender to be in instant contact with any Telex or telephone subscriber in the world. Therefore, reliable ship-to-shore or shore-to-ship communication (Telex, cablegram, data, facsimile), as well as international land-to-land communication, can take place. The maritime satellite system is called MARISAT and consists of three satellites in geostationery orbit over the Atlantic, Pacific, and Indian Oceans.

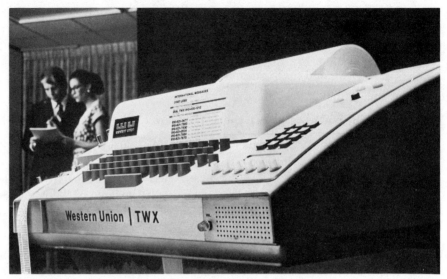

A Western Union TWX keyboard (Courtesy Western Union)

SATELLITE TELEVISION SERVICE

Much of Western Union's satellite (Westar) capacity is used for television and radio broadcasting. Western Union satellites are multi-function; they transmit communication messages and are also used for relaying radio and television broadcast signals. For example, the Apollo moon flights, Wimbleton tennis, and International Olympic Games have been transmitted via satellite.

Computer-based message system (CBMS) *People communicate from computer to computer.*

Miller very ably describes a computer-based message system (CBMS) as follows:

> A CBMS is a computer network, either self-contained or part of another communications network, that uses a computer and special software for store-and-forward message handling. Users have CRT terminals, some with hardcopy output. The software is written specifically for message handling, using familiar English words as commands, and a typical "office memo" format on the CRT screen.
>
> Such a system holds messages and "mail" in a sender's electronic mailbox or specific area within the computer and sends mail on command to the recipient's mailbox or to multiple mailboxes if carbon copies are needed, or if more than a single other user is a recipient.[6]

[6]Miller, p. 38.

246

facsimile

Exxon Office Systems' Qwip 1200 is a desk facsimile unit that lets users send and receive pictures and letters over the telephone nationwide in four to six minutes. (Courtesy Exxon Enterprises)

Computer-based message systems (CBMS) are cost saving. "In a study done by Citibank in New York City, it was estimated that a $10 million CBMS servicing 4,000 executives resulted in a cost avoidance of $15 million."[7]

Communicating word processors (CWP) *Word processors that communicate with each other.*

The communicating word processor is a text editing unit with communicating equipment. CWPs can communicate with other CWPs or with computers, and they can transmit copy to phototypesetters. "Because both DP and WP equipment use the same electronic technology, the joining of the two into information processing and communications networks is inevitable."[8] In the future, CWPs will be hooked up to intelligent copiers. Copies will be made from electronic impulses.

About one in three word processing units has communications capabilities. CWPs communicate rapidly over phone lines about fifteen to twenty times the speed of facsimile. Also, they are less expensive than facsimile.

The CWP electronic mail system works as follows:

1. Copy is keyboarded on a small computer with a CRT screen.

[7]Miller, p. 38.

[8]"Electronic Mail Systems," *Administrative Management*, XXXIX, no. 8 (August, 1978), 37.

Xerox 8010 Star information systems enables users to create, change, store, and retrieve text, graphics, and records. Users can distribute documents via electronic mail. (Courtesy of Xerox Corporation)

2. The message is edited, if necessary, and transmitted electronically to a single or multiple location.

3. The message appears on the recipient's CRT screen where it can be viewed or received as hard copy.

Electronic computer-originated mail (E-COM) *like mailgram but it is used by big company*

E-COM is a new electronic service offered by the U. S. Postal Service to speed the delivery of automated messages. Mailgram offers overnight service; E-COM provides delivery within two business days anywhere in the contiguous United States. E-COM enables high-volume commercial mailers—customers must send a minimum of 5,000 messages a month, at least 200 messages to a batch—to send material either by telecommunications carriers or telephone to twenty-five designated post offices for delivery as regular first-class

248

facsimile

The Xerox Telecopier 485 can send or receive a typical one-page business letter in about one minute. (Courtesy Xerox Corporation)

mail. E-COM has been instituted by the U. S. Postal Service to prevent any further loss of first-class mail business to private electronic-message services.

INTELPOST   *like mailgram too, only messages go overseas internationally.*

INTELPOST is an international electronic service of the U. S. Postal Service. The Communications Satellite Corporation is assisting in the development of this mail-via-satellite service. Mail delivered to the Postal Service headquarters in Washington, D. C. or to the World Trade Center in New York City will be transmitted electronically to the Comsat earth station at Etam, West Virginia. Messages will be sent via satellite to INTELPOST centers in foreign countries (Argentina, Belgium, France, Iran, the Netherlands, the United Kingdom, and West Germany). At these centers, the messages will be printed and delivered to addressees as regular mail. Messages can be sent from these foreign countries to the Postal Service headquarters in Washington, D. C. or to the World Trade Center in New York City for delivery.

Datapost ~ Competitor of mailgram. It is not run by Government

Datapost is a Mailgram competitor. Datapost receives messages by telecopier and facsimile in Chicago and distributes them to the U. S. Postal Service for delivery to 25 cities the next day. Datapost uses a telegram/Mailgram look-alike format.

Facsimile will boom in future

At times, it is essential to transmit hard copy, such as letters, financial statements, and orders, to a distant point in seconds or minutes. This is an impossible task using regular delivery systems such as mail and express. Facsimile transceivers are the answer; they make quick and accurate hard copy communication possible by combining digital technology with existing telephone lines.

Facsimile is a major form of electronic mail in use today. A light-sensing device scans an image (printed copy, diagrams, graphs, pictures, tables, and the like), which is transmitted over telephone lines to the receiver. The recipient's transceiver reproduces a hard copy of the exact image. A major advantage of facsimile is that the sender retains the original while the receiver gets a copy. Although facsimile is relatively expensive, some executives think its high-speed image transmission capabilities are well worth the cost. (See Figure 13–3.)

Alexander Bain of Scotland is credited with first proposing a facsimile transceiver in 1842. He proposed a stylus swinging from a pendulum. The stylus explored a shellacked picture on a metal base. The electric current from the stylus's contact with the metal was to be sent over telegraph lines to a receiver, where the image would be reproduced by another pendulum on chemically treated paper.

It is interesting to note that radiophoto and wirephoto services had the first commercial facsimile systems. Facsimile is becoming an integral part of the modern electronic office.

To state the procedure simply, it can be compared to the making of a photocopy of a document and having the copy appear at a distant point in seconds or minutes.

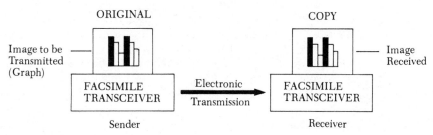

FIGURE 13–3. Facsimile transmission system

Facsimile is commonly called *fax* in the business world. Other terms used are:

facsimile

- Phototelegraphy
- Telecopier
- Radiophoto
- Wirephoto
- Telephotography
- Telephoto

Facsimile communication is generally employed as follows in the business world: A facsimile transceiver uses a light-sensing device to scan the original document for electronic transmission over telephone lines. An exact copy is printed at the destination point.

Since facsimile is a form of electronic mail, facsimile machines are sometimes called "electronic mail machines" by one manufacturer. A company can have electronic written communication with branch offices, customers, suppliers, and so on using graphic transceivers connected to regular telephone lines. Documents from a word processing unit can be fed to the facsimile transceiver for communication.

The operation of newer facsimile machines is simple; no special training is required. The set is turned on, a switch is moved to the SEND or RECEIVE modes, the telephone number is dialed, a "ready" light goes on, and a start button is pressed.

Newer, unattended facsimile transceivers are designed to send and receive documents automatically. Automatic transmission can take place from a word processing center by storing the message in computer memory. As many as one hundred documents can be transmitted and received unattended, day or night. Some of the newer facsimile machines have the ability to "store" a document on magnetic tape until it is transmitted.

Since telephone rates vary throughout the day, peak hour transmission is more expensive than night transmission. *Automatic, unattended facsimile systems can save considerable money by functioning after regular business hours.*

Some of the newest automatic transceivers have automatic phone answering capabilities. When document preloaded, they will respond to a telephone command from a compatible machine to send or receive a document.

Manufacturers are experimenting with improved equipment that will speed up transmission time and further reduce the cost of manual and automatic operation.

Special facsimile equipment is used to make stencils and offset masters. A scanner reproduces an exact copy of a document on a stencil or offset master.

PORTABLE TRANSCEIVERS

Completely portable units can be used anywhere there is a telephone connection. This portability is ideal for many business situations. For example, an executive at a convention in a foreign country can send vital information to the home office immediately, or a salesperson can send in order forms while on the road. Some unattended portable models can receive documents and business communications day and night.

DESKTOP FACSIMILE TRANSCEIVERS

Easy to operate desktop facsimile transceivers can send images at selectable speeds of 2, 3, 4 or 6 minutes over conventional telephone lines. Variable-speed transmission permits compatibility with other transceivers. Communication with all other kinds of transceivers is important for it expands the facsimile network to include *all* transceivers.

Desktop models are attractive, compact units, about the size of a portable typewriter. In addition to transmitting hard copy, it is possible to hold regular telephone conversations using desktop facsimile transceivers. Resolution quality can be controlled. Automatic features include document loading, margin adjustment, document ejection, and return to "ready."

SOPHISTICATED FACSIMILE TRANSCEIVERS

Large, sophisticated transceivers can transmit a document in 20 seconds or less. Some models feature automatic answering, receiving and disconnect mechanisms so that documents can be handled unattended day or night. Night transmission allows lower phone rates. Also, new transceivers send and receive images simultaneously.

Automatic feeders accept originals of various thicknesses, from onion skin to card stock. Mixed sizes of paper can be accepted, up to 8½ by 14 inches.

Some transceivers have automatic redialing features. For example, if a

line is busy or if there is a faulty connection, the number is automatically re-
dialed.

Special codes are used for security reasons. An unauthorized operator
cannot intercept a document.

When excellent document transmission is required, special facsimile
transmitters with no receiving capabilities may be used.

ADVANTAGES

The advantages of facsimile transmission are numerous:

- Transmission can be to any place where there is a telephone and a
  transceiver, worldwide.
- Hard copy messages can be transmitted rapidly in seconds or minutes
  faster than by messenger, mail or express.
- A document can be transmitted simultaneously to one hundred differ-
  ent destination points.
- Copy that is as large as 8½ by 14 inches can be transmitted.
- Costs are generally lower than by messenger, mail, or express.
- Automatic, unattended transceivers permit night transmission when
  telephone rates are lower.
- Portable units facilitate transmission from any telephone.
- Transceivers can send and receive simultaneously.
- Coding devices make it impossible for unauthorized operators to "in-
  tercept" documents.
- Operation is simple; special operators are not necessary.
- Fully automatic features such as automatic feeder, automatic margin
  adjustment, and automatic redial simplify operations.
- Communication is accurate, since an exact duplicate is received. The
  error potential of TWX and Telex is eliminated.
- There is a choice of resolution quality.
- Originals can be as thin as onion skin paper or as thick as a card.
- The original copy is retained by the sender.

Summary

Electronic mail offers an enticing advantage over regular mail, speeding up
time-critical communications. Electronic mail takes seconds or minutes to
transmit; mail may take several days. Electronic mail is a communications

system which entails the transmission of information or messages in electronic form. In its broadest interpretation, the telephone and telegraphic services are forms of electronic mail. The following communications systems are considered to be forms of electronic mail:

- Telegraphic services (telegrams and Mailgrams)
- Telex and TWX
- Satellite services
- Computer-based message system (CBMS)
- Communicating word processors (CWP)
- Electronic computer-originated mail (ECOM)
 - INTELPOST
- Datapost
- Facsimile (fax)

The telegram is the most widely used telegraph service. There are full-rate and overnight telegrams; there are also personal opinion telegrams and telegraphic money orders. The Mailgram utilizes the services of Western Union and the U. S. Postal Service. A message is sent to Western Union and transmitted to the post office nearest to the addressee for delivery. Various international telegraph services are available, such as: international full-rate telegrams, international letter telegrams, international Telex, leased channel service, international money orders, and database service.

Many large businesses, in addition to having their own internal teletype-writer systems, employ Telex and/or TWX. Telex and TWX are teletypewriter networks operated by Western Union.

In a computer-based message system, a computer is used for store-and-forward message distribution.

The communicating word processor is a text-editing unit with communicating equipment. Presently, about one in three word processing units has communications capabilities.

Electronic-computer-originated mail service is offered by the U. S. Postal Service. E-COM enables high-volume mailers to send messages to twenty-five designated post offices for delivery as first class mail. INTEL-POST is an international electronic service of the U. S. Postal Service. Datapost is a Mailgram competitor.

Facsimile, a form of electronic mail, is very popular today. Images of diagrams, printed copy, graphs, pictures, tables, and the like can be transmitted over telephone lines to the receiver. The recipient's transceiver reproduces a hard copy of the exact image transmitted.

With a facsimile capability, a company can have electronic written communications with branch offices, customers, suppliers, and so on using graphic transceivers connected to regular telephone lines. Documents from a word processing unit can be fed to the facsimile transceiver for communication.

Newer, unattended facsimile transceivers are designed to send and receive documents automatically. Portable units can be used anywhere there is a telephone connection.

Desktop facsimile transceivers can send images at selectable speeds. This permits compatibility with other kinds of transceivers.

Sophisticated transceivers can transmit a document in twenty seconds or less, have receiving and disconnect mechanisms, permit night transmission, send and receive images simultaneously, accept various thicknesses of originals, and have automatic redialing features. There are numerous advantages of facsimile transmission.

Discussion

1. Explain the major advantages and disadvantages of electronic mail in contrast to traditional mail. *faster, but more expensive*
2. What is the United States Postal Service doing to combat the mounting competition of electronic mail?
3. Explain how facsimile is used as a form of electronic mail.

Study questions

1. What are the reasons for the increased popularity of electronic mail? *faster*
2. What is electronic mail? *transmission of communication in electronic form*
3. List nine forms of written electronic mail services. *pp. 254*
4. What is the major advantage and disadvantage of the telegram? *Retain copy of message, proof of message, yet declining due to expensiveness.*
5. List six ways to transmit communications to the telegraph company.
6. What are the two basic types of telegrams? *full-rate and overnight*
7. What is a personal opinion telegram?
8. Explain telegraphic money orders.
9. Explain Mailgram service.
10. List seven international services.
11. List the five international carriers.

12. What function does a teleprinter serve?

13. Many large corporations, in addition to having their own internal teletypewriter systems, have one or two teletypewriter systems operated by Western Union. List them.

14. MARISAT is an acronym for what service?

15. What is much of Westar's capacity used for?

16. Briefly describe a computer-based message system (CBMS).

17. What is a communicating word processor (CWP)?

18. How does electronic computer-originated mail (E-COM) differ from Mailgram?

19. What is INTELPOST?

20. What is Datapost?

21. What is "facsimile"?

22. Who is credited for the first proposal of a facsimile transceiver?

23. Who had the first commercial facsimile systems?

24. What is facsimile commonly called in the business world?

25. How many documents can be transmitted and received unattended, day and night?

26. Can special facsimile equipment be used to make stencils and offset masters?

27. How rapidly can large, sophisticated transceivers transmit?

28. To how many destination points can a document be transmitted simultaneously?

29. Can some transceivers send and receive simultaneously?

30. What has a higher error potential, facsimile or TWX and Telex?

Activities

1. Compose a full-rate telegram message (not to exceed fifteen words) extending congratulations to a friend.

2. Compose a personal opinion telegram message (not to exceed fifteen words) to the President of the United States voicing your opinion about a current problem.

3. Compose a night letter message (not to exceed one hundred words) to a domestic automobile manufacturing company. Tell what you like or dislike about the automobiles manufactured by the company.

4. Describe in writing some of the newest features of facsimile com-

munication equipment. The yellow pages of your telephone directory list the names of facsimile dealers. Sales representatives will be able to assist you in your research. Also, current articles in periodicals can provide you with this information.

ACHIEVEMENT OF LEARNING GOALS

Check the appropriate boxes to determine whether you have or have not achieved the learning goals of this chapter.

I Can:

		YES	NO
1.	Comprehend what electronic mail entails.	☐	☐
2.	Recognize the relative advantages of electronic mail.	☐	☐
3.	Understand the various electronic mail systems and equipment currently in use.	☐	☐
4.	Describe facsimile equipment and procedures.	☐	☐
5.	Explain the role facsimile plays in electronic mail systems.	☐	☐

If any of your responses were "no," it is suggested that you review pertinent chapter parts.

III

NONWRITTEN COMMUNICATIONS

Oral Presentations/Listening

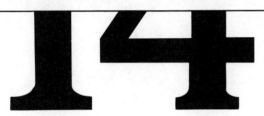

LEARNING GOALS

1. Understand the importance of effective oral communication.
2. Identify the various informal and formal oral communication situations that exist in the business world.
3. Ascertain the activities undertaken during the precommuniation, communication, and post-communication periods.
4. Comprehend fully nonverbal communication signals.
5. Know how messages are verbalized.
6. Recognize the reciprocal relationship between the speaker and the audience, feedback.
7. Differentiate between hearing and listening.
8. Understand the barriers to effective listening.
9. Recognize the techniques for improving listening skills.

Oral presentations

The word "oral" is derived from the Latin word *os,* which means "mouth." Oral communication is the interchange of ideas, thoughts, or information by speech. Human speech is audible language, a series of sounds and periods of silence. The sounds vary in volume, rhythm, length, and pitch.

Historically, oral communication preceded written communication. Although oral communication is universal, about one-third of the people in the world (over 800 million) are illiterate. UNESCO projects that by 1990, there will be 884 million illiterates worldwide!

Most people spend more time communicating orally (speaking and listening) than writing or reading. However, very often oral communication is garbled, inaccurate, and difficult to comprehend. William Safire, the well known political columnist, was asked, "What is most responsible for corrupting the English language?" His response is interesting:

> The telephone. A couple of generations ago people wrote letters to each other. Not anymore. We have become an oral society; we've forgotten how to write. After you forget how to write, you forget how to read; then you forget how to speak. That results in conversation studded

with "like, I mean, you know, wow"—a form of grunting that would be familiar to cavemen. I don't consider *cavemen* sexist either. I include cavewomen under the rubric cavemen.[1]

To be successful in the business world, it is critical that an individual be able to articulate thinking orally.

Oral communication in the business world can be divided into two parts, informal and formal. Generally, informal presentations are made to individuals and formal presentations are made to groups.

must be able to express yourself well orally

INFORMAL ORAL COMMUNICATION   *—talk to people*

Much of the oral communication in the business world is informal, person-to-person. These communications are generally conversational, with instantaneous feedback. Most conversations are a rapid give-and-take of information and ideas. Explaining procedures to an employee is an example of informal, conversational communication.

FORMAL ORAL COMMUNICATION

Formal oral communication in the business world takes the form of public or presentational speaking. A speaker communicates to a number of people simultaneously, on a group basis. There are, of course, obvious advantages to speaking to a group of people. It avoids duplicity of effort, saves time, and permits a polished presentation. At times, there is a question-and-answer period after a formal oral presentation. Many group oral presentations are in a formal setting.

These are some of the situations which call for formal oral presentations in business organizations:

- Speeches/addresses
- Oral reports
- Lectures
- Presentations
- Meetings
- Forums
- Symposiums

- Panels
- Conferences
- Discussions
- Orientations
- Training sessions
- Banquets

Three Speech-Making Activities. Generally, there are three distinct periods of activity in the speech-making continuum:

Test ques

---

[1]William Safire, "In His Own Words," *People*, 15, no. 8 (March 2, 1981), 60–61.

Interval of Time	*Activity* Test Question
Precommunication period	Preparation
Communication period	Delivery
Post-communication period	Evaluation

A number of steps are involved in each of these periods (Table 14–1).

THE PRECOMMUNICATION PERIOD (PREPARATION)

Preparation
Delivery
Evaluation

The average business executive is not a polished public speaker; therefore, considerable time should be spent preparing for a speech. Techniques of delivery should be studied and mastered. The executive who can give an interesting and informative speech is usually on the road to advancement.

Most people are frightened at the prospect of speaking before a group. For introverts, it may prove to be a rather traumatic experience. The following are suggestions for overcoming the fear of public speaking (called "laliophobia"): — fear of giving speech.

Test 1) Preliminary
      2) Delivery
      3) Evaluation

1. To bolster confidence, know the subject thoroughly; have a greater knowledge than the audience. Prepare yourself by developing a well-structured presentation. Your talk should have an introduction, body, and summary.

2. Speak before groups of people as often as possible. Some people have

Precommunication Period (Preparation)	Communiucation Period (Delivery)	Post-Communication Period (Evaluation and "Clean Up")
1. Identify the topic	1. Nonverbal communication	1. Evaluative techniques
2. Determine the purpose	Appearance	Forms
	Eye contact	Individuals
3. Ascertain the time allowance	Gestures	Personal appraisal
4. Study the audience	Posture	Analyze questions
5. Research the subject thoroughly	Facial expressions	Review tapes
6. Organize the presentation	Mannerisms	
	Paralanguage	2. Follow through on commitments made
7. Determine audiovisual aids	Body movement	
8. Structure the delivery	2. Verbal communication	3. Return special equipment used
Memorized	Voice quality	4. Extend thanks
Textual	Pitch	5. File research and notes
Extemporaneous	Rate	
	Volume	6. Note specifics
9. Prepare notes	Resonance	
	Pronunciation	
10. Check the physical arrangements	Enunciation	
11. Rehearse the speech	3. Language skills	
12. Prepare for evaluation	4. Audience feedback	

found it beneficial to join the Toastmasters Club, an organization formed to improve the membership's public speaking ability. Assume a leadership role in group activities (clubs, discussion groups, classes, etc.) whenever possible.

3. Learn to speak extemporaneously from notes. Avoid reading or memorizing a speech unless it is absolutely essential, for you may lose your spontaneity. Try to be conversational. Talk to individuals in the audience and maintain eye contact with them. Don't tell jokes if it makes you uncomfortable. A silent audience after a joke can be devastating. Also, avoid offensive remarks that antagonize.

4. Take a few deep breaths before speaking. This will help to relax you. Do not rush to the podium.

helps calm you down

5. Use visual aids. If the audience is looking at a poster or screen, not the speaker, this will temporarily relieve tension.

6. Be animated and dynamic while speaking (gesturing, moving towards the audience to emphasize a point, etc.) will also help to release anxiety and tension.

7. Rehearse the speech, ideally in the location where it will be presented. Familiarize yourself with the use of the microphone if one will be used. Practice the use of audiovisual equipment. This will help to reinforce your confidence.

It is important to prepare carefully for a presentation. An analysis of many variables, such as audience, audiovisual aids, and physical arrangements help to ensure a smooth, articulate presentation. Mastery of speaking technique will help to bolster confidence. The steps below should be kept in mind during the precommunication period:

Steps in Preparing to Deliver a Speech

1. Identify the topic precisely.
2. Determine the purpose of the presentation.
3. Ascertain the time allowance.
4. Study the audience.
5. Research the subject thoroughly.
6. Organize the presentation.
7. Determine the kinds of audiovisual aids to be employed.
8. Structure the delivery.
9. Prepare notes.
10. Check the physical arrangements.
11. Rehearse the speech.
12. Prepare for evaluation.

Identifying the Topic. Be certain that you know the precise topic of your oral presentation. If assigned the topic orally, write it down and read it back for verification. If possible, request a written statement of the topic from the program chairperson or the administrator assigning the speech to you. A brief title may be vague. Be sure you understand the ramifications and/or subdivisions of the topic. It would be very costly to the company (and to your career opportunities) if you were to go off on a tangent or present the subject with the wrong emphases.

Determining the Purpose. It is essential for the speaker to determine the purpose(s) and objective(s) of the presentation. Is it to transmit information, explain, persuade, describe, narrate, entertain, stimulate, actuate, inquire? What changes, if any, are you attempting to make in the psychology and thinking of the listener? The content of the speech should be structured by the intent or purpose; for instance, an entertaining speech may be sprinkled with humorous stories and jokes while an informative presentation will be specific, accurate, factual, and clear.

Ascertaining the Time Allotment. Find out the time allowed for your presentation. A speech that is too short or too long can disrupt an entire program. Going over a half hour may raise havoc with chefs preparing a banquet. The president of the company is not going to be pleased if the soup is cold or if a later appointment is missed!

You can indicate on your notes at what point you should be at a specific time: one quarter, one half, three quarters, finished. You may have to slow down or speed up. Have a friend in the audience assist you by holding up warning countdown signs: "five minutes left," "two minutes left," "one minute," "time!" A stopwatch on the lectern next to your notes is also of assistance.

Disregarding time is inconsiderate and can tarnish your personal image. The speaker who rambles on, insensitive to others, is committing a major speaking blunder. A good business speaker is brief, to the point, and knows when to be seated!

Studying the Audience. If communication—the transfer of ideas, thoughts, and information—is to take place, it is imperative that you know your audience. Draw up a profile of the audience. The program chairman may be able to provide you with information about the audience. What is the average experience, interest, age, sex, mood, knowledge, vocabulary level, attitude, socioeconomic standing, educational background, occupation, affiliation, expectation, of your audience? Who is attending the oral presentation (managers, production workers, etc.)? What is the size of the audience? Does the audience have previous knowledge of your subject?

The manner of presentation may be relative to the size of the audience. Speaking to a large audience is usually a more formal situation than speaking to a small audience. What are the interests, expectations or needs of the audience? Do you have a captive audience, an audience directed to listen to you? If you can clearly visualize your audience, you can structure the message (content, language level, etc.) appropriately.

Researching the Subject. Know the subject thoroughly. Do your homework. Research the topic and its subdivisions carefully, accurately, and completely. Discern the main points or issues. Be sure your findings are current. Check the dates of your sources of information. For example, current financial data may be very important. Gather as much information as possible from various sources: library, specialists, files, primary research, and so on. General libraries are an excellent source of secondary information. Many companies have their own specialized libraries; for example, a chemical company may have an extensive library of chemistry books.

Consult with specialists, but remember to give credit to individuals who provide information. (Not giving credit when credit is due can make you very unpopular. Also, there may be legal implications.) Before using company files, be sure you have permission and are not revealing confidential information. Remember, an objective, factual, concrete presentation is usually preferred in business.

If you do not know a subject thoroughly, it may be wise to decline an invitation to speak on it. You may fall flat on your face if you do not know the subject well. It is very precarious to speak to an audience that is more knowledgeable than you are on a particular subject, especially if there are going to be questions following.

Another word of caution. Be careful about accepting repeated speaking engagements on the same subject. You may exhaust the subject and go stale. Some individuals may be boxed into hearing your presentation two or more times. You may get a reputation as a bore.

Organizing the Presentation. In order to develop your presentation so that there is a smooth articulation of ideas and a smooth transition between component parts, organize your presentation logically. Usually, the more formal the situation, the more methodical the plan. There are three component parts of an effective speech:

- Introduction
- Body of main ideas
- Summary, conclusions, recommendations

Some presentations may end with a summary and omit conclusions and/ or recommendations. At times, the summary, conclusions, and recommendations will appear before the facts or details.

The Introduction. The purpose of the introduction is to state the subject and, hopefully, to capture the interest of the listeners. The introduction may contain historical perspectives, a statement of the problem, definition of terms, and so on. Jokes or anecdotes (stories) are often told at this point of the presentation. They can help to capture and sustain the attention of the audience; however, they should be related to the topic being discussed. If not introduced, or if there is not a program listing speakers, the speaker should identify himself or herself and identify the topic of the speech:

> Good afternoon! I am John R. Travis, Traffic Manager. I am going to speak about plans for a new parking garage.

The Body. The body of the presentation contains the substance of the speech: ideas, facts, details, statistics, information, and analysis.

The Summary. The closing section of a speech is very important, for it is the part most often remembered. Usually, it is best to end with a clear summary of the entire presentation; however, if the presentation is complex and long, a summary can appear at the end of each major section also.

Since many people are poor listeners, the summary serves an important function. It repeats and reinforces what has been previously said. It is a synopsis of the entire presentation. If the summary is well constructed, it could stand alone; that is, if a person were to hear only the summary, all the important ideas of the presentation would have been conveyed.

Recommendations and Conclusions. At times, the speaker is expected to draw conclusions and to make recommendations. In the concluding remarks, the speaker draws together ideas and presents decisions, judgments, or opinions. The recommendations of the speaker suggest specific courses of action.

When organizing the presentation, decide if you want to use a *direct approach* (present the main ideas first, then give details) or an *indirect approach* (present details first, then give the main ideas). An informative presentation is generally best suited for a direct approach while a persuasive presentation is generally best suited for an indirect approach.

Drawing up an outline of your speech is an aid to effective organization; the logical sequence of key ideas is critical. If the sequence is illogical, the content may be confusing, disjointed, incomprehensible to the listener. The outline can be in word, phrase, or sentence form; phrase form is preferred since it facilitates drawing up notes for an extemporaneous presentation.

If your subject is very complex, it may assist the audience to see the outline. You can project the outline on a screen, distribute printed copies, or have it on a poster or flip chart.

Determining the Audiovisual Aids to be Used. The word "audiovisual" pertains to hearing and sight. "Audiovisual aids" are materials of instruction that are heard or seen, such as slides which accompany a lecture. Fred R. Barnard wrote in 1927, "One picture is worth a thousand words."[2] This is certainly true when discussing audiovisual aids, for they clarify.

Audiovisual aids can enhance an oral presentation; the learning process is more effective when multi-sensory stimuli are used. Hosie and Mayer state, "People generally remember only 20 percent of what they hear but 50 percent of what they hear and see."[3] The spoken word alone may not have a mental impact. However, reinforcement by vision, a picture for example, may stimulate interest and foster retention. Audiovisual aids help make the complex simple. They provide visual reinforcement of the spoken word. Data or statistics can be boring when related orally; however, a graph containing the same data, projected on a screen, may prove to be more interesting. A movie or slides can "perk up" a presentation. Audiovisual aids should be pertinent, skillfully integrated, and attractive.

Be sure to make arrangements for audiovisual equipment. In some situations you can request assistance, such as an operator for a movie projector. Check to see if the equipment is in operative condition. Be sure you know how to use the equipment. Rehearse using the equipment. Make arrangements for the return of equipment after the presentation.

There are numerous audiovisual aids that a speaker can employ to improve the presentation. Some of the more commone ones are:

• Chalkboards	• Handouts	• Posters
• Diagrams	• Magnetic boards	• Radios
• Easel displays	• Maps	• Records
• Felt boards	• Models	• Slides
• Film strips	• Movies	• Tables
• Flannel boards	• Opaque projectors	• Tape recordings
• Flip charts	• Overhead projectors	• Television
• Graphs	• Pictures	• Videotape

When planning the use of audiovisual materials, be certain that they can be heard and / or are visible to everyone in the audience. Also, they should be simple, understandable, and pertinent to the discussion. The printing on a poster or chalkboard should be legible from the rear of the room. Be sure lighting is adequate. Some companies have graphic artists (located in a graphics department) that draw attractive posters, make colored transparencies, and so on. Check the audiovisual materials for correctness and accuracy. A spelling error can be very distracting. Be sure your body is not obscuring a

---

[2]Burton Stevenson, *The Macmillan Book of Proverbs, Maxims, and Famous Phrases* (New York: The Macmillan Company, 1968), p. 2611.

[3]William A. Hosie and Barbara Mayer, "Which Audiovisual Aid for which Situation?," *Public Relations Journal*, XIX, no. 12 (December 1963), 4.

poster or screen; write high on a chalkboard. A combination of audiovisual aids can be used effectively if well coordinated.

Structuring the Delivery. There are two basic kinds of delivery: *impromptu* and *planned*.

Impromptu delivery. An impromptu delivery is usually brief and given without advance thought or preparation. It is presented on the spur of the moment, improvised. For example, a person at a conference is unexpectedly called to the podium to accept an award. The recipient gives an offhand, spontaneous acceptance speech.

Impromptu speeches give the speaker the opportunity to reveal quick thinking. If the response is poor, important ideas may be inadvertently omitted, incorrect words may be used, thoughts expressed may be disjointed, and so on. Since there is always the possibility that an executive will be called upon for an impromptu speech, it is wise to anticipate being asked to speak and to be as informed as possible at all times. Avoid drawing a blank. Keep in mind some anecdotes or jokes that would be appropriate for various occasions, such as a retirement party, a sales convention, and so on.

Planned delivery. There are three basic planned deliveries:

1. A *memorized delivery* requires committing the material to memory. It permits precise wording and eye contact; however, there is the danger of forgetting or omitting facts, data, and so on. It generally creates tension for the speaker and the presentation suffers from lack of spontaneity. Some people find memorizing difficult. A very long memorized presentation may be an arduous task for a busy executive.

2. A *textual delivery*, also called a manuscript speech, is read verbatim, word by word in its entirety. There is an inherent hazard to a read delivery—boredom. Few people can read a speech with vitality. This form of presentation may be necessary when vital information is being conveyed. It should be reserved for special purposes only, when it is critical that a presentation be precise and accurate.

   If a speech is going to be read aloud in a business situation, it might be better to have the speech printed and distributed instead. This may save considerable time and not tie up a group of people all at once.

3. An *extemporaneous delivery* is not completely written or memorized. The speaker occasionally refers to notes containing key words or thoughts. Generally, an extemporaneous speech is chosen for its elements of naturalness and spontaneity. The speaker's personality has an opportunity to reveal itself, and it affords the speaker favorable circumstances to express thoughts in a conversational manner. An extemporaneous presentation also affords the speaker the opportunity for eye contact with the audience. The

speaker can ad lib and react to the nonverbal messages the audience conveys (smiles, frowns, nods, and so on). Readjustments in the presentation can be made in response to audience feedback. This flexibility helps the speaker make the presentation more pertinent and informative.

A key to presenting a good extemporaneous speech is excellent notes. The notes usually outline the presentation: introduction, presentation of information, summary, conclusions and recommendations. The notes should be typed on index cards and be easy to see while standing.

The method of delivery may be predetermined by the circumstances. For example, a person may have little or no choice when asked to make an impromptu delivery. The same may be true when a very precise statement of complex subject matter must be made, it should be read word by word in its entirety. Although the statement could be memorized, this alternative is frought with the ever looming danger of forgetting something. Generally, the best kind of presentation is the extemporaneous one. It affords the speaker flexibility, as well as the opportunity to be spontaneous, natural, animated, and interesting. The personality of the speaker can "shine through." The danger of monotony is lessened. It takes more courage to give an extemporaneous presentation than it does to give a textual one. However, if you want to be a success in the business world, you should have the capability of giving extemporaneous presentations. Careful preparation and continual practice in giving extemporaneous presentations will help to allay your fears.

Preparing Notes. Most speakers use cards (3 by 5 inches, 4 by 6 inches, or 5 by 8 inches) or sheets of paper (8½ by 11 inches) for notes. Cards are generally preferred since they can be held in a hand and permit freedom of movement away from a lectern. The notes should be legible and visible from a distance; the reading distance while standing is usually greater than while seated. Notes can be typed in all capital letters or with large primer or primary type (each letter about a half inch tall) to ensure readability. Notes can be personalized with cues; for example, words to be emphasized can be underlined, circled, or typed in red. You can indicate pauses by writing "PAUSE" in parentheses. Also, you can note appropriate gestures, point up where audiovisual aids should be used, indicate time, and so on. (See Figure 14–1.)

Checking the Physical Arrangements. Since familiarity with your surrounding may bolster your confidence, preview the physical arrangements. Check the size of the room and acoustics. Stand on the podium, so that you get a "feel" of the physical environment. Is there a lectern, necessary tables? Check the lighting, microphone, electrical outlets, room temperature, audiovisual equipment. What is the seating capacity of the room? Are the seats comfortable?

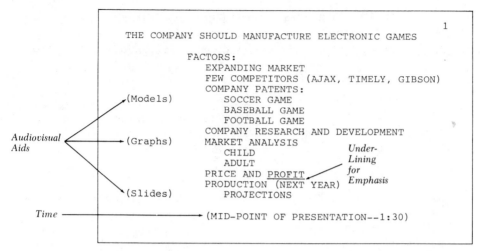

```
                                                                    1
        THE COMPANY SHOULD MANUFACTURE ELECTRONIC GAMES

                    FACTORS:
                       EXPANDING MARKET
                       FEW COMPETITORS (AJAX, TIMELY, GIBSON)
                       COMPANY PATENTS:
          (Models)        SOCCER GAME
                          BASEBALL GAME
                          FOOTBALL GAME
                       COMPANY RESEARCH AND DEVELOPMENT
          (Graphs)    MARKET ANALYSIS        Under-
                          CHILD              Lining
                          ADULT              for
                       PRICE AND PROFIT      Emphasis
                       PRODUCTION (NEXT YEAR)
          (Slides)        PROJECTIONS

    Time                  (MID-POINT OF PRESENTATION--1:30)
```

Audiovisual Aids

FIGURE 14-1. 4-by-6-inch note card with cues

The mind of the listener may be willing, but not the bottom, especially if your presentation is long! Can the room be darkened for audiovisual presentations?

Pay particular attention to the voice amplification system. Adjust the microphone to the correct height. Speak over the microphone to check the volume. Make sure your speaking distance from the microphone is correct.

Rehearsing the Speech. Self-confidence in public speaking usually comes from repetitive speaking experiences. It is for this reason that many elementary school educators urge the participation of children in "show-and-tell" situations. Some managers have found it beneficial to join social groups that provide opportunities for public speech making.

Rehearsing a speech will add to your confidence as a speaker, for "practice makes perfect." Rehearse repeatedly, until your presentation is smooth, articulate, and well-coordinated. There are two stages of rehearsal:

1. Study your notes carefully. Understand the content and purpose of the presentation.
2. Rehearse aloud, until you have a smooth delivery. Try to speak assertively with confidence. If possible, rehearse the speech in the same room that the presentation is to be made. Practice using audiovisual equipment. Get friends, spouse, or associates to appraise your rehearsal. Self-analysis is also important. Practice your speech before a mirror. Observe your posture, gestures, facial expressions. Tape record the speech and listen critically for enunciation, pronunciation, vocabulary, rate, pitch, volume, and so on. A videotape would provide both audio and visual performance feedback. Time the rehearsal. Remember, in a real situation you may be nervous and

272

tend to speak rapidly. Extra material for this eventuality may be wise.

Preparing for Evaluation. During the preconference period, it is wise to make provisions for evaluation of your presentation. These are some of the evaluative techniques that can be employed:

1. Prepare an evaluative form for distribution to the audience.
2. Invite selected people in the audience to appraise your presentation.
3. Arrange to have the speech taped (audio/visual).

THE COMMUNICATION PERIOD (DELIVERY)

When the initial preparation has been completed, the speaker is ready for the delivery of the message. An effective delivery encompasses many factors that will now be reviewed:

1. Nonverbal communication — *without use of words; eye contact*
2. Verbal communication
3. Language skills
4. Audience feedback

Nonverbal Communication. In addition to the spoken message that is being communicated during an oral presentation, nonverbal communication is also taking place. Nonverbal communication consists of the following:

1. Personal appearance
2. Eye contact
3. Gestures
4. Posture
5. Facial expressions
6. Mannerisms
7. Body movement

The *nonverbal signal* should be in agreement with the *verbal signal* being transmitted. The nonverbal signal positively reinforces the verbal one if used correctly. If the verbal and nonverbal signals are in disagreement, the listener tends to believe the nonverbal message. If the nonverbal signal contradicts the verbal one, it leads to disbelief and confusion. The personal integrity of the communicator is subject to challenge.

During the famous Nixon–Kennedy debates, nonverbal communication played an important role. Nixon wore heavy makeup, was very serious, and perspired. Kennedy appeared poised and confident. Nixon lost the debates. A similar situation occurred during the Carter-Reagan debate. Carter was intense, scowling, taut, and frowning. Reagan appeared poised, confident, smiling. Although some thought that Carter was better technically, Reagan won the debate and was subsequently elected president.

Various body movements, commonly called *body language,* can aid communication if used effectively. We convey messages by the movements of our bodies. For example, biting fingernails is an indication of nervousness; crossing arms presents a firm, perhaps hostile stance; clenching a fist indicates anger; and sitting close to a person indicates friendliness. Let us examine some of the facets of nonverbal communication.

Personal appearance. Consider carefully your appearance during the presentation, for it may have a definite impact on your success or failure. The speaker should be clean, neat, and well groomed. The attire should be appropriate for the audience being addressed; it should not be distracting, for this may result in poor listening. The author remembers attending a conference at which a lady spoke wearing a large orange hat with a long, colorful peacock feather. As the lady spoke, the feather moved back and forth. Soon, the attention of the audience was focused on the hat and little attention was paid to what was being said. The hat had a mesmerizing effect!

The speaker's dress should also be relative to the occasion. A plaid shirt may be appropriate for the speaker at the company picnic; however, it may be totally inappropriate for the after-dinner speaker at a formal banquet.

Eye contact. It is very disconcerting to see a speaker looking continuously at a far wall, the ceiling, the floor, or out a window. The speaker should maintain eye contact with the audience. Looking at the audience is very important; eye contact stimulates interaction between the speaker and the audience. Instantaneous feedback can help structure the presentation. Also, direct eye contact conveys a cordial feeling. The person who does not look you square in the eye is considered to be shifty, untrustworthy. A smile, a nod, or a frown may be very significant feedback to the speaker.

To maintain good eye contact, select individuals at random in the audience. Don't neglect people in the rear, corners, or sides. Speak to one person for a few seconds, then to another momentarily, and so on. When speaking to a large audience, it is not necessary to maintain eye contact with everyone, just selective individuals.

Gestures. Gestures are body movements used for expression while speaking. A pointed finger, a clenched fist, a thumb pointed downward, are all examples of common gestures. Gestures should appear spontaneous, not forced. They reinforce or emphasize what is being said. Unnatural gesturing, such as continuous arm waving and lectern pounding, can prove to be distracting and very negative. The repetitive use of the same gestures can be annoying. Gestures should be varied to create the impact desired. Timing is

Using gestures (Courtesy of CIGNA Corp.)

critical. The gesture should coincide with what is being said. A delay can be devastating.

Gestures help to make the speaker appear animated, alive. One of the dangers of not using gestures is monotony. A steady droning voice without gestures can put the audience to sleep. Another danger is that a gesture may have multiple meanings and, therefore, be misinterpreted. For example, circular motion with a finger may be interpreted as "around the subject," "more and more," or "come to me."

Posture. Generally, a speaker should stand up. Poor posture conveys a poor image. The speaker who is slumped over the lectern or leaning on his/her elbow may not project confidence. The speaker should be alert, comfortably poised (feet firmly on the floor and slightly apart), stand tall, evince trust, be energetic. Good posture commands attentiveness. The hands can be a source of problems. Some speakers keep them in side pockets (while jiggling coins); place them in hip pockets (and leave them there for most of a talk).

Your posture while walking to and from the lectern will convey confidence or insecurity.

Facial expressions. The human face is very expressive and communicates messages. A smile, a raised eyebrow, or a scowl communicates the emotions of the speaker. Since many facial expressions are spontaneous, there is danger that a smile during a sober presentation may cause the audience to distrust the speaker. At times, the speaker must mask his emotions and be certain that facial expressions are matching what is being stated. The credibility of a speaker can be questioned if unconscious facial expressions are communicating a different nonverbal message from what is being stated.

Avoid objectionable mannerisms. There are objectionable mannerisms that can be very distracting and should be avoided. One college speaker has been known to do all of the following:

- Take off his glasses and place them in his coat pocket.
- Remove his wrist watch and place it on the lectern.
- Take off his jacket.
- Loosen his tie.
- Unbutton the top buttons on his shirt.
- Roll up his sleeves.

Fortunately, the talk and the "strip tease" eventually come to an end! By that time, the attention of the students is focused on what is coming off next, rather than on what is being said!

These are some of the particularly objectionable nonverbal mannerisms to avoid:

- Tapping a pen or pencil.
- Pacing back and forth.
- Scratching.
- Playing with jewelry, eyeglasses, coins, and so on.
- Cracking knuckles.

don't do it excessively

Paralanguage. Interjecting pauses with sounds such as "uh" and "um" can be very annoying. These extra sounds are *paralanguage.*

One speaker discovered some tacks in his pocket while speaking. The speaker lined the tacks on the lectern one by one! Soon, the attention of the audience was focused on the tacks, not on what was being said. After the tacks were lined up, the speaker returned the tacks to his pocket, one by one. You guessed it—out from his pocket came the tacks again, and again.

Body Movement. Moving can relieve some of the tension inherent in public speaking. The speaker who stands rigidly behind the lectern will come across as cool and detached. A simple movement to the left or right of the lectern may help to emphasize a point; however, care should be taken about not moving away from a fixed microphone. At times, when not using a lectern, movement towards the audience will emphasize a point. Obviously, too much walking, pacing back and forth, or awkward motion can be distracting.

Verbal Communication. The verbalization of the message, speaking, is a very critical aspect of the entire process of oral communication.

Voice. A person's voice consists of the sounds uttered by the vocal organs. Each of us has characteristic speech sounds influenced by pitch, rate, volume and resonance. We may not all have good vocal qualities; however, through training we can improve the quality of our voices.

1. *Pitch.* The pitch of one's voice pertains to the highness or lowness of the sound emitted. There are breathing exercises to vary the pitch of a voice. Raising one's voice when excited may cause shrill sounds. A desirable pitch is one that is not too low or too high. If the range of pitch is limited, a person has a tedious voice, commonly called monotone. A person speaking in a monotone can put members of the audience to sleep. Variation in pitch makes a speaker interesting. It is an excellent way to emphasize a point.

squeeky voice

2. *Rate of Delivery.* We can speak about 120 words per minute (two words per second). Time yourself as you read aloud to determine how many words per minute you are speaking. Taping your voice will expedite studying your delivery rate. By varying the rate of speaking, you can accentuate ideas. Pausing or slowing down draws attention.

120 words per minute

The shifting of tempo helps make the speaker more dynamic and animated. It aids in emphasizing key ideas. If the content is complex, slow down a bit. If it is simple and understandable, you can speed up the delivery rate.

It is very irritating to listen to a speaker who is droning along very slowly; it is equally irritating to strain to listen to the speaker who is revealing complex ideas and information at a rapid clip. Pauses between some words will help vary the delivery rate. Pause when the audience applauds or laughs. There is a danger inherent in pausing; speaker's have a tendency to fill the speaking gaps with vocalized sounds (paralanguage) such as "ah," "uh," "OK," "er," "right," "you know," and "um." There seems to be an aversion to any interval of time when there is silence.

3. *Volume.* The intensity of sound (loudness) is called volume. Speaking too softly (mumbling) or too loudly (shouting) may be irritating to a listener. Try to make your voice interesting by alternating its volume. Breath control is an important factor. You can emphasize a point by either increasing or decreasing volume. The volume of a speaker's voice should be relative to such factors as the size of the room and background noises. The volume should be strong enough so that every person in the audience hears the speaker clearly, without straining. Many listeners will "tune out" a speaker if they have to strain to listen. Is voice amplification needed? If so, is a stationary microphone or mobile amplification needed? When using a microphone, it is not necessary to speak very loudly. A clear speaking voice is a definite asset in the business world.

4. *Resonance.* The richness of a voice is its resonance. Try to eliminate harsh nasal tones which can be irritating. A pleasant voice is an advantage in the business world. People prefer to listen to a person with a rich, melodious voice.

5. *Pronunciation.* The manner of pronouncing words is called pronunciation. Many speakers unknowingly speak a "sub-language" rather than standard English. "Hi ya buddy.. Whatcha doen tonight? Gunna go ta da dance? etc...." If a speaker mispronounces words, it may prove very distracting. The audience may question the expertise of the communicator. There may be a question in the minds of listeners about the education of the speaker. Mispronouncing the following words will convey a poor image of the speaker:

brung (brought)	dis (this)
da (the)	doen (doing)
dey (they)	edjacate (educate)

er (or)

fer (for)

gimme (give me)

gotta (got to)

gunna (going to)

hasta (has to)

havta (have to)

idears (ideas)

jist (just)

ketch (catch)

kin (can)

kinda (kind of)

liberry (library)

looken (looking)

lotta (lot of)

piture (picture)

riden (riding)

somethen (something)

ta (to)

tryen (trying)

twoney (twenty)

wanna (want to)

yer (your or you are)

youse (you)

If you are unsure about the correct pronunciation of a word, consult a dictionary.

6. *Enunciation.* The way we articulate words is called "enunciation." Words should be spoken distinctly so that they are understandable.

Language Skills. The language used should be appropriate for the situation and the audience.

Casual Language: Used when conversing with friends. Includes slang, joking, common phrases, and so on.

Informal Language: Used in most business conversations.

Formal Language: Used in public speaking.

The English used should be correct and understandable. Standard English is the hallmark of an educated person; nonstandard English is generally used by uneducated people. The use of words such as "youse," "gotta," and "gunna" are examples of nonstandard speech. Grammatical construction and pronunciation in business oral communications should be correct. The college student deficient in language skills should take appropriate English courses. Speech courses are helpful.

Profanity is offensive to many people and should be avoided in all business communications. The profane person will create a poor image in the minds of many listeners. Also, profanity may be shocking, vulgar, and distracting to some.

Audience Feedback. In a viable speaking situation, there is a reciprocal give-and-take relationship between the speaker and the audience. Many of the signals sent from the audience are nonverbal, such as a smile, a frown, laughter, a puzzled expression, and applause. This interaction is critical to the speaker. It indicates the reception of the message. Also, it indicates the speaker's effectiveness. A famous comedian was asked the key to his success. He said that he kept testing his routine. The jokes that received sustained applause and laughter were retained; those that were not well received were dropped. Eventually, he had an excellent routine of tested jokes!

An experienced speaker will scan the audience for feedback clues. By analyzing these clues, the speaker can make adjustments to improve the presentation.

Questions from the audience are a special consideration during the precommunication period. Should the audience be permitted to question? If so, should the questioning be permitted during the presentation or after? Questioning during a presentation may upset the train of thought of the speaker. Generally, people in the audience are expected to raise questions. The speaker should anticipate questions and have answers. Tell the audience in advance when questions may be asked. Generally, questioning at the end of major sections of a presentation is better, since it helps clarify the message being conveyed.

What do you do when asked a question you cannot answer? Be honest. You might casually say that it is an interesting question that you failed to research. You can offer to look up the answer; ask if someone in the audience knows the answer.

Remember your time limitations. Try to answer questions briefly and concisely. You may have to close off questions by stating, "There is time for only two more questions." Don't be tripped by "sharpshooters" in the audience. Maintain your composure. Generally, speaker hostility or anger will have a negative effect.

THE POST-COMMUNICATION INTERVAL

After the speech has been delivered, the speaker should evaluate the performance. These are some evaluative techniques:

1. If the audience was asked to complete evaluative forms, review them critically.
2. If individuals in the audience were invited to evaluate the presentation, meet with them. Be receptive to criticism.
3. Try to objectively appraise your performance. Was the message communicated effectively? Were there any "goofs?" Were the audiovisual aids smoothly integrated? What was the attitude of the audience—interested, bored, hostile, aggressive, receptive?
4. Analyze the type of questions asked. Did you answer them precisely, clearly?

√5. If the presentation was taped (audio/visual), study your platform
style, gestures, enunciation, and so on.

Other Tasks. Follow through on any commitments made during the presentation; for example, you may have stated that a report would be distributed. If
so, distribute the report.

Be sure that all special equipment needed for the presentation (voice amplification, audiovisual aids, etc.) are returned. Also, the room should be
restored to its original appearance; room darkening curtains should be
opened, extra chairs on the podium should be returned, and so on.

Thank people who assisted you, such as the program chairman, people
who operated the audiovisual equipment, custodians, graphic artists, and so
on, personally or by writing thank-you notes.

File your research findings and notes. You may be asked to deliver the
same speech to a different audience, or present a similar talk to the same
audience. Also, if you have been asked to introduce a speaker or speakers, file
the *vita* (autobiographical sketch) for future reference.

Note specifics about the speech, topic, date, place, audience, so that the
information can be added to your personal resume of activities.

Listening   *Test question*

Attentive listening is critical in the communication process. There is a
difference between hearing and listening. Hearing is the perception of aural
stimuli, called "sound." Listening entails hearing with attention, meaning,
thoughtfulness. We may hear a speaker make sounds but not comprehend
what is being said.

Rankin discovered that white-collar people spend about 45 percent of
their time listening. Actually, more time is spent listening than reading,
writing, or speaking.[4] Some individuals, such as interviewers, counselors, and
psychologists, may spend higher percentages of their time listening.

Unfortunately, very few people receive training in listening. It is some-
what paradoxical that educators generally emphasize reading, writing, and
speaking, even though listening is the major communicating skill. In the
business world, where errors can be very costly, training in listening is critical.
Instructions must be followed precisely; ideas and facts must be transmitted
completely and accurately.

Marginal listeners are a serious concern in the business world, for they
may be the weakest link in the communciation process.

[4]Paul T. Rankin, "Listening Ability: Its Importance, Measurement and Development,"
Chicago School Journal, 12 (June 1930) pp. 177–179, 414–420.

Much of the time spent listening involves person-to-person situations. These are the private, interpersonal conversations we all participate in, the rapid exchange of thoughts. There are, however, formal public listening situations as well, such as listening to a lecture or oral report. During the formal listening situation, the listener plays a less active role. The listener is the recipient of information, thoughts, and ideas. The listener may not, in some circumstances, contribute to the dialogue by speaking. The listener must, of necessity, be attentive and receptive.

There may be barriers to effective listening, such as distractions, hearing disabilities, mind wandering, lack of interest, preconceptions, prejudices and bias, the connotations that words have, abstract language, semantics, and so on.

The business manager must make a concerted effort to receive communications. Since the manager is in a position of leadership, directions or orders are commonly issued. People in lower echelons must listen to the manager. However, it is vital that the manager be a good listener if upward communication is to take place in a business. The ability to listen is an important communicative tool of the effective manager; if listening does not occur, the manager may become insulated to vital information.

Listening ability can be improved by following these suggestions.

TECHNIQUES FOR IMPROVING LISTENING SKILLS

Concentrate. Listen actively, attentively, alertly, critically. Concentrate on the speaker's message, not on the speaker. Do not take mental excursions—daydreaming is particularly hazardous. A boring speaker may require more attentiveness than usual. Your mind is capable of racing ahead more rapidly than the speed of words being received. Robbins expressed this concept by stating:

> The reason for poor listening is easily explained. The average person speaks at the rate of approximately 150 words per minute, whereas we have the capacity to listen at the rate of over 1,000 words per minute. The difference obviously leaves idle brain time and opportunities for mind wandering. And people who do not have good listening skills are flagrant mind wanderers.[5]

Take Notes: Jot down the key ideas, facts, conclusions, and recommendations of the speaker. Do not attempt to write verbatim the entire presentation or every detail. This effort will bog you down, so that you miss important concepts. If possible, formulate an outline of the speaker's presentation. Is

[5]Stephen P. Robbins, *The Administrative Process* (Englewood Cliffs, N.J.: Prentice-Hall, Inc., 1980), p. 361.

there a logical sequence or flow of ideas? Written notes are generally better than mental notes, especially if the subject is complex.

Listen with an Open Mind. Preconceived notions can cause a listener to resist or reject new ideas. Listen for content.

Tape Complex Oral Presentations. Because of the rapidity of speech (usually over two words per second), it may be very difficult to assimilate pertinent facts and ideas, especially if the material is involved or complex. Receive permission before taping any conversation or speech. There may be legal implications.

Observe the Speaker's Nonverbal Communication. Notice if the speaker's gestures, body language, and facial expressions are attuned to what is being said. Remember, the message conveyed nonverbally may be more significant and convincing than what is being stated.

Analyze the Motives of the Speaker. Is it to convince, convey information, motivate action, persuade, or provide solutions? Is the speaker sincere, rational, objective, competent, factual and correct; or, is the speaker propagandizing, subjective, emotional, omitting facts? A flamboyant delivery may be masking the meaning of a message. Discern the motives of the speaker.

Be Wary of Distractions. Distractions such as the speaker's accent, command of English, physical appearance, or manner of delivery may cause a listener to tune out. For example, a speaker has an unusual tie. This visual distraction interferes with listening. Attention is focused on the tie, not on what is being said. Multi-stimuli received simultaneously may divert attention.

Be Alert to Language Barriers. The level of language used by the speaker may be above or below the level of the listener. Listen for meaning, stated or implied. Your connotations of words may differ from the speaker's.

Create a Good Listening Environment. Try to create a good physical environment conducive to listening, an environment free from distractions. The radio blaring in the background can be shut off; windows can be closed to shut out noise. Many business offices have conference rooms that provide a pleasant physical environment for listening: comfortable chairs, soundproofing, pads for note taking, and so on.

Avoid Distracting the Speaker. The listener can inadvertently distract the speaker and create a disjointed presentation. A question asked at the wrong time, an inappropriate siege of coughing, or other distractions can disrupt the logical transition of ideas. The listener should look alert, sit erect. Nothing is as disconcerting to a speaker as a yawning listener! Basic courtesy is a prerequisite to good listening. A good listener is attuned to the speaker. Eye contact is desirable. Feedback to the speaker in the form of a smile, frown, or nod, may help the speaker fathom the impact being made by the talk and, thereby, aid in structuring remarks.

Be Mentally Prepared. Preliminary preparation may be necessary for effective listening, especially if the subject is complex. Research the topic as well as you can. For example, if you are going to hear a talk about the automated office, you should familiarize yourself with terms such as coded keyboards, electronic blackboard, electronic mail computers, word-processing terminals, microelectronic circuits, and high-speed printers.

do your homework

Be Physically Prepared. You should be in good physical condition to listen effectively. It may be physically taxing to attend a long oral presentation. Don't skip lunch and attend a conference. Have you had enough sleep? This is not the time for cat napping! A drink before a lecture can cloud the listener's mind.

don't be tired alert metaly

Recapitulate. After hearing the speaker, immediately review your notes. If there are any discrepancies or inaccuracies, it may be possible to check with the speaker. Assess the value of the presentation by making your own value judgments. Recapitulation will help to reinforce what has been said and facilitate retention. It is interesting to note that about half of the message is generally lost immediately after it has been transmitted!

Summary

Oral communication is the interchange of ideas, thoughts, or information by speech. Oral communication in the business world can be divided into two parts: informal and formal. Generally, informal presentations are made to individuals and formal presentations are made to groups.

There are three distinct periods of activity in the speech-making continuum: preparation, delivery, and evaluation.

Most people are frightened at the prospect of speaking before a group. The fear of public speaking can be overcome by knowing the subject thoroughly, speaking before groups of people as often as possible, learning to speak extemporaneously, taking a few deep breaths before speaking, using visual aids, being animated and dynamic while speaking, and rehearsing the speech.

The steps in preparing to deliver a speech are:

- Identify the topic precisely.
- Determine the purpose of the presentation.
- Ascertain the time allowance.
- Study the audience.

- Research the subject thoroughly.
- Organize the presentation.
- Determine the audiovisual aids to be employed.
- Structure the delivery.
- Prepare notes.
- Check the physical arrangements.
- Rehearse the speech.
- Prepare for evaluation.

An effective delivery includes many factors: nonverbal communications, verbal communication, language skills, and audience feedback. Nonverbal communication encompasses the following: personal appearance, eye contact, gestures, body language, posture, facial expressions, mannerisms and body movement.

The proper verbalization of the message, speaking, is a critical aspect of the process of oral communication. Through training, we can improve the quality of our voices. Each of us has characteristic speech sounds influenced by pitch, rate, volume, and resonance.

If a speaker mispronounces words, it may be very distracting. The audience may question the expertise of the communicator. Words should be spoken distinctly, so that they are understandable. The language used by a speaker should be appropriate for the situation and the audience. The English used should be correct. Profanity is offensive and should be avoided.

In a viable speaking situation, there is a reciprocal relationship between the speaker and the audience. An experienced speaker will scan the audience for feedback clues. By analyzing these clues, the speaker can make adjustments to improve the presentation.

The speaker should evaluate the performance afterwards by reviewing evaluative forms, discussing the performance with individuals preselected for evaluative purposes, personally appraising the performance, analyzing the types of questions asked, and studying audio/visual tapes of the presentation.

Other post-communication activities consist of the following:

- Following through on commitments made during the presentation.
- Returning special equipment used.
- Restoring the room to its original state.
- Filing research findings and notes.
- Recording specifics about the speech for future reference.

Attentive listening is critical in the communication process, especially since white-collar people spend about 45 percent of their time listening.

Unfortunately, very few people receive training in listening, even though listening is the major communicating skill.

Marginal listeners are a very serious concern in the business world. Listening errors can prove to be very costly.

There are barriers to effective listening, such as distractions, hearing disabilities, mind wandering, lack of interest, preconceptions, prejudice and bias, the connotations that words have, abstract language, semantics, and so on.

Listening can be improved by following these suggestions:

1. Concentrate.
2. Take notes.
3. Listen with an open mind.
4. Tape complex oral presentations.
5. Observe the speaker's nonverbal communication.
6. Analyze the motives of the speaker.
7. Be wary of distractions.
8. Be alert to language barriers.
9. Create a good listening environment.
10. Avoid distracting the speaker.
11. Be mentally prepared.
12. By physically prepared.
13. Recapitulate.

It should be noted that aside from major business implications, good listening habits are essential in a social environment.

Discussion

Why is effective oral communication so critical in the business world?

Study questions

1. Define the following terms:
   Oral communication — *interchanging of ideas, thought and infor*   Eye contact
   Speech ◄   Gestures — *body movements*
   Verbal —   Objectionable mannerisms
                                        tapping

Informal communiation   Rate of delivery

Formal communication   Pitch

Captive audience   Volume

Company library   Resonance

Impromptu speech   Pronunciation

Memorized delivery   Enunciation

Textual delivery   Standard English

Extemporaneous delivery   Nonstandard English

Nonverbal communication   Audience feedback

Body language

2. List situations for formal oral presentations in business organizations.

3. What are the three distinct periods of activity in the speech-making continuum? Specifically, list the three time intervals and the activity that takes place during each period. *Prep. Delivery Evaluation*

4. List the twelve steps in preparing to deliver a speech.

5. List the three component parts of an effective speech. *Introduction Body, Summary*

6. Explain the <u>direct</u> and <u>indirect</u> approaches used when organizing a presentation.

7. Cite some of the audiovisual aids used by speakers.

8. Discuss casual language, informal language, and formal language.

9. What is the difference between hearing and <u>listening</u>? *hearing with attention*

10. According to Rankin, what percentage of the time of white-collar people is spent listening? *45%*

11. List some of the barriers to effective listening.

12. List the techniques for improving listening skills.

Activity

Prepare an extemporaneous speech to be presented to your class. Your instructor will designate the length of the presentation. Allow for a question-and-answer period at the end of your speech.

To make your presentation interesting to the class, prepare an original audiovisual aid—flip chart, transparency, poster, and so on.

A list of topics for written and oral reports appears at the end of Chapter 6. Ideally, use the same topic for both your written and oral reports. Only one student in a class should select a particular topic, for it may be boring to hear a talk on the same topic repeatedly.

ACHIEVEMENT OF LEARNING GOALS

Check the appropriate boxes to determine whether you have or have not achieved the learning goals of this chapter.

I Can:

	YES	NO
1. Understand the importance of effective oral communication.	☐	☐
2. Identify the various informal and formal oral communication situations that exist in the business world.	☐	☐
3. Ascertain the activities undertaken during the precommunication, communication, and post-communication periods.	☐	☐
4. Comprehend fully nonverbal communication signals.	☐	☐
5. State how messages are verbalized.	☐	☐
6. Explain the reciprocal relationship that exists between the speaker and the audience, feedback.	☐	☐
7. Differentiate between hearing and listening.	☐	☐
8. Explain the barriers to effective listening.	☐	☐
9. Recognize the techniques for improving listening skills.	☐	☐

If any of your responses were "no," it is suggested that you review pertinent chapter parts.

Meetings Via
Electronic Media

LEARNING GOALS

1. Recognize the need for effective, inter-echelon communication and participatory meetings.
2. Differentiate between meetings and conferences.
3. Plan an effective meeting or conference.
4. Comprehend the order of business at a committee meeting and parliamentary procedures.
5. Structure post-conference activities.
6. Understand modern electronic conferencing systems.

In some business organizations there is minimal communication among the individuals at various levels. Clear channels of communication are essential if information is to be shared and problems are to be defined and solved. In a democratic administration, provisions are made for shared responsibility in formulating company policy. In an autocratic administration, those in the higher echelons dictate policy. Often, the perception of problems is limited because the executive at the top of the hierarchy is isolated.

Meetings or conferences provide for inter-echelon communication. There are many advantages to participatory meetings:

1. There is superior input. Group input for complex problem solving is generally better than individual input.
2. Those involved in a decision-making process are more likely to be committed to the outcomes.
3. There is a favorable work climate. Goodwill is generated by cooperative efforts.
4. Individuals grow by direct involvement in research, appraisal, controversy, and the free exchange of ideas.

A *meeting* is a coming together of people. A *conference* is a formal meeting at which discussions and consultations are held, decisions are made, information is exchanged, policy is determined, and appraisals are conducted. There is a broad spectrum of formality, ranging from brief, informal meetings that are generally instructional to very formal, structured conventions where large numbers of delegates congregate to analyze complex problems. (See Figure 15–1.)

FIGURE 15–1.   The continuum of meeting formality

Informal meetings

An informal meeting takes place when an executive calls together a small group of people to discuss a problem, seek solutions, share information, or recommend a course of action.

The meeting is usually held in an executive's private office. A telephone call or written notice (note or memo) informs the participants of the topic, location, date, and time. (See Figure 15–2.)

```
MEMORANDUM

     TO:  Ching Fu              November 10, 19--
          Richard Galli
          Diana Molloy
          Mary Rubin
          Jose Santos                          •

   FROM:  Ellen Nolan

SUBJECT:  Department Meeting


A department meeting will bc held at 10:00
a.m. on November 20 in my office (Room 304)
to discuss the implementation of new account-
ing procedures.

Please review the accounting procedures
manual, which will be updated at this
meeting.

                E.N.
```

FIGURE 15-2. Notice of a department meeting

During the informal meeting, the business at hand is discussed while a secretary takes notes. If a secretary is not available, one of the individuals attending the meeting is delegated to recording notes. This is not a desirable practice, for the person taking the notes finds it difficult to contribute or participate in the discussion. The proceedings of some informal meetings are tape recorded for future reference.

The summary of the meeting is distributed to the participants and any person concerned about the meeting.

291

An informal meeting

Committee meetings

A committee consists of a group of people delegated to give consideration to a specific matter or to perform a specific task or tasks. Committee meetings are more structured than informal meetings.

THE AGENDA — *tells what in store for meeting/conference*

An *agenda*, a plan of activities for a meeting, is distributed well in advance of the meeting. In addition to citing the activities of the meeting, the agenda lists the order of business. The bylaws of a committee usually state when the agenda must be received by the participants—usually a week or two before the meeting. The agenda is distributed to each committee member and to other concerned people. The agenda is prepared by the chairperson, and committee members are encouraged to submit agenda items for inclusion. Generally, only items on the agenda are discussed at a meeting. This keeps the meeting on track and helps to avoid digressions. (See Figure 15–3.)

Test question

Tells whats going to happen during meeting

must be submitted 2 weeks ahead of time

292

FIGURE 15-3. An agenda

REED AND SCOTT CORPORATION

AGENDA FOR THE MEETING OF THE MANAGERIAL
COMMUNICATIONS COMMITTEE

May 1, 19--

1. Call to Order . . . .   Howard A. White

2. Roll Call . . . .   Sara F. Murphy

3. Minutes of the April 1 Meeting   Alisan T. Carter

4. Reports of Officers:
    Chairperson . . . .   Howard A. White

5. Reports of Committees:
    Telecommunications . . . .   Mary R. Zocci
    Dictation Equipment . . . .   Thomas C. Denny
    Reprographics . . . .   Kevin D. Rogers
    Micrographics . . . .   Karen B. Rosenberg

6. Old Business:
    The "Paperless Office" . .   J. Dale O'Sullivan

7. New Business:
    Computer Conferencing . . .   Jennifer C. Brown
    Teleconferencing . . . .   Nathaniel T. Barker

8. Announcements:
    Editing Typewriters . . . .   John N. Christie
    Typesetting . . . .   Nancy R. Paige

9. Adjournment

The order of business at a committee meeting is generally as follows:

1. The meeting is called to order by the presiding officer, usually called the chairperson or chair.
2. The role is called.
3. Minutes of the previous meeting are read, amended or corrected if needed, and approved.
4. Reports are heard from officers and committees.
5. Old or unfinished business is discussed.
6. New business is discussed.
7. Announcements are made.
8. The meeting is adjourned.

Parliamentary procedures from *Robert's Rules of Order Newly Revised* provide a structured order of discussion for large, formal meetings:

- A committee member speaks only when recognized by the leader.
- Motions are made and must be seconded before they receive the consideration of the group.
- Discussion of the motion follows and the motion is put to a vote.
- The leader announces the results of the vote.

THREE TYPES OF COMMITTEES

There are three types of committees: *standing committees, special committees,* and *ad hoc committees.* Standing committees are permanent committees, special committees are temporary committees that deal with special problems or issues, and ad hoc committees are temporary committees that are charged with resolving noncontroversial problems. Usually, ad hoc committees are small in size.

The committee leader, called a "chairperson" or "chair," should be a qualified person with leadership attributes. The people serving on a committee should be contributing members; therefore, they should be selected with care.

Usually, a company conference room is reserved for committee meetings. A secretary takes the *minutes,* an official report of the proceedings, in shorthand. If needed, a verbatim (word for word) transcript can be obtained by tape recording the meeting.

After the committee meeting is over, the minutes are transcribed (typed from notes) by the secretary and submitted to the participating members and any other concerned individuals. Minutes are filed and become permanent company records. (See Figures 15–4a and 15–4b)

FIGURE 15–4a. Minutes of a committee meeting, page 1

Official

REED AND SCOTT CORPORATION

MINUTES OF THE MEETING OF THE
MANAGERIAL COMMUNICATIONS COMMITTEE

May 1, 19--

ATTENDANCE

The monthly meeting of the Managerial Communications Committee was
held at 2:00 p.m. in the company conference room. Mr. Howard A.
White, Director of Managerial Communications, presided at the
meeting.

The following members were present:

Nathaniel T. Barker, Jennifer C. Brown, Alison, T. Carter,
John N. Christie, Thomas C. Denny, Sara F. Murphy, J.
Dale O'Sullivan, Helen R. Paige, Kevin D. Rogers, Karen
B. Rosenberg, Howard A. White, Mary R. Zocci.

MINUTES OF THE PREVIOUS MEETING

The minutes of the April 1 meeting were approved without amend-
ment or change.

REPORTS

Chairperson Howard A. White reported that a junior officer has been
added to the managerial communications staff.

Reports from the telecommunications, dictation equipment, reprographics, and micrographics committees indicate that substantial
progress has been made in updating equipment. Fifty thousand
dollars has been expended to date on new dictation equipment for
the Word Processing Center.

OLD BUSINESS

The Committee pledged its support for movement towards a totally
electronic, paperless office.

NEW BUSINESS

Jennifer C. Brown motioned and Karen B. Rosenberg seconded the
motion that computer conferencing be studied by an ad hoc committee. Discussion indicated that many savings would be made by
implementing computer conferencing. The motion passed unanimously.

FIGURE 15–4b. Minutes of a committee meeting, page 2

Minutes of the Managerial Communications Committee
Page 2
May 1, 19--

Nathaniel T. Barker motioned and Mary R. Zocci seconded the motion
that teleconferencing be studied by an ad hoc committee. Discussion
followed about the relative merits of audio and visual electronic
communications. The motion passed unanimously.

ANNOUNCEMENTS

John N. Christie stated that two editing typewriters would be
delivered on May 15. He offered to demonstrate the new equipment
upon arrival.

Helen R. Paige announced that new typesetting equipment would
not be purchased until next year because of budget restrictions.

ADJOURNMENT

The meeting adjourned at 3:30 p.m.

Mary T. Trimble
Mary T. Trimble, Secretary

Distribution:
    President
    Vice President
    Treasurer
    Secretary
    Committee Members

At times, a committee will pass a *resolution,* a formal expression of group will or opinion. For example, Figure 15–5 illustrates a resolution commending an employee for a job well done.

Test question

FIGURE 15–5.   Resolution

Resolution

Adopted May 12, 19--

WHEREAS   Rebecca Rich has been a trustworthy
            member of the Reed and Scott Corpor-
            ation since its inception twenty
            years ago and has served faithfully
            in various administrative capacities;
            and

WHEREAS   Rebecca Rich is retiring on June 1;
            be it

RESOLVED   that she be commended for her out-
            standing contributions to the success
            of the Reed and Scott Corporation.

Gail R. Parker
Gail R. Parker
Secretary

P. J. Williams
P. Jay Williams
Chairperson
Personnel Committee

Formal conferences

The conference is a more structured, formal meeting on a specific topic. These formal meetings are an integral part of a business's operations. (*Note.* Since the terms "meeting" and "conference" may be used interchangeably by some people in the business world, it should be noted that some executives call small, informal meetings "conferences" too.)

Formal conferences entail three steps:

1. Planning the conference
2. Holding the conference
3. Post-conference activities

PLANNING THE CONFERENCE

Define the Topic and State the Purpose. If a conference is to succeed, the topic for discussion should be a meaningful one to the participants. Only knowledgeable individuals who can contribute to the dialogue should be invited to participate as conferees. Many conferences have been dismal failures because of a lack of interest and motivation on the part of the participants. The topic should be clearly defined and be a viable one. The purpose of the conference should be formulated and clearly stated. Most conferences are problem solving and/or informational.

Conference Leader. An individual should be selected as conference leader or conference coordinator. The conference leader selects the conferees, prepares the agenda, and determines the time and place of the gathering. The leader usually assumes a neutral role and only discards this neutrality when asked by members to state specific opinions or attitudes.

Committee Selection. If the conference is a large one, the conference leader selects conference committees for the following:

1. Invitations and registration (make name tags)
2. Facilities (conference rooms)
3. Publicity (coverage by news media)
4. Program (conference agenda)
5. Guest speakers (invitations, travel accommodations)
6. Refreshments (coffee breaks, meals)
7. Housing (for guests coming a long distance)
8. Exhibitions (equipment, materials, and so on)
9. Audiovisual equipment (projectors, chalkboards, and the like)
10. Entertainment (tours, entertainers, and so on)

The conference leader should be an accommodating, objective, capable, knowledgeable person. The person with the highest administrative rank may not be the best qualified individual to lead the conference. The conference coordinator should be encouraged to prepare adequately for the meeting. If the meeting is formal, the leader should review rules of parliamentary procedure by referring to reference books in the library, such as *Robert's Rules of Order Newly Revised* and Sturgis's *Standard Code of Parliamentary Procedure.* Most business meetings, however, are informal and parliamentary law is not followed.

Test question

The leader should keep the discussion on track and encourage participation by all conferees. The conference leader should create a pleasant atmosphere for the free give-and-take of ideas, opinions and information.

The conference leader helps in the decision-making process by asking for votes or determining the majority or consensus of the thinking of members. Also, the conference leader offers clarification and summarizes.

Conference Participants. Care should be taken in selecting conference participants. Only individuals who can make a contribution and are closely concerned with the topic being discussed should be invited to participate. Each participant works actively with the leader and other group members in the decision-making process. An effective participant is a good listener, a person who helps to resolve problems.

Notification. Conference participants should be notified of the subject, location, other people attending, and time of the conference. For small meetings, a telephone call will suffice; for large conventions, formal, written notification is desirable. The conference participants should be directed to appropriate background materials or resources (files, library resources, data, and so on).

Agenda. An agenda should be prepared and distributed well in advance. The participants should have an opportunity to schedule the conference, that is, mark their calendars. Also, they must have adequate time to prepare for the conference, do their "homework."

Assembling Materials. It is a common practice at conferences to distribute materials. These materials are usually assembled in *packets.* Reports, articles, data, graphic aids, and pamphlets are examples of the diversified materials contained in packets.

distribute materials

Facilities. Adequate physical facilities for a conference are essential. Small, informal meetings can be held in an executive's private office. Larger, formal conferences are held in conference rooms, in an auditorium, or off the company premises—at a convention hall, restaurant, hotel, and so on.

The following arrangements are usually made:

Test question

1. *Reserving the room.* A room with adequate seating, a podium, and lectern is usually preferred for a large conference. For a smaller conference, a room with a large conference table is adequate. If a meeting is held in a private office, a reservation is usually not required. However, if it is held elsewhere (conference room, auditorium, restaurant, and so on), a reservation is required.

2. *Voice-amplification equipment.* In large rooms, provisions must be made for the amplification of voices. Usually, a microphone is at the lectern; in some circumstances a hand-held microphone provides more mobility for a speaker who wishes to move about.

3. *Audiovisual aids.* Equipment should be provided for the use of audiovisual aids, such as a chalkboard, slide and film projectors, an overhead projector, and so on.

4. *Furniture.* Provision should be made for adequate seating. Tables are often needed for display purposes, for the people registering conference guests at the door, or for the conference speakers on the stage.

5. *Refreshments.* Arrangements must be made for serving refreshments. For a short meeting, a pitcher of cool water and glasses suffice.

6. *Name cards.* If the conferees are not close business associates, name cards are helpful.

7. *Miscellaneous.* If the conference is held in a conference room, arrangements should be made for note taking. Paper and pencils are usually provided for each participant.

Recording the Conference. Arrangements should be made for recording the meeting. A secretary can be assigned this task. The dialogue can be recorded by shorthand or tape. If the meeting is not recorded, the conferees should take individual notes.

HOLDING THE CONFERENCE *knowledgeable (Good like person) - don't like this expression he uses*

The Coordinator's Role. The conference coordinator welcomes people to the conference and states the procedures to be followed. The coordinator tells the conference participants the topic and purpose of the meeting. At some meetings, the conference coordinator is an active participant in the dialogue; at other meetings, the coordinator only presides over the meeting.

Speakers are introduced by the conference coordinator. The effective conference coordinator expertly guides (follows the agenda) and stimulates relevant discussion, to provide information and to resolve problems. Individuals who try to monopolize the conversation or digress from the topic at hand must be controlled; reserved individuals should be encouraged to participate.

Unless the meeting is open-ended, the coordinator must be mindful of the time.

At the end of the discussion period, the coordinator usually summarizes the findings or main ideas and proposes courses of action.

The conference atmosphere should be a friendly one. The conference coordinator should be democratic, well-mannered, competent, considerate, and cordial. The conferees should be encouraged to work collectively. The coordinator resolves disagreements and keeps the conversation on track. The coordinator may summarize major points during the conference (as well as at the end). At some meetings, votes are taken and results recorded.

The Conferees. The conferees should contribute to the dialogue and not engage in irrelevant discussions. An effective conference member is a good listener, alert, courteous, and informed. Each member should try to make a positive contribution to the proceedings.

POST-CONFERENCE ACTIVITIES

After the conference, minutes of the meeting—or a summary—are distributed to conferees and other concerned individuals. The conference coordinator should determine whether proposals made have been implemented. The coordinator may suggest a follow-up meeting. Letters of appreciation (enclosing honoraria) are sent to invited speakers.

Formal conventions

A convention is a formal meeting of people who are all usually members of the same group or organization. Delegates may be sent to a convention. Although the structures of formal conventions varies, they are often associated with a formal meal or banquet. Because of the need for large food facilities, reservations are often made at a hotel or large restaurant. A facility with conference rooms is essential. Delegates from a wide geographic area may require lodgings. Usually, formal meetings are held and guest speakers are invited.

GUEST SPEAKERS

Since guest speakers must be introduced, they should submit biographical sketches. These sketches are also used for publicity releases. A guest speaker usually receives an *honorarium* for speaking. Honorariums are payments to professional persons. Propriety forbids setting a price. Honorarium are usually thought of as gifts for services rendered. It should not be confused with a fee, which is a fixed payment for a service rendered. A fee is thought of as a predetermined charge.

a gift for services rendered.

The convention leader may serve as toastmaster at the banquet, or another person may be selected to serve this function. The toastmaster should have a pleasant personality and set the proper tone. The toastmaster usually tells some jokes, introduces invited guests, and introduces speakers.

Electronic conferencing systems

on Test

There are obvious advantages to traditional, personal conferencing systems, such as meeting people face-to-face, establishing rapport, observing body language, and so on. However, this may well be a luxury few businesses will be able to afford in the future. One of the major drawbacks of traditional face-to-face meetings or conferences is that participants must physically congregate, often from diverse, geographically separated areas. A company may have branches located in distant cities in the United States or foreign countries. A great deal of time and money may be spent in traveling. It is not uncommon for executives to spend several days attending a conference or convention; therefore, the high-echelon officers of a business may be devoting all of their time to a convention, when other business activities are pressing.

Modern telecommunications, made possible by semiconductor technology, have provided an alternative to the traditional conference. Conferees need not meet face-to-face. A meeting can be held electronically in an executive's office by *computer conferencing, teleconferencing,* and *videoconferencing.* (See Figures 15–6 and 15–7 for illustrations of traditional conferences and electronic conferences.)

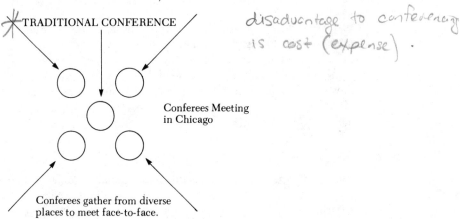

disadvantage to conferencing is cost (expense).

FIGURE 15–6. Traditional conference

Citing the frustration and fatigue of an executive returning from a convention, Prince states, "Now the same executive can simply press a button and let modern technology do the rest. He need never leave his desk. More-

ELECTRONIC CONFERENCING SYSTEMS

Disadventage
cost by the phone
bill .

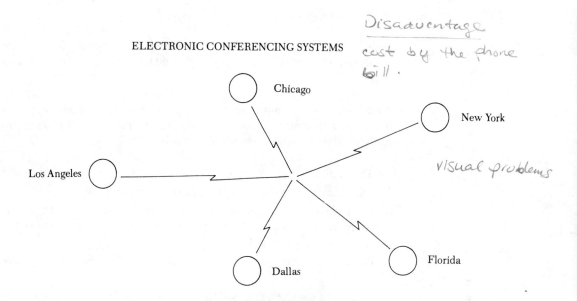

visual problems

Conferees remain at their locations
and are interconnected by computer,
telephone or telephone/television.

FIGURE 15–7. Electronic conferencing system

over, his co-workers need not leave theirs either, even if they are thousands of miles apart, as long as there is access to a phone or terminal."[1]

The savings are very considerable. The Atlantic Richfield Co. is designing a teleconferencing system that "is expected to save $50 million to $60 million annually in travel costs."[2]

 ## COMPUTER CONFERENCING

In a computer conference, there is an electronic exchange of information among the conferees. Computer information can be entered and accessed by the conference participants at their convenience. Since the information or message is stored by the computer, access can be at a later time if more convenient. However, with computer conferencing, instantaneous response is possible. This may be invaluable when time is a critical factor in the decision-making process.

Prince describes computer conferencing as follows:

Users input messages to other group participants on standard computer terminals linked by telephone to a national or international compu-

[1]Jeffrey S. Prince, "Conference Systems in the 80's" *Administrative Management*, XLI, no. 4 (April 1980), 65–66.
[2]Christopher Byron, "Now the Office of Tomorrow," *Time*, 116, no. 20 (November 17, 1980), 80.

ter network. All participants can 'talk' via terminals or review what has transpired from entry information retrieved from a shared data base and react.[3]

In addition to the major advantage of conferees not having to by physically present at a designated meeting place and the capability for instantaneous or delayed communication, there are other advantages.

1. The system is confidential.
2. There is a retrievable record of information entered.
3. Conference participants need not, if inconvenient, interact with the computer at the same time as a group. Individuals can check with the computer at their convenience.
4. Participants can have computer access by dialing a telephone number.
5. Computer conferencing systems are easy to use and do not require extensive training.

TELECONFERENCING

Electronic conferences can be held by using *Speakerphones* which are attached to regular phones. The Speakerphone permits the controlled amplification of the speaker's voice. An omnidirectional microphone makes voice pickup from across a room possible. The telephone need not be held. Conference calls connect conferees who can speak on the same line. This permits a dialogue among individuals who may be in different cities and eliminates the need for face-to-face conferencing. A major disadvantage of teleconferencing is that there is no visual input. To compensate for this, *facsimile machines* can be used to transmit hard copies of documents, tables, diagrams, pictures, graphs, textual material, and so on among conferees. (See Chapter 13 for details about facsimile transceivers.)

Visual Contact. Also, visual input can take place during a teleconference by using an *Electronic Blackboard*. The Electronic Blackboard is a rapid means of electronic visual communication. It is usually used during teleconference calls. The electronic blackboard works as follows: A person writes or draws on the Electronic Blackboard with chalk—similar to writing on a regular chalkboard. The words or pictures are instantly transmitted over telephone wires to a video screen at another location.

The Electronic Blackboard consists of two sheets of Mylar with pressure sensitive gas between. Chalk strokes are converted to digital data for

---

[3]Prince, "Conference Systems in the 80's," 66.

Gemini^tm 100, an Electronic Blackboard, sends both graphics and two-way voice communications over telephone lines to distant locations. (Courtesy Southern New England Telephone Co.)

electronic transmission over telephone lines. The data are converted to images for viewing on a TV monitor. The Electronic Blackboard can be erased in part or in whole, so that additional information can be transmitted. (See Figure 15–8.)

VIDEOCONFERENCES

The *videoconference* combines the audio and visual aspects of communication. It should be noted, however, that in the business world, the term "teleconference" is used at times interchangeably with the word "videoconference."

The *videophone* is more sophisticated than the Speakerphone, for it is a combination television/telephone communications system. Diagrams,

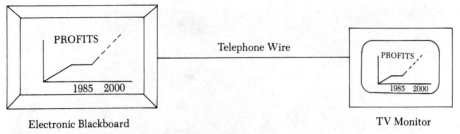

Electronic Blackboard   TV Monitor

FIGURE 15-8. Electronic blackboard

pictures, graphs, illustrations, and written text can be transmitted instantaneously and viewed on a screen. If hard copies are needed, facsimile machines can be used in conjunction with videophones.

Members of each participating group can be seen and heard. Televised conferences can be arranged among people in distant cities. Charles R. Brown, Chairman of American Telephone & Telegraph Company describes a videophone conference as follows:

> Generally, the conference takes place in a room furnished by the phone company where cameras are already set up. The cameras are voice activated; they focus on each member as he or she talks. The room also has facilities for one group to send the other a copy of a piece of paper—say, a chart or a graph—so everyone can study it at the same time.[4]

Some businessess have conference rooms equipped for videophone conferences.

Videoconferencing networks can link distant locations by satellite. Signals are transmitted to a communications satellite orbiting the earth. The signal is amplified by satellite and returned to the receiving station on earth. A satellite disk picks up the signal and it is displayed on a TV set. Aetna Life & Casualty in Hartford, Connecticut has a satellite link with its Chicago, Illinois office. Visual images from satellite hookups are projected on wall-sized screens. Figure 15-9 is a diagram of the Aetna Life & Casualty videoconference room.

It is interesting to note that there are two modes of picture reception in use: full motion and freeze frame. In freeze frame, the picture remains stationary for 10 to 70 seconds; however, normal conversation continues.

There are proposals to integrate by satellite the areas of communication that are presently being used as separate entities: data communications,

---

[4]Interview with Charles L. Brown, "The Phone in Your Future: What's in Store," *U.S. News & World Report*, LXXXVI, no. 6 (February 12, 1979), 63–64.

facsimile, voice communications, teleconferencing, and videoconferencing.[5] When this is accomplished, conferees will be able to hear, see, and exchange hard copy effortlessly.

Summary

Meetings or conferences provide for interchange of information and ideas among the individuals at various levels of a company. A *meeting* is a coming together of people. A *conference* is a formal meeting at which discussions and consultations are held, decisions are made, information is exchanged, policy is determined, and appraisals are conducted. There is a broad spectrum of formality to meetings, from small meetings of individuals to formal conventions.

A *committee* consists of a group of people delegated to give consideration to a specific matter or to perform a specific task or tasks. An *agenda*, a plan of activities for the meeting, is distributed well in advance of the meeting. Parliamentary procedures provide a structured order of discussion for large, formal meetings. A secretary takes the *minutes*, an official report of the proceedings.

At times, a committee will pass a *resolution*, a formal expression of group will or opinion.

Formal conferences entail three steps:

1. Planning the conference,
2. The conference itself, and
3. Post-conference activities.

In planning the conference, the topic should be defined and the purpose stated. An individual should be selected as conference leader or conference coordinator. Care should be taken in the selection of conference participants. Only individuals who can make a contribution and who are closely concerned with the topic being discussed should be invited to participate. Conference participants should be notified of the conference and given pertinent details. An agenda is prepared and distributed in advance. Also, various materials are assembled. Attention is given to securing adequate physical facilities (room, voice-amplification equipment, audiovisual aids, furniture, refreshments, name cards, etc.). Arrangements should be made for recording the conference.

At the conference, the coordinator welcomes people, states the topic and

[5]"Spreading the Word—and the Data," *Dun's Review*, 114, no. 2 (August 1979), 76.

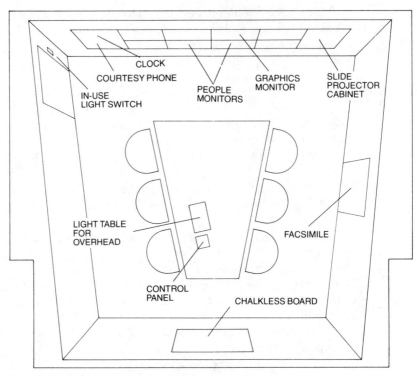

FIGURE 15-9. A videoconference room layout
(Courtesy of Aetna Life & Casualty)

purpose of the meeting, participates in the dialogue at some meetings, and presides over the meeting. At the end of the discussion period, the coordinator usually summarizes the findings or main ideas and proposes courses of action.

After the conference, minutes of the meeting—or a summary—are distributed. Letters of appreciation are sent to invited speakers.

Conventions are the most formal of business meetings. Delegates may be sent to a convention. Conventions are often associated with a formal meal or banquet.

Modern telecommunications have provided an alternative to the traditional conference. A meeting can be held *electronically* in an executive's office by computer conferencing, teleconferencing, and videoconferencing. Electronic conferencing networks can be linked by satellite to cross long distances.

Discussion

1. Why is communication essential among individuals at various administrative levels?

2. Differentiate between a meeting and a conference.
3. Explain some of the advantages of electronic conferencing systems.

Study questions

1. What is a conference? *formal meeting of people*
2. Meetings cover a broad spectrum of formality. Please describe this range. *Informal → some meetings conference convention → formal*
3. What are the four advantages of participatory meetings?
4. Describe an informal meeting.
5. What is an agenda? *Tells whats in store for meeting*
6. Explain the order of business at a committee meeting. *pg 294*
7. Explain the parliamentary procedures followed at a meeting.
8. What are the three types of committees? *standing, special, ad hoc*
9. What are minutes? *an official report of proceedings in shorthand*
10. When are the proceedings of a meeting tape recorded?
11. What is a resolution? *formal expression of group will or opinion.*
12. Describe the personal qualifications of a conference leader.
13. In order to follow parliamentary procedures, the conference leader usually refers to one of two reference books. List one of these reference books. *Roberts Rules of order Newly Revised*
14. Generally, two basic qualifications are required of conference participants. Please list them. *299*
15. What are the physical arrangements that generally must be made for a conference?
16. What must be done after a conference?
17. What is a convention?
18. What does the term "telecommunications" encompass?
19. List three major electronic conferencing systems.
20. What are Speakerphones?
21. What is an Electronic Blackboard?

Activities

1. *Preparing an Agenda:* Assume that you are the chairperson of a conference of college students designated to discuss student center activities. Prepare an agenda.
2. *Preparing a Resolution:* Karen Tyler has completed a major study for the Parker Company which will be used as a basis for instituting a

word processing center. Prepare a resolution commending Karen Tyler for her major contribution to the Parker Company.

3. *Planning a Conference:* Assume that you are a conference coordinator. Student delegates will arrive from other colleges to discuss the new technology in business (editing typewriters, facsimile machines, dictation machines, and so on). Explain the arrangements you have to make (keeping your college facilities in mind)—invitations, registration, facilities, publicity, speakers, refreshments, housing, exhibitions, audiovisual equipment, and entertainment.

ACHIEVEMENT OF LEARNING GOALS

Check the appropriate boxes to determine whether you have or have not achieved the learning goals of this chapter.

I Can:

	YES	NO
1. Recognize the need for effective, inter-echelon communication and participatory meetings.	☐	☐
2. Differentiate between meetings and conferences.	☐	☐
3. Plan an effective meeting or conference.	☐	☐
4. Comprehend the order of business at a committee meeting and parliamentary procedures.	☐	☐
5. Structure post-conference activities.	☐	☐
6. Understand modern electronic conferencing systems.	☐	☐

If any of your responses were "no," it is suggested that you review pertinent chapter parts.

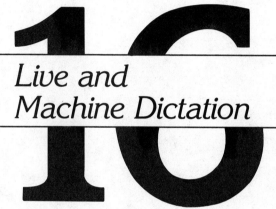

Live and
Machine Dictation

LEARNING GOALS

1. Explain the methods of effective dictation and the equipment used.

2. Master the dictation process.

Dictation - fast way of transmitting info or ideas to paper. the act of speaking words to another person or machine for transcription.

Transcription - conversation of speech or shorthand notes into typewritten copy.
Person dictating the call is known as the ~~dictator~~ author, principle or word originator.

Dictating vocabulary and methods

on
Test !

Although rough drafts of business communications can be written in long-hand—a long, arduous and tedious task for an executive—and given to a secretary for typing, most business communications are dictated. *Dictation* is an expeditious way of transmitting information or ideas to paper. Dictation is the act of speaking words to another person or to a machine for *transcription*. Transcription is the conversion of speech or shorthand notes into typewritten copy. In the modern office, the person dictating is called the "principal," "word originator" or "author." In the traditional office, the term "dictator" is commonly used. The terms "principal" and "dictator" will be used in this chapter. *Live dictation* entails speaking to another person; *machine dictation* entails speaking to a machine.

FOUR METHODS OF DICTATION

Dictation can be conducted in four ways:

1. to a typist,
2. to a secretary or stenographer,

312

Live dictation - means speaking to a person
Machine dictation - means speaking to a machine

3. to a machine, and

4. to a voice-operated typewriter.

Dictation to a Typist.   The principal speaks directly to the typist. As the principal speaks, the words are typed immediately. Of course, the principal must not speak too rapidly—a good typist can type one word per second; the normal rate of speaking is about two words per second. This method of dictation is usually reserved for brief messages that must be sent out immediately, such as telegrams. However, it has been used for lengthy copy outside the business world. The outstanding example is Winston Churchill's dictation of *The Second World War,* consisting of six volumes, directly to his secretary seated at a giant primer typewriter. As Churchill spoke, he could *see* the words. It is interesting to note that Churchill received the Nobel Prize for Literature for this voluminous publication.

[margin note: Common in business world.]

DICTATOR   TYPIST

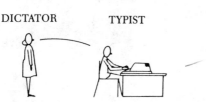

[handwritten note: Winston Church Hill won noble Price for Lit dictating "The Second World War".]

FIGURE 16–1.   Dictation to a typist

Usually, the typist taking dictation types at a rough-draft rate of speed. Errors are corrected after the dictation is completed. A final draft is typed from the rought-draft copy.

Dictation to a Secretary or Stenographer.   In a traditional office, an executive (dictator) dictates to a personal secretary or to a secretary or transcriptionist in a stenographic pool, a shared secretary. The secretary knows shorthand, an abbreviated symbolic method of writing words, or uses a stenographic machine (touch shorthand).

[margin note: Short-hand written (simple writing)]

Shorthand systems were used by the Greeks, Romans, Persians, and Egyptians and date back to 103 B.C. when Marcus Tullius Tiro was secretary to Cicero.[1] The Gregg and Pitman systems are used most widely today. Both systems use symbols to represent letters or words. Words are written phonetically, the way they sound.

Touch shorthand is used mainly in courts where dictation is taken at 150 to 250 words per minute on a stenotype machine. The machine has twenty-two keys. It was invented in 1910 by Ward Stone Ireland, a court stenographer in Dallas, Texas. As keys are depressed, consonants and vowels are printed on paper. Although touch shorthand is faster and more accurate than

[1]Caleb W. Davis, "Shorthand," *Collier's Encyclopedia* (1968), 20, 703.

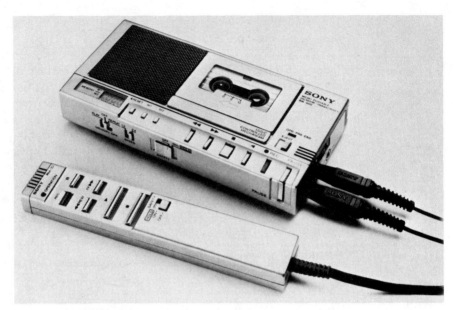

Sony dictator/transcriber.

written shorthand, it has some disadvantages: it is difficult to revise notes, and the machine must be carried by the secretary. The shorthand notes must be transcribed; that is, converted from phonetic symbols to typewritten form. Secretaries are usually employable if they can take dictation at a minimal speed of 80 words per minute for five minutes with 95 percent accuracy. An expert secretary can take dictation at two words per second (120 wpm) and upward. Some secretaries employ speedwriting methods (abbreviated standard words).

DICTATOR   STENOGRAPHER   STENOGRAPHER

Message recorded   Transcribes
by stenographer   message on
in shorthand (or   a typewriter.
touch shorthand).

FIGURE 16–2. Dictating to a secretary/stenographer

As explained in the chapter on word processing, there is a major disadvantage to live dictation: two individuals must be present at the same time.

This is very costly, for two salaries are being consumed simultaneously. Also, a secretary may not be available at all times.

However, some executives prefer the luxury and prestige of a secretary. It is usually more pleasant relating to a person rather than to a microphone. Feedback during face-to-face dictation is instantaneous and corrections can be made easily. Also, confidentiality is safeguarded by live dictation to a personal secretary rather than a typist in a pool.

Dictation to a Machine. Machine dictation is gaining in popularity, for it is generally more economical, convenient, and rapid than live dictation methods. Dictation is done via a microphone or telephone.

A dictation machine records sounds electronically on a belt, disc, or cassette. The sounds are played back and transcribed by a secretary. (It is interesting to note that in word processing systems, correspondence secretaries need not know stenography.)

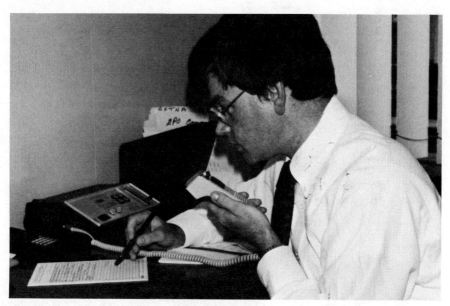

Machine dictation with a desk-top unit (Courtesy Connecticut General Corp.)

A major advantage of machine dictation is its availability. An executive can have a portable recording unit at home, in the car, or on a train or plane. Thoughts can be recorded when they occur.

Dictating machines are an integral part of modern word processing systems. Messages can be telephoned to units in a word processing center twenty-four hours a day. This is very convenient for an executive away from the

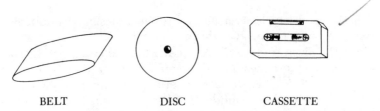

| BELT | DISC | CASSETTE |

FIGURE 16–3. Dictation may be stored on belts, discs, or cassettes

office. The chapter on word processing details the many advantages of machine dictation (lower cost, faster dictation rates, efficient scheduling of personnel, and so on).

MACHINE DICTATION

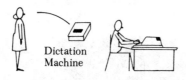

DICTATOR   CORRESPONDENCE
                   SECRETARY

FIGURE 16–4. Dictation to a machine

TYPES OF MACHINES *Test question on Thomas Edison!*

Thomas Edison, inventor of the phonograph, invented the first dictation machine in 1888. A needle recorded sound by cutting into a cylinder made of wax. Presently, there are three broad categories of dictating machines using magnetic media (belts, discs, and cassettes):

1. portable units,
2. desktop units, and
3. centralized units.

disadvantage! no record in print.

Portable Units. Portable units are battery operated. They can be held in a hand and are lightweight. They are particularly convenient while outside the office. Portable tapes should be compatible with inside-the-office equipment.

Desk-Top Units. Desk-top units are designed for dictation in an office. These units are highly sophisticated and feature tone, volume, and speed controls. There are two broad classifications of desk-top units:

1. *Universal.* Can be used both for dictating and transcribing.
2. *Specialized.* Separate units for dictating and transcribing.

316

desk Top units two types:
Universal :- can be used for dictating and transcribing
Specialized - separate units for dictation and transcribing

The executive speaks directly into a microphone which is attached to the unit.

Centralized Units. Central dictation units are classified as single-unit media (belts, discs, cassettes) or endless loop systems. Endless loop systems are popular since they eliminate the handling of media. They are available twenty-four hours a day, seven days a week. Input by telephone is an outstanding feature. Within an office, input is through desk phones.

It should be noted that an executive may speak to a dictating machine, remove the recorded message, and mail the cassette in a mailing carton to the correspondent (Figure 16-5). This eliminates the need for a stenographer or correspondence secretary to transcribe the message. The recipient merely listens to the message that has been recorded.

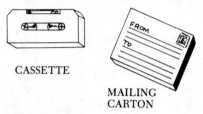

CASSETTE

MAILING
CARTON

FIGURE 16–5. Cassettes may be mailed

Executives can exchange cassettes which can be reused. This system of communication is particularly effective for visually impaired individuals.

Voice-Operated Typewriters. Highly sophisticated *voice-operated typewriters* have been invented. These machines "recognize" most words spoken (about 95 percent). A CRT (cathode ray tube) screen displays the message as it is being spoken. What about the 5 percent of words the machine does not recognize? These have to be typed, either by the executive or a secretary. Voice-operated typewriters will require excellent dictation: clarity, preciseness, and command of language. (See Figure 16–6)

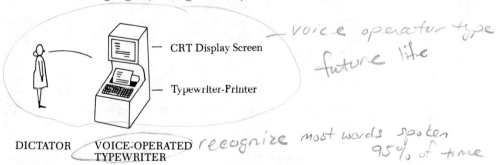

CRT Display Screen

Typewriter-Printer

DICTATOR   VOICE-OPERATED
            TYPEWRITER

FIGURE 16–6. Dictation to voice-operated typewriter

The dictating process

The techniques for effective business writing and those for dictation are similar. First, determine the purpose of the communication (inform, persuade, goodwill, etc.). Next, visualize the recipient of your communication. The language level will depend on this.

The following steps are suggested:

preparing for dictation

1. *Gather the necessary information.* Assemble pertinent information from company files and other sources needed. Usually, there is a file folder for people who correspond regularly with the company. Have your secretary withdraw this folder from the files. After dictation, give this folder to your secretary for reference and filing.

2. *Determine the order of dictation.* Decide which message is to be dictated first, second, third, and so on.

3. *Plan the message.* Prepare a logical plan of the message content. An outline, mental or written, is usually helpful. When replying to correspondence, some executives jot notes directly on the original letter received or on notepaper. (See Figure 16–7.)

4. *Schedule the dictation.* Usually, it is best to designate a specific time each day for dictation. Some executives prefer the morning, after the mail has been reviewed. Ideally, it should be a time when there will not be interruptions. Some executives will hold telephone calls and make no appointments during dictation time.

Dictating techniques

IDENTIFICATION

Assign a number to each message dictated. When using a dictating machine, the person dictating should be identified by name, title, department, and telephone extension.

PRELIMINARY INSTRUCTIONS

Tell the stenographer or correspondence secretary as much as you can about the communication:

- The kind of communication (letter, memo, telegram, report, speech, and so on)

318

- Specify whether the message is to be typed in rough draft or finished form
- The kind and size of stationery to be used (letterhead, bond paper, memo form, personal stationery, and so on)
- Designate mailing instructions (registered, special delivery, certified mail, air mail and so on)
- Specify on-arrival handling instructions (confidential, personal attention, and so on)
- When the job must be completed. Identify priority of items. Certain communications may be rushed
- The name, title, and address of the correspondent
- If applicable, the attention line
- The salutation or greeting (Dear Sir, Dear Ms. Carpenter, and so on)
- If applicable, the subject line
- Enclosure information
- The number of carbon copies or photocopies and the recipient(s) of copies
- The length of the message

    Short letter (Under 100 words)
    Medium letter (100–200 words)
    Long letter (Over 200 words)

All preliminary instructions must be given before dictating when using a machine.

DICTATING THE MESSAGE

Your voice must be audible, capable of being heard, while dictating. Speak naturally, evenly. Each word must be enunciated distinctly at a reasonable rate of speed. The rate of dictation is relative to the method employed (see Tables 16–1, 16–2, 16–4, 16–6).

Speak more slowly than you would normally while conversing. Avoid any actions that will physically interfere with clear communications: speaking with cigarette or pipe in the mouth, hands in front of the mouth, chewing gum, eating, pencil in mouth, and the like. Face your secretary, otherwise your voice will be difficult to hear. Don't speak to a wall or window.

When dictating to a secretary, watch the writing rate. If the secretary is having difficulty, adjust your dictation speed accordingly. You may be dictating complex material at a rapid rate of speed.

A good communicator anticipates secretarial errors. Dictate any me-

Dear Mrs. Rosenbaum:

Your advertisement in <u>Reel Talk</u> shows a picture of a new rod and spinning reel combination, model X21.

Since I am considering buying this combo, please answer the following questions:

1. Does the reel have stainless steel ball bearings? *YES*

2. What is the length of the rod? *6½ FEET*

3. What is the price of the combo? *$39 + STATE TAX*

4. What is the action of the rod? *MEDIUM ACTION*

5. What is the gear ratio of the reel? *4:9:1*

6. What is the weight of the combo? *3 LBS.*

Since fishing starts in one week, an immediate reply would be very much appreciated.

Sincerely,

Cathy Sullivan

FIGURE 16–7. Letter with dictation notes

chanics needed, such as the spelling of difficult words and names, unusual punctuation, paragraphing, and so on. Repeat any important figures. Don't dictate obvious information; for example, the addresses of individuals corresponded with on a regular basis.

Homonyms. *Homonyms* are words that sound alike and have different meanings. When dictating, it may be wise to spell out the homonyms in Table 16–2 and others you may come across.

TABLE 16–1. Relative dictating speeds

Situation	Speed
Dictating to a person writing in longhand	*Very slow*—about 24 words a minute.
Dictating to a typist	*Slow*—35–60 words a minute. Exceptional typists can type over 100 words a minute.
Dictating to a stenographer using shorthand	*Moderate–fast*—80–140 words a minute. Average is about 100 words a minute.
Dictating to a secretary using touch shorthand	*Fast*—150–250 words a minute required for a court stenographer.
Machine dictation	*Fast*—120–140 words a minute is average talking speed.

TABLE 16–2. Homonyms

ad, add	miner, minor
allowed, aloud	pain, pane
altar, alter	pair, pare, pear
ascent, assent	passed, past
bare, bear	peace, piece
billed, build	presence, presents
brake, break	principal, principle
calendar, calender	rain, reign, rein
cite, sight, site	raise, raze
coarse, course	rap, wrap
complement, compliment	right, rite, write
council, counsel	role, roll
fair, fare	shear, sheer
foreword, forward	stake, steak
forth, fourth	stationary, stationery
guarantee, guaranty	to, too, two
higher, hire	their, there, they're
hoard, horde	threw, through
holy, wholly	vain, vane, vein
incite, insight	vary, very
it's, its	waive, wave
knew, new	ware, wear, where
know, no	weak, week
lean, lien	weather, whether
lessen, lesson	who's, whose
loan, lone	your, you're

Confusing Words. Some words are very confusing since they sound similar to other words. Enunciate such words clearly (Table 16–3). Spell them if you think it will help avoid errors.

321

TABLE 16–3. Confusing words

accede, exceed	disapprove, disprove
accept, except	disburse, disperse
access, excess	disinterested, uninterested
adapt, adept, adopt	dual, duel
adverse, averse	elicit, illicit
advice, advise	emigrate, immigrate
affect, effect	eminent, imminent
allude, elude	era, error
allusion, illusion	eraser, erasure
appraise, apprise	formally, formerly
biannual, biennial	incidence, incidents
canvas, canvass	later, latter
cease, seize	loose, lose
censor, censure	marital, martial
census, senses	moral, morale
choose, chose	personal, personnel
coma, comma	practicable, practical
consul, council, counsel	precede, proceed
continual, continuous	quiet, quite
credible, creditable	reality, realty
decent, descent, dissent	residence, residents
desert, dessert	respectfully, respectively
device, devise	than, then
	weather, whether

Two Norelco dictation machines (Courtesy Norelco)

Worn Expressions. The English language is full of worn, trite expressions. They make dictation lengthy and costly. Avoid the words shown in Table 16–4.

TABLE 16–4. Worn expressions

a large number of	first and foremost
according to our records	for better or worse
acknowledge receipt of	for the purpose of
after all is said and done	for your convenience
allow me to	for your information
along this line	fully cognizant of
am of the opinion	goes without saying
as a matter of fact	hereby acknowledge
as of this date	hit the nail on the head
as per your order	if and when
as regards	in a satisfactory manner
as stated above	in accordance with
as the case may be	in answer to your
as you know	in due course
assuring you of our	in my opinion
appreciation	in other words
at an early date	in receipt of
at hand	in regard to
at the present time	in the amount of
at your earliest convenience	in the event that
attached hereto	in the final analysis
attached please find	in the meantime
avail yourself of the	in the near future
opportunity	in this day and age
be good enough to	it has come to my attention
beg to differ	it goes without saying
better late than never	it stands to reason
bring to your attention	in view of the fact that
by means of	kind enough
by return mail	last but not least
consensus of opinion	let me call your attention to
continued patronage	long period of time
deem it advisable	looking forward to
despite the fact that	
don't hesitate to write	
due to the fact that	
easier said than done	
enclosed herewith	
enclosed please find	
feel free to	
few and far between	

(continued on next page)

TABLE 16-4. Worn expressions (cont.)

make an adjustment	thank you kindly
meet with your approval	thanking you in advance
my personal opinion	this day and age
needless to say	this is to acknowledge
nick of time	receipt
on behalf of	this is to advise you
on the ball	this is to inform you that
open-and-shut case	to date
our check in the amount of	to make a long story short
over a barrel	to the bitter end
over and done with	under separate cover
permit me to say	upon reviewing our records
plain as day	we are in receipt of
please be advised that	we are in the opinion that
please contact us	we regret to inform you
please do not hesitate to	we take pleasure in
write	we wish to acknowledge
quick as a flash	we wish to express our
reason is because	gratitude
receipt is acknowledged	wish to advise you
recent date	wish to call your attention to
regarding your letter of	the fact
replying to your letter of	wish to inform you
rest assured	with regard to
slowly but surely	without further ado
take pleasure	your check in the amount of
take the liberty of	
take this opportunity	
take under consideration	
thank you for your	
patronage	

Redundancies. *Redundancies,* saying the same thing two or more times also make dictation lengthy. Avoid the phrases in Table 16-5.

Pauses. If you must pause while using a dictating machine, stop recording. A long pause or interruption (such as phone ringing) while dictating to a secretary may necessitate having the secretary read back the last few sentences.

Try to strip your speech of all paralanguage, such as "um," "ah," "anduh," and "uh." These tend to confuse the person transcribing the message. Also, when using a dictating machine, speak directly into the microphone; hold it two or three inches from your mouth.

Be careful about adding any extraneous remarks, statements that are irrelevant. Extraneous remarks tend to confuse the stenographer taking the dictation or the correspondence secretary typing the message.

If you must make a change when speaking to a secretary, say "correction," then dictate the change. When using a dictating machine, say "oper-

TABLE 16–5. Redundancies

above mentioned	industrious, hard-working
and etc.	meet together
annual, yearly meeting	modern, up-to-date
at about	near to
basic fundamentals	new and innovative
circulated around	over with
close proximity	personal opinion
congregated around	rarely ever
consensus of opinion	reason is due
continue on	rebate back from
each and every	refer back
exact same	repeat again
exactly identical	rules and regulations
first and foremost	same identical
full amount	tired and exhausted
full and complete	to regain again
fundamental basics	true facts
future potential	united together
in my opinion I believe	up above

ator, correction," or use the secretary's name, "Terry, correction." Mark the correction on the indicator slip.

When dictating to a machine, indicate the end of a communication by saying "end of telegram," "end of memo," "end of letter," or "end of report."

Cues. Cues assist your secretary (see Table 16–6). A typical dictation to a secretary is shown in Figure 16–8. The procedures for machine dictation differ a bit from those for face-to-face dictation. In Figure 16–9, the underscored parts represent instructions to the typist, and they are not to be typed. Figure 16–10 shows the transcribed letter as it comes out of the typewriter.

TABLE 16–6. Cues

Cue for	Say
Paragraphing	(Paragraph)
Punctuation:	
Quotation	(Quote) a substantial profit (Unquote)
Comma, period,	(Comma), (Period),
question mark,	(Question mark),
exclamation point,	(Exclamation point),
semicolon, colon	(Semicolon), (Colon)
Capitalization	(Capital) Ajax *or* (Cap) Ajax
Spelling	(Y-a-b-l-o-n-s-k-i)
Correction	(Correction)
Correction (when using a dictating machine)	(Operator—Correction) or (Terry—Correction)

*At the start of
dictation, tell
the secretary:*
1. *The number of
   the letter*
2. *The number of
   carbon copies*
3. *Special mailing
   instructions*
4. *Kind of station-
   ery*
5. *Name and address
   of the correspon-
   dent*

Terry, please send letter number five, requiring
two carbon copies, special delivery, on letterhead stationery. The letter is to Ms. Lois A.
Clay (C-L-A-Y), Forty (F-O-R-T-Y) Elm Street,
Kalamazoo (K-A-L-A-M-A-Z-O-O), Michigan, four-
nine-zero-zero-two.

Dear Ms. Clay: Subject: Radio Repair
I am happy to inform you that the electronic
digital (D I G I T A L) clock phonograph
(Correction--) radio has been repaired without
charge (Exclamation point, paragraph) The
defective fluorescent (F-L-U-O-R-E-S-C-E-N-T)
display light and doze (D-O-Z-E) button have
been repaired. (Paragraph) We are very pleased
(comma) indeed (comma) to learn that you like
the wake (hyphen) to (hyphen) music and alarm
settings. Thank you for informing us of this.
(Paragraph) Your repaired radio should give
you many years of satisfactory service.
Sincerely, Penny Adams, Manager, Customer
Relations.

Terry, please enclose a copy of our new advertising flyer. Send a blind carbon copy to Mr.
Reed Scott in Quality Control.

*When making a change,
say "correction"*

*Dictate:
Difficult punctua-
tio, spelling, and
paragraphing*

Blind Carbon Copy:
• *No notation
  on original copy.*
• *Recipient of letter
  does not know carbon
  copy has been sent.*

FIGURE 16–8. Typical dictation to secretary (special directions to typist in parentheses)

Try to avoid frequent readbacks during dictation. This is usually an indication of poor preparation for dictation.

If the message is complex, upon completion of dictation you may want it read back in part or its entirety to be sure it has been recorded accurately. If the message has been recorded on a dictating machine, play back the message.

Ask the secretary if there are any questions when dictation of a message has been completed.

After dictation has been completed, it is customary to hand the file to the secretary. It is helpful to the secretary to refer to the file for specific aids, such as the spelling of names, addresses, zip codes, figures, and the like.

326

Operator, this is Penny Adams, Manager of
Customer Relations, extension seven-two-four-
zero. This is a short letter, number five, requiring
two carbon copies. Please use letterhead
stationery and mail the letter special delivery.
The letter is to Ms. Lois A. Clay (C-L-A-Y), Forty
(F-O-R-T-Y) Elm Street, Kalamazoo (K-A-L-A-M-A-
Z-O-O), Michigan, four-nine-zero-zero-two.

Dear Ms. Clay: Subject: Radio Repair
I am happy to inform you that the electric
digital (D-I-G-I-T-A-L) clock phonograph
(Operator: correction--) radio has been
repaired without charge   (Exclamation point,
paragraph) The defective fluorescent (F-L-U-O-
R-E-S-C-E-N-T) display light and doze (D-O-Z-E)
button have been repaired. (Paragraph) We are
very pleased (comma) indeed (comma) to learn
that you like the wake (hyphen) to (hyphen)
music and alarm settings. Thank you for
informing us of this. (Paragraph) Your
repaired radio should give you many years of
satisfactory service. Sincerely, Penny Adams,
Manager, Customer Relations.

Operator, please enclose a copy of our new
advertising flyer. Send a blind carbon copy
to Mr. Reed Scott in Quality Control. End of
letter number five.

FIGURE 16–9

CHECKING THE TRANSCRIPT

The principal is responsible for the accuracy of the document. Before signing
or approving the transcript, check the following:

1. *Appearance.* Has the proper format been used? Is the appearance attractive? Have corrections been made neatly?

2. *Correctness.* Have all your instructions been followed correctly (carbon copy notations, enclosures, and so on)? Is the message free from
   error (typographical, spelling, punctuation, grammar, and the like)?
   Double check figures for accuracy. Undetected errors can be very

PARAMOUNT RADIO, INC.

23 Sioux Lane
St. Louis, MO 64504–4432

February 13, 19--

Ms. Lois A. Clay
Forty Elm Street
Kalamazoo, Michigan 49002

Dear Ms. Clay:

SUBJECT: RADIO REPAIR

I am happy to inform you that the electric digital
clock radio has been repaired without charge!

The defective fluorescent display light and doze
button have been repaired.

We are very pleased, indeed, to learn that you
like the wake-to-music and alarm settings. Thank
you for informing us of this.

Your repaired radio should give you many years of
satisfactory service.

Sincerely,

Penny Adams

Penny Adams, Manager
Customer Relations

tk
Enclosure

Note. Blind carbon copy notation (bcc) does not appear on the orig-
inal. It appears on carbon copies only. The illustrated letter is an
original.

FIGURE 16–10

costly to a company. Check the message for completeness. If the corrections are minor, light pencil marks should be used. This will avoid the necessity for retyping the entire paper.

Remember, the final responsibility for the accuracy of dictated material lies with the principal. This responsibility cannot be sloughed off. The person who signs the document is responsible for proofreading and editing its contents! If the final draft contains errors (in format, language, mechanics, or elsewhere), it casts a negative image on the principal and the company.

SIGNING

Some documents, such as a letter, require a complete signature. The signature should be written in pen. Some memos are signed; however, most are initialed. A word of caution: Some executives delegate the signing activity to subordinates or a secretary. This can be "hazardous" if the individual is not capable. When the authority to sign has been delegated, the person writes his or her initials under the signature in lower case letters:

Summary

Most business communications are dictated. *Dictation* is the act of speaking words to another person or to a machine for transcription. *Transcription* is the conversion of speech or shorthand notes into typewritten copy. In the modern office, the person dictating is called the "principal," "word originator" or "author." In the traditional office, the term "dictator" is commonly used.

Live dictation entails speaking to another person; *machine dictation* entails speaking to a machine.

The methods of dictation are:

1. Dictation to a typist
2. Dictation to a secretary or stenographer
3. Dictation to a machine
4. Dictation to a voice-operated typewriter

The techniques for effective business writing and those for dictation are similar. First, determine the purpose of the communication; next visualize the recipient of your communication.

The following steps are suggested when preparing for dictation:

1. Gather the necessary information.

2. Determine the order of dictation.
3. Plan the message.
4. Schedule the dictation.

The following are suggested techniques for dictation:

1. Identify each message dictated.
2. Provide the stenographer or correspondence secretary with preliminary instructions.
3. Dictate the message audibly, naturally, evenly. Speak slower than you would normally while conversing. Dictate any mechanics needed, such as spelling, punctuation, paragraphing, and so on. Repeat any important figures. Spell out homonyms and confusing words. Avoid dictating worn, trite expressions and redundancies.
4. Check the transcript for appearance and accuracy.
5. Sign a document with a complete signature if required, using pen or ball point. Most memos are initialed. Be careful about delegating the signing activity to subordinates or to a secretary. This can be "hazardous" if the individual is not capable.

Discussion

1. Explain why the executive should master dictation techniques.
2. Tell why machine dictation is gaining in popularity.

Study questions

1. Define the following terms:
   - Dictation - act of speaking words to person or machine
   - Transcription - conversion of notes into typewriter form
   - Homonyms - words that sound same,
   - Trite expressions -
   - Redundancies - repetitive words
2. In the modern office, the person dictating is called by what names (list three)? author, principal, dictator
3. What are the four methods of dictation? typist, stenographa, machine, voice
4. Who invented the dictation machine? When? Thomas Edison 1888
5. What are the three broad categories of dictating machines?
   Portable units
   Desktop units
   Centralized units

[handwritten margin notes: Plan message / schedule dictation]

6. What are the four steps in preparing for dictation? *[handwritten: Gather info, determine order of dic.]*

7. List the preliminary instructions that are given to the secretary when dictating?

8. Rate the following methods of dictation from a speed standpoint:
   - Dictating to a typist at a typewriter *[handwritten: fast]*
   - Dictating to a stenographer using shorthand *[handwritten: slower]*
   - Dictating to a secretary using touch shorthand *[handwritten: -fast]*
   - Machine dictation *[handwritten: fast]*

9. Before signing or approving a transcript, tell what should be checked by the principal. *[handwritten: all]*

10. Explain the implications of signing a letter.

Activities

1. Read the sample dictated dialogues on pp. 326–327 silently if in class or aloud if in an appropriate place. Try to familiarize yourself with correct dictating technique.

2. The following passage contains many homonyms. Rewrite the passage, selecting the proper homonyms.

   The Beaty Corporation has (waived, waved) (it's, its) (principal, principle) (rights, writes). It has (passed, past) (miner, minor) rules (threw, through) (it's, its) legal department that will change the (coarse, course) of business activities.

3. The following passage contains words that sound alike and cause confusion. Rewrite this passage, selecting the correct words.

   The supervisor, wishes to (appraise, apprise) you that we cannot (accede, exceed) to your request for it will (affect, effect) company policy. Please (accept, except) our (consul, council, counsel) rather (than, then) contesting the matter.

4. The following passage is cluttered with worn expressions. Please rewrite it.

   According to our records, we *wish to inform you* that your bill is delinquent. It has been a *long period of time* since payment has been made. *Let me call your attention to the fact* that payment was due on November 24. *To make a long story short, be good enough* to pay the enclosed invoice for $30.50. *Thanking you in advance.*

5. The following passage contains many redundancies. Please rewrite it.

It is the *consensus of opinion of each and every member* of the committee that we should *meet together* on Friday. *First and foremost,* we want *to regain again* our leadership in the field. *United together* we can *continue on* with our *new and innovative* programs. If we are *industrious and hard working,* we can *repeat again* our *modern up-to-date* program.

ACHIEVEMENT OF LEARNING GOALS

Check the appropriate boxes to determine whether you have or have not achieved the learning goals of this chapter.

I Can:

	YES	NO
1. Explain the methods of effective dictation and the equipment used.	☐	☐
2. Demonstrate mastery of the dictation process.	☐	☐

If any of your responses were "no," it is suggested that you review pertinent chapter parts.

Telephone Communications

LEARNING GOALS

1. Master correct telephone technique.
2. Recognize and use effective telephone services.
3. Identify modern telephone systems and equipment.

The telephone reproduces and conveys sounds over distances by converting sound into electronic signals that are transmitted by wire. At the destination point, the electric signal is reconverted to the original sound.

The telephone is a very popular form of oral communication because:

1. it is convenient and easy to use;
2. it is a rapid means of communication; and
3. there is a worldwide network of interconnected telephones.

Taken for granted

Alexander Graham Bell filed a patent application for the invention of the telephone in 1876. Since that time, the telephone has become an essential mode of communication in the business world.

Test Question 1876 Definatly

Presently, a whirl of activity is taking place in the "new" telephone industry. In 1968, a Federal Communications Commission decision (Carterfone Case) permitted competition in an industry that once was a monopoly. Business communications systems, equipment, and long distance services are now being offered by many companies other than the Bell System.

Broke-up Bell Telephone Co. that had monopoly.

The days of plain old telephone service are over. Key decisions of the Federal Communications Commission recently cleared by the courts have opened to bruising competition vast sectors of the once-staid, $44 billion telephone industry and the $10 billion equipment manufacturing business it supports. Scores of new competitors are barging in—ranging from tiny beginners to such industrial giants as IBM, TRW, Southern Pacific, 3M and Rockwell International. By offering new products and services, many of them hope to carve out billion-dollar segments of the nation's market.[1]

To further complicate matters, the new technology is bringing forth a flood of new equipment.

And not only competition but also new technology—a complex mixture of semiconductors, computers, optics, and space satellites—is working radical change in the market place. New phone gadgetry may be the most visible for now, but key developments in facsimile, data transmission, and integrated voice-data-video systems are shaking the telephone industry right down to its buried cables.[2]

Telephone technique

Since the telephone is such an important communication device, it is essential that the business executive exploit it to its maximal effectiveness. Executives commonly receive and place calls. The following are suggested techniques for using the telephone.

*Draw
list of notes
before you call*

Prepare for the Call. Before dialing, draw up notes of pertinent points. These notes can be in outline form or simply listed by number. To expedite matters, responses can be jotted down on the same sheet. (See Figure 17–1.)

Take Notes. Keep a pad and pencil readily available for taking notes: accurate information is very important. Jot down pertinent ideas and information. At times, it is necessary to request spelling or the repetition of data.

---

[1]"COMMUNICATIONS—The New Telephone Industry," *Business Week*, no. 2521 (February 13, 1978), p. 68.
[2]"COMMUNICATIONS—The New Telephone Industry."

```
Questions                                    Responses

1.  Price of electric typewriter,           $700
    model X278?

2.  Repeating keys--hyphen, X,              Yes
    underscore?

3.  Colors available?                       Beige, Blue

4.  Elite type?                             Yes

5.  Touch and impact adjustments           Yes

6.  Changeable type keys?                   Yes

7.  Full-range tabulation?                  Yes

8.  Visible margin controls?               No

9.  Cartridge ribbon system?               Yes

10. 88-character keyboard                   Yes
```

FIGURE 17-1. Notes in preparation for a phone call

Making notes during a telephone conversation (Courtesy Connecticut General Corp.)

List Frequently Dialed Numbers. You can speed up the telephoning process by having a listing of frequently used telephone numbers. These numbers can be listed on a sheet of paper or they can be located in a card file. Listings of telephone numbers are particularly helpful when calling individuals with unlisted telephone numbers. If the same numbers are dialed repeatedly, an automatic dialing device can be used. These devices are explained later in the chapter.

Study the Company's Telephone Directory. The company's telephone directory is usually prefaced with general instructions such as:

- Long-distance calls
- Collect calls
- Transfer calls
- Third-party calls
- Conference calls
- Call limitations (time)
- Recording of WATS and long distance calls
- *Emergency Numbers*

- Personal calls
- Repair service

This telephone directory usually states the policies of the company concerning the use of the telephone. It is important for company personnel to review and to adhere to these policies.

Identify Yourself. Executives commonly receive and place calls. When receiving a call from within the company, identify yourself—"Advertising Department, Nathan Carter speaking." Very often, the company switchboard operator identifies the company, so it is not necessary to repeat the company name when an outside call is received. If you are receiving a call directly from outside the company (without an operator intervening) say Advanced Technologies Corporation, Nathan Carter of Advertising speaking."

When telephoning someone inside the company, introduce yourself—"Good afternoon, this is Nathan Carter of the Advertising Department." When telephoning someone outside the company say—"Good afternoon, this is Nathan Carter of Advanced Technologies Corporation. May I speak to . . ."

Answer Promptly. The telephone should be answered promptly, by the second or third ring.

By second or third ring

Speak Clearly. Do not speak too rapidly or slowly, a moderate rate is best. When presenting complex data or technical information, slow down. Pronounce words distinctly in a normal conversational tone of voice. Avoid being verbose. Use words that are understandable.

conversational tone

Your voice should be loud enough to be heard, but not so loud that it is harsh. Hold the mouthpiece of the telephone about an inch from your mouth so that your voice is audible.

Be a Good Listener. The telephone involves two basic communication skills, speaking and listening. It is important to listen attentively and to avoid interrupting. Ask for confirmation if you are in doubt about what is being stated.

listen attentively repeat things on phone

At the end of the conversation, the listener may summarize details, to be sure the message was encoded and decoded accurately. For example, "Therefore, Mr. Parker, legal action will be taken on May 1, if the bill is not paid in full by April 30."

Be Courteous. Use words such as "You're welcome," "May I," "Thank you," and "Please" in your telephone conversations. Be pleasant, friendly and solicitous, answering calls promptly and giving explanations if you must keep the caller waiting. Whenever possible, use the caller's name—most people enjoy hearing their own names. Terminate calls graciously.

May I? Thank you

TABLE 17-1. Long-distance area codes for some cities

Alabama			*Georgia*			*Maine*	
all locations	205		Atlanta	404		all locations	207
Alaska	907		Augusta	404		*Maryland*	
			Macon	912		all locations	301
Arizona			Savannah	912		*Massachusetts*	
all locations	602		*Hawaii*	808		Boston	617
Arkansas			*Idaho*			Framingham	617
all locations	501		all locations	208		New Bedford	617
Bahamas	809		*Illinois*			Northampton	413
			Alton	618		Pittsfield	413
California			Belleville	618		Springfield	413
Fresno	209		Bloomington	309		Worcester	617
Los Angeles	213		Champaign	217		*Michigan*	
Sacramento	916		Chicago	312		Ann Arbor	313
San Diego	714		Joliet	815		Detroit	313
San Francisco	415		Peoria	309		Grand Rapids	616
San Jose	408		Rockford	815		Jackson	517
Santa Barbara	805		Springfield	217		Kalamazoo	616
Santa Rosa	707		Waukegan	312		Lansing	517
Canada						Marquette	906
Ontario			*Indiana*			Muskegon	616
Ft. William	807		Bloomington	812		Pontiac	313
London	519		Elkhart	219		Saginaw	517
Ottawa	613		Evansville	812		Sault Ste. Marie	906
Sudbury	705		Indianapolis	317		*Minnesota*	
Toronto	416		Kokomo	317		Duluth	218
			South Bend	219		Minneapolis	612
Quebec						Rochester	507
Montreal	514		*Iowa*			St. Paul	612
Quebec	418		Cedar Rapids	319		*Mississippi*	
Sherbrooke	819		Council Bluffs	712		all locations	601
			Davenport	319			
Colorado			Des Moines	515		*Missouri*	
all locations	303					Columbia	314
			Kansas			Joplin	417
Connecticut			Hutchinson	316		Kansas City	816
all locations	203		Lawrence	913		St. Joseph	816
			Topeka	913		St. Louis	314
Delaware			Wichita	316		Springfield	417
all locations	302						
			Kentucky			*Montana*	
District of			Ashland	606		all locations	406
Columbia			Lexington	606			
Washington	202		Louisville	502		*Nebraska*	
			Owensboro	502		Lincoln	402
Florida						Omaha	402
Clearwater	813		*Louisiana*			Scottsbluff	308
Daytona Beach	904		Baton Rouge	504			
Ft. Lauderdale	305		Monroe	318		*Nevada*	
Jacksonville	904		New Orleans	504		all locations	702
Miami	305		Shreveport	318			
Tampa	813						

Source: Telephone Directory 1981–1982, Hartford, Connecticut, Southern New England Telephone Company, 1981, p. 14.

339

TABLE 17–1. Long-distance area codes for some cities

New Hampshire		Ohio		Tennessee	
all locations	603	Akron	216	Chattanooga	615
		Cincinnati	513	Memphis	901
New Jersey		Cleveland	216	Nashville	815
Atlantic City	609	Columbus	614	Texas	
Camden	609	Dayton	513	Amarillo	806
Hackensack	201	Mansfield	419	Austin	512
Morristown	201	Springfield	513	Dallas	214
Newark	201	Toledo	419	El Paso	915
New Brunswick	201	Youngstown	216	Fort Worth	817
Paterson	201	Oklahoma		Galveston	713
Trenton	609	Lawton	405	Houston	713
Vineland	609	Muskogee	918	San Antonio	512
Woodbury	609	Oklahoma City	405	Waco	817
		Tulsa	918	Utah	
New Mexico		Oregon		all locations	801
all locations	505	all locations	503	Vermont	
				all locations	802
New York		Pennsylvania		Virgin Islands	
Albany	518	Allentown	215	all locations	809
Binghamton	607	Altoona	814		
Buffalo	716	Bradford	814	Virginia	
Cortland	607	Easton	215	Alexandria	703
Elmira	607	Erie	814	Arlington	703
Hempstead	516	Harrisburg	717	Charlottesville	804
Hudson	518	Indiana	412	Newport News	804
Ithaca	607	Lancaster	717	Norfolk	804
Lockport	716	Lebanon	717	Richmond	804
Monroe	914	Norristown	215	Roanoke	703
Mount Vernon	914	Philadelphia	215	Washington	
New York City	212	Pittsburgh	412	Seattle	206
Niagara Falls	716	Pottstown	215	Spokane	509
Peekskill	914	Reading	215	Tacoma	206
Poughkeepsie	914	Rochester	412	West Virginia	
Rochester	716	Scranton	717	All locations	304
Schenectady	518	Sharon	412	Wisconsin	
Syracuse	315	Stroudsburg	717	Beloit	608
Troy	518	Warren	814	Eau Claire	715
Utica	315	Washington	412	Madison	608
White Plains	914	Wilkes-Barre	717	Milwaukee	414
		Puerto Rico		Racine	414
North Carolina		all locations	809	Wausau	715
Asheville	704	Rhode Island			
Charlotte	704	all locations	401	Wyoming	
Greensboro	919	South Carolina		all locations	307
Raleigh	919	all locations	803	Wide Area Tel. Serv.	
Winston-Salem	919			all locations	800
North Dakota		South Dakota			
All locations	701	all locations	605		

Source: Telephone Directory 1981–1982, Hartford, Connecticut, Southern New England Telephone Company, 1981, p. 14.

Long-distance calls — *Calls outside your service area*

Calls outside the local service area are *long-distance calls.* There are two basic types: station-to-station and operator-assisted (Table 17–1).

STATION-TO-STATION — *avoid operator*   *DDD is used to avoid operator assistance*

Station-to-station calls are relatively inexpensive because you dial the call yourself without help of a telephone company operator. Dial station-to-station if you are willing to speak to anyone who answers the telephone.
Direct Distance Dialing (DDD) calls are made as follows:

- DDD calls within your area: Dial 1 + telephone number
- DDD calls outside your area: Dial 1 + area code + telephone number

Charges begin the moment the telephone is answered when a station-to-station call is placed.

OPERATOR-ASSISTED CALLS — *When ever you can avoid the operator*

Operator assisted calls are those which require a telephone company operator to assist you in completing the call. Basically, three calls require operator assistance:

1. *Bill to a third number.* A caller may place a call and transfer the charge to another telephone. However, the billed party must authorize the charge. The operator records the number to be billed.
2. *Credit card calls.* Some people have telephone credit cards. The caller tells the operator that a credit card call is being placed and gives the credit card number. The caller is billed for the call. There is no charge for obtaining a credit card; however, credit card calls are more expensive than Direct Distance Dialing (DDD) calls. There are several advantages to placing credit card calls: cash is not needed; there is a monthly record (bill) which identifies credit card calls made; the company can be billed for calls. This service is of particular value to the business person away from the office.
   Expanded Direct Distance Dialing (EDDD) is used to get the operator on the line to assist with person-to-person, collect, and credit card calls. DIAL 0 plus area code plus telephone number.
3. *Person-to-person calls.* These are the most expensive long distance calls. However, charges begin only when a particular person or extension number is reached. If the individual or extension is not reached, there is no charge. For person-to-person calls within your

341

area, dial 0 plus seven-digit number; for person-to-person calls outside your area, dial 0 plus three-digit area code number plus seven-digit number. When the operator comes on the line, say "I am placing a person-to-person call." Tell the operator the name of the person being called.

It is generally a good idea to mention at the start of your call that you are calling long distance. This will prompt the person you are calling to avoid needless small talk or chatter and save considerable money. For example: "Good afternoon Mrs. Sung, this is Mr. Rodriguez, in New York City, calling."

TIME ZONES   *4 Time Zone Areas*

There are four time zones in the United States (Pacific, Mountain, Central, and Eastern), and five in Canada (Pacific, Mountain, Central, Eastern, Atlantic). When it is 1:00 p.m. in Los Angeles, it is 4:00 p.m. in New York City. Check with the operator to determine the time in foreign countries.

Highest rates are for calls Monday through Friday between 8 a.m. and 5 p.m. Since there are lower rates in effect from 5 p.m. to 8 a.m., you can save money when you call to a time zone in the west after 5 p.m. during the week (Figure 17–2).

TIME AND CHARGES

To determine the time and charges of a long-distance call, ask the operator to provide you with this information when the call is completed.

COLLECT CALLS

The charges for station-to-station and person-to-person calls can be reversed, if the party called agrees to accept the charges. This is called a collect call. Tell the operator you are placing a collect call and give your name. The operator will leave the line when the person called agrees to accept the charges.

OVERSEAS CALLS   *— call beyond the contiguous*

Test question

With the use of communicating satellites, it is now possible to telephone remote places in the world. Calls within the 48 contiguous states and Canada

FIGURE 17–2. Area codes and time zones

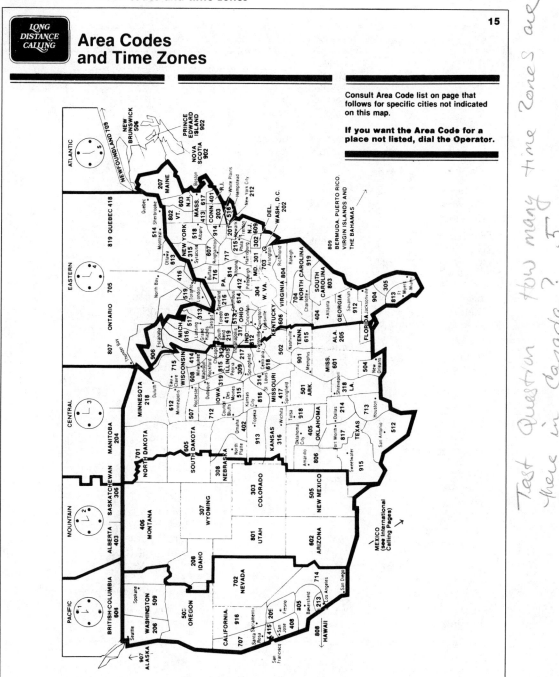

Test Question How many time zones are there in Canada? 5

Source: Telephone Directory 1981–1982, Hartford, Connecticut, Southern New England Telephone Company, 1981, p. 14.

TABLE 17-3. Codes for many countries and cities

Andorra	33*	*France*	33	*Norway*	47
all points	078†	Bordeaux	56	Bergen	5
Australia	61	Marseille	91	Oslo	2
Melbourne	3	Nice	93	*Philippines*	63
Sydney	2	Paris	1	Manila	2
Austria	43	*Germany, Federal*		*Portugal*	351
Innsbruck	5222	*Republic of (West)*	49	Lisbon	19
Vienna	222	Berlin	30	*Singapore, Republic of*	65
		Bonn	228	routing codes	
Belgium	32	Frankfurt	611	not required	
Antwerp	31	Munich	89	*South Africa,*	
Brussels	2	*Greece*	30	*Republic of*	27
Brazil	55	Athens	1	Cape Town	21
Brasilia	61	Rhodes	241	Pretoria	12
Rio de Janeiro	21	*Guatemala*	502	*Spain*	34
Sao Paulo	11	Guatemala City	2	Barcelona	3
Chile	56			Las Palmas	
Santiago	2	*Ireland, Republic of*	353	(Canary Is.)	28
Valparaiso	31	Dublin	1	Madrid	1
Costa Rica	506	Galway	91	Seville	54
routing codes		*Israel*	972	*Sweden*	46
not required		Haifa	4	Goteborg	31
		Jerusalem	2	Stockholm	8
Cyprus	357	Tel Aviv	3	*Switzerland*	41
Nicosia	21	*Italy*	39	Berne	31
Denmark	45	Florence	55	Geneva	22
Aalborg	8	Naples	81	Lucerne	41
Copenhagen	1 or 2	Rome	6	Zurich	1
		Venice	41	*Taiwan*	86
Ecuador	593	*Japan*	81	Tainan	62
Cuenca	4	Hiroshima	822	Taipei	2
Quito	2	Tokyo	3	*United Kingdom*	44
El Salvador	503	Yokohama	45	Belfast (N. Ire.)	232
routing codes		*Netherlands*	31	Cardiff (Wales)	222
not required		Amsterdam	20	Edinburgh (Scot.)	31
		Rotterdam	10	Glasgow (Scot.)	41
Fiji	679	The Hague	70	Liverpool (Eng.)	51
routing codes		*New Zealand*	64	London (Eng.)	1
not required		Auckland	9	*Vatican City*	39
Finland	358	Wellington	4	all points	6
Helsinki	0				

*Numbers beside countries are "Country Codes."
†Numbers beside cities are "Routing Codes."

Source: Telephone Directory 1981–1982, Hartford, Connecticut, Southern New England Telephone Company, 1981, p. 14.

are considered to be long distance calls. Calls to Alaska, Hawaii and foreign countries, other than Canada, are classified as overseas calls.

Most overseas calls can be dialed directly. This service is called international direct distance dialing (IDDD):

DIAL 0 (international access code)	plus 11	plus country code	plus	city or call code	plus number

For example, to call Munich, Germany, dial 011 + 49 + 89 + local number. If the call cannot be placed by IDDD, an operator will assist the caller. Because of differing time zones, the caller should check with the operator for the time at the destination point.

CONFERENCE CALLS

A conference call consists of three or more people tied in on the same line. At times, it is more convenient to make conference calls than to speak to people individually. The telephone company conference operator can arrange such calls (from a business or home phone). The number of people that can confer at a time is relative to the geographic location. For example, in Connecticut, thirty people can confer at once! The charge is at the person-to-person rate. There is a separate charge for each person on the line. If there were thirty conferees, the charge would be for thirty separate person-to-person calls. It is usually wise to notify the conferees in advance of the date and time of the proposed conference call.

ASKING FOR CREDIT

If you have difficulty completing the call (poor connection, cutoff, or wrong number), report this promptly to the operator and ask for credit, so that your company will not be charged for the call.

LOG LONG-DISTANCE CALLS

Keep a record of all long-distance calls made. Verification of long-distance calls may be required. Some offices provide printed forms for logging long-distance calls. Usually, the following are recorded:

- Date
- Time
- Caller

- Person called
- City and State
- Number
- Type of call (station-to-station, person-to-person, etc.):

Telephone systems and equipment

It is beyond the scope of this book to entirely detail this "new" telephone industry and its technology. However, the modern executive should be familiar with the following telephone systems and equipment:

- Automatic dialers
- Automatic call distributor — *music in background*
- Automatic recording services - *take on message for you*
- Multiple-line or push-button telephone - *handles 12-34 lines*
- Central exchange (Centrex) - *what we have at central*
- Push-button telephone system *(outside calls)* — *main switch board.*
- Computerized branch exchange (CBX) - *large offices 800 #s*
- Key telephones - *2-6 push button #s.*
- Private automatic branch exchange (PABX) - *switch boards system*
- Private branch exchange (PBX) - *special telephone service*
- Hand-free telephone — *canonce - operate without holding coupler*
- Tie lines -
- Touch-tone telephones - *replaces dial phone*
- Wide Area Telephone Service (WATS) - *company pays for all calls 1-800-*

AUTOMATIC DIALERS

Automatic devices, such as the Touch-A-Matic Dialer, can be used to speed up dialing. This equipment eliminates the need for manually dialing numbers that are called frequently and eliminates dialing errors.

The Touch-A-Matic Dialer allows the caller to press a button for automatic dialing. Names of the persons or businesses to be called appear next to the bottom.

AUTOMATIC CALL DISTRIBUTOR

This device is used to switch incoming calls to the next available operator. Calls are held when phones are busy. Background music is played during the hold period. Calls are released when phones become free.

AUTOMATIC RECORDING SERVICES

These devices use a tape to deliver a message and to record a response. This is especially valuable after regular business hours. The caller can record a message after hearing the initial announcement and waiting for a starting "beep."

MULTIPLE-LINE OR PUSH-BUTTON TELEPHONE

This device is similar in operation to a key telephone; however, it handles 12 to 29 lines. It can be connected to a switchboard, be used as an intercom system and for paging, or be used to play music in the background while a caller is on "hold."

CENTRAL EXCHANGE (CENTREX)

This system is popular in organizations with numerous telephone extensions, for it permits direct dialing by individuals, without going through a switchboard. Using Centrex, a caller can directly dial an office extension number within the organization without the aid of an operator. Also, calls outside the business organization, local and long distance, can be dialed without operator assistance.

Each telephone has a seven-digit number; for example, 728–7240. Using Centrex, an outside caller can reach a telephone station without the aid of a company operator by dialing the company prefix and the extension number: 728 + 7240.

If calling within an organization, simply dial the extension number, 7240, to reach your party. Many companies publish their own telephone directories that list various Centrex stations (Figure 17–3).

When 728–0000 is dialed, the company operator replies. If someone outside the organization wishes to speak to Joyce Larson, 728–7461 is dialed; if someone inside the organization wishes to speak to her, 7461 is dialed.

To dial a number outside the organization, follow the unique dialing instructions for that particular Centrex system.

```
            COMPANY OPERATOR 728-0000


    Department      Director/Administrator     Ext.

    Accounting          Jose Rivera            7288

    Administrative      Joyce Larson           7461
      Service

    Budgeting           Louise Kowalski        7271

    Cashier             Linda Dunn             7345
```

FIGURE 17–3. Part of an illustrative telephone directory

PUSH-BUTTON TELEPHONE SYSTEM

This permits outside calls, music on hold, intercompany calls, loudspeaker paging, conferencing and intercom. The Push-Button Telephone System is being replaced by multi-line, conferencing and intercom.

COMPUTERIZED BRANCH EXCHANGE (CBX)

This system is designed for large offices having up to 800 stations. CBX's microcomputer automatically selects circuits to use and holds call requests.

KEY TELEPHONES

These telephones, equipped with two to six pushbuttons, permit the making or taking of multiple calls simultaneously on the same telephone. Buttons are pressed to control calls. For example, you can press a hold button to keep a caller waiting while speaking to another person. A key telephone usually has six pushbuttons at its base. The hold pushbutton is at the left; keys 2 through 6 are used for receiving and making outside calls.

When an incoming call is received on a key telephone, one of the buttons flashes. To answer the call, simply depress the flashing button and speak into the receiver. The button will remain lighted as long as the line is in use. To place a call, depress an unlighted button and dial the number. An intercom button permits using the telephone as an intercom system.

PRIVATE AUTOMATIC BRANCH EXCHANGE (PABX)

These telephone exchanges are classified as:

1. *Cord switchboards.* An operator using plugs and jacks makes the connections for calls.
2. *Cordless switchboards.* These switchboards may be attended or unattended by an operator.

PRIVATE BRANCH EXCHANGE (PBX)

This private switchboard is used to provide telephone services. A company telephone switchboard operator assists with outgoing calls, incoming calls, and calls within the organization. The system may be a dial or nondial one.

Dial PBX. The user dials other extensions.

Nondial PBX. The switchboard operator makes all connections.

HAND-FREE TELEPHONE

This is a combination telephone, microphone, and loudspeaker. It is not necessary to pick up the receiver; simply press a button and speak aloud. Hand-

348

free telephones have sensitive, omnidirectional microphones with a wide range for voice pickup. The caller's voice comes over an adjustable loud-speaker. The hand-free telephone permits the busy executive to move about a room and handle papers while telephoning. The hand-free telephone is commonly used for telephone conferences.

TIE LINES

This service permits a company to have a direct, telephone line connection with its branches or other offices. The company avoids the delays that may occur when using regular long-distance lines. Tie lines are also used for the transmission of machine data.

TOUCH-TONE TELEPHONES

These telephones have buttons in place of a rotary dial. Ten buttons are used for placing calls; "#" and "*" are for special services. In addition to regular telephone service, the Touch-Tone telephone permits the tone transmission of data to computers. Touch-Tone telephones are replacing rotary-dial telephones in many offices because they are easier to use.

WIDE AREA TELEPHONE SERVICE (WATS)

Companies may subscribe to this special long distance service. Rather than being billed for individual calls, there is a monthly flat fee for service (either full-time or part-time). Inward WATS makes it possible to call a subscribing company (by using area code 800) toll free. For example: 1–800–telephone number.

Before placing a long-distance call, check with the nationwide directory assistance operator by dialing: 1–800–555–1212. Also, some companies list toll-free WATS (800) numbers in the telephone directory.

Other telephone services such as radio signaling service, the electronic blackboard, teleconferencing, videophone, facsimile, and mobile and marine telephones are discussed in other sections of this book.

Summary

The telephone is an instrument or system that reproduces and conveys sounds over distances. The telephone is very popular because of its convenience, ease of use, rapidity, and worldwide networks.

The following are suggested techniques for using the telephone:

1. Prepare for the call by drawing up notes of pertinent points.
2. Take notes during the telephone call.

3. List frequently dialed numbers.

4. Study the company's telephone directory.

5. Identify yourself when receiving or placing a call.

6. Answer promptly, by the second or third ring.

7. Speak clearly.

8. Be a good listener.

9. Be courteous.

10. Know the various long distance call services.

11. Understand billing to a third number.

12. Avail yourself of credit card services.

13. Familiarize yourself with time zones.

14. Ask the operator to provide you with information about the time and charges of a long-distance call, when this information is needed.

15. Place collect calls, if the party called agrees to accept the charges.

16. Overseas calls can be made world-wide. Most overseas calls can be dialed directly.

17. Make conference calls when you wish to speak to two or more people simultaneously.

18. Ask for credit for poor connections or wrong numbers.

19. Keep a record of all long-distance calls made. Verification of long-distance calls may be required.

The modern executive should be familiar with telephone systems and equipment, such as automatic dialers, automatic call distributor, automatic recording services, multiple-line or pushbutton telephone, central exchange, pushbutton telephone system, computerized branch exchange, key telephones, private automatic branch exchange, privatge branch exchange, hand-free telephone, tie lines, touch-tone telephones, and wide area telephone services.

Discussion

1. What are the apparent advantages and disadvantages of telephone communications?

Study questions

1. Why is the telephone such a very popular form of oral communication?

1) Convenient
2) Easy to use
3) fast
4) World wide network of connections

2. Who invented the telephone? When did he file a patent? *Alexander Graham Bell 1876*

3. When did the Federal Communications Commission permit competition in the telephone industry? *1968*

4. Under the FCC regulations, can you now supply your own telephone or other terminal equipment? *Yes*

5. How can you prepare for a call? *Take notes draw notes before you call, list numbers*

6. What are some of the general instructions the company's telephone directory include? *long distance calls, collect calls, Transfer calls, third party calls, conference calls*

7. When telephoning someone inside the organization, how do you introduce yourself? *Good Afternoon, this is ____ of the ___ Dpt.*

8. By what ring should you answer the telephone? *2 or third*

9. How many time zones are there in the United States? Canada? *4 in US. 5 in canada*

10. Is there a charge for obtaining a telephone credit card? *No*

11. Under what circumstances can you ask the operator not to be charged after completing a long distance call? *When party is not there*

12. What are the two basic types of long distance call services available? *Station - to - station, Operator assist.*

13. What is a collect call? *When the other party agrees to pay for charges*

14. How are charges determined for a conference call? *charge for each person on line*

15. List a device used for automatic dialing. *Touch-a-matic-dialer*

16. What is the major advantage of Centrex? *do not have to go through switchboard.*

17. How many buttons does a key telephone have? *two - to six push buttons*

18. What is a combination telephone, microphone, and loudspeaker?

19. In addition to regular telephone service, what does the Touch-Tone telephone permit? *permits tone transmission to computers.*

20. What is the telephone number of the nationwide directory assistance operator? *1-800-555-1212*

Activities

1. Assume that you are preparing to make a telephone call to a store to inquire about a new print/display calculator for your office desk. Draw up an enumerated list of questions you will ask.

2. Assume that you are in New York City and it is 4:00 p.m. What time is it in the following cities: (Refer to the map in this chapter showing time zones.)

   Miami, Florida
   Dallas, Texas
   Denver, Colorado

New Orleans, Louisiana
San Diego, California
Cincinnati, Ohio
Las Vegas, Nevada
Cheyenne, Wyoming

Assume it is 10:00 a.m. in Los Angeles, California. Would you be wise to place a station-to-station call to Duluth, Minnesota?

Assume it is 3:00 p.m. in Seattle, Washington. Would it be wise to place a station-to-station call to Boston, Massachusetts?

ACHIEVEMENT OF LEARNING GOALS

Check the appropriate boxes to determine whether you have or have not achieved the learning goals of this chapter.

I Can:

	YES	NO
1. Demonstrate mastery of correct telephone technique.	☐	☐
2. Recognize and use effective telephone services.	☐	☐
3. Identify modern telephone systems and equipment.	☐	☐

If any of your responses were "no," it is suggested that you review pertinent chapter parts.

18

Interviews

very critical!

LEARNING GOALS

1. Recognize the many types of interviews conducted in the business world.
2. Prepare for an interview, both as an interviewer and as an interviewee.
3. Master interviewing techniques.
4. Know what activities are undertaken during the post-interview period by the interviewer and interviewee.
5. Identify the legality of certain questions asked during employment interviews.
6. Understand how an interviewee creates a favorable impression during an employment interview.

In the business world, an interview is a structured, formal face-to-face meeting at which purposeful information is exchanged and, on many occasions, evaluations are made. Although people generally think of an interview as a meeting of two people, it may consist of several people or a group of people. For example, a group of people may interview an applicant for a position.

Many types of interviews are conducted in the business world:

- Appraisal or evaluation interview
- Counseling interview
- Disciplinary or reprimand
- Employment or hiring interview
- Exploratory or discussion
- Goal-setting
- Grievance or complaint
- Improvement
- Information or instructional interview
- Investigative

- Job analysis
- News
- Orientation interview
- Problem solving
- Progress
- Promotion
- Retirement
- Sales
- Termination, separation, or exit interview
- Training interview
- Transfer

 The three steps in the interviewing process are:

1. Preparing for the interview
2. The interview proper   *Know this*
3. The post-interview period

Preparing for the interview

 NEED FOR STRUCTURE

If an interview is to be effective, attention must be given to planning. The interview should be structured. The effective interviewer gives attention to the following:

Determining the Purpose. The purpose of the interview should be clearly stated, so that the conversation is not rambling. A list of objectives should be developed.

Establishing Criteria. If criteria are needed, they should be established; for example, in employment interviews the educational level and number of years of experience preferred should be determined.

Researching. The interviewer should gather and study information pertinent to the interview. For a job interview, background information about the job, such as the duties, salary, and so on must be known by the interviewer. The credentials of the individual being interviewed for a position, the resume, letters of recommendation (usually three or four), and application form, should be carefully reviewed and verified for accuracy. In some instances, consultations with others may be helpful.

Drawing up a List of Questions. The interviewer should draw up a list of questions to be asked. The questions should help the interviewer achieve the objectives of the interview. A list of questions is especially important when interviewing many candidates for a position. If each candidate is asked the same questions, there is a basis for comparative analyses of responses. The list of questions can be on a form with space provided for jotting down responses.

Scheduling the Interview. Adequate time should be allocated for an interview, enough time to ask pertinent questions and allow for input by the interviewee. An open-end interview can be held; however, most interviews are scheduled for a half hour.

Inviting Participants to the Interview. Individuals who can make a contribution to the interview should be invited to participate. For example, during an appraisal interview, supervisory personnel can be invited.

Planning the Physical Arrangements. The interviewer must select appropriate surroundings for the interview. Usually, a comfortable, quiet, private place is preferred. Interruptions should be kept at a minimum during an interview. Tell your administrative secretary to hold calls that are not important.

An executive in an East Coast company prefers to observe the table manners of an applicant for executive positions. Therefore, part of the interview is conducted while eating lunch. Many nonverbal messages can be communicated while eating (manners, personality, and so on).

Recording the Interview. Provisions can be made to have an interview taped (video and/or audio) or recorded by a secretary in shorthand. This should be done only with the permission of the interviewee.

The interview proper

At the start of the interview, it is important to establish good rapport between the interviewer and the interviewee. There is usually some tension during an interview; therefore, an experienced interviewer will try to break the ice at the very inception of the interview by being cordial. Usually, this is accomplished by exchanging social pleasantries.

At the start of an interview, an executive may rise from behind his or her desk, walk to the candidate with hand out-stretched, shakes hands, and extend a cordial greeting. Next, the executive and the candidate may sit on a comfortable couch and begin the dialogue. If the executive were to remain seated behind the desk and the candidate had to walk alone across the room, a frosty atmosphere would prevail. The candidate would be cast in an inferior position. The executive should immediately create a friendly, cordial atmosphere.

State the Purpose Immediately. The interviewer should state the purpose and subject of the interview immediately. The first question should be innocuous,

to set the interviewee at ease. A typical dialogue during a promotion interview
follows:

> Good afternoon Mrs. Carpenter. I am pleased to learn that you are
> interested in a new position. This is a screening interview conducted
> with candidates for the position of word processing supervisor. Would
> you like a cup of coffee before we begin?

— specific response *→ ramble on about details*

Test
question

1) Direct
2) Open

Use Direct and Open Questions. The communication during an interview
consists of a series of questions and answers, a probing dialogue with
immediate feedback. Questions fall into two broad categories: direct and
open. Direct questions require a specific response. For example, "What
college degree or degrees do you hold?" Open questions, on the other hand,
require a broad response: "What are your goals in life?" Open questions are
generally used to gain insights into the personality of the interviewee. Both
direct and open questions can be asked to determine the knowledge of the
interviewee.

It is important that the interviewer, who is in a superior position by
controlling the dialogue, not dominate the conversation. Usually, more than
half the talking should be done by the interviewee who should be encouraged
to participate, to ask questions, state opinions, and so on. It is essential that
there be interaction between the interviewer and interviewee, a structured
dialogue.

The art of listening

The effective interviewer is an experienced listener, and observer. Both verbal and nonverbal insights are obtained. The effective interviewer is objective, rational, and evaluative.

During a lengthy interview, it is a good practice to jot down notes. The list of questions, Figure 18–1, that were prepared prior to the interview can be listed on a rating sheet and responses checked.

rating sheet

```
RATING SHEET                        APPLICANT: _____
INTERVIEW DATE: _____     POSITION:  _____
INTERVIEWER: _____
WHAT SALARY WOULD YOU CONSIDER FOR THIS
POSITION?
              $15,000 ___
               16,000 ___
               17,000 ___
               18,000 ___
               19,000 ___
               20,000 ___

              OTHER _____

WOULD YOU BE WILLING TO TRAVEL?
              YES ___
              NO  ___
              COMMENTS  _____
                        _____

WHY DID YOU APPLY FOR A POSITION AT THE
PEARSON COMPANY?

     ___ REPUTATION OF COMPANY
     ___ OPPORTUNITIES TO "GROW"
     ___ LOCATION OF COMPANY
     ___ OTHER _____
```

FIGURE 18–1. Interview rating sheet

There is a hazard in conducting an interview that is too structured. The interviewee should have the opportunity to elaborate on questions and reveal the dimensions of his or her personality.

Terminate the Interview Tactfully. An interview can be terminated tactfully by a secretary who reminds the executive of another appointment, or the interviewer can end an interview by rising and graciously thanking the person for attending the interview.

usualy interview lasts 30 min.

The applicant should be apprised of the next step in the evaluative process: testing, additional interviews, and so on. The interviewee should be informed how and when notification of the employment decision will be made.

The post-interview period — hours of reading

During the post-interview period, judgments are made about the relative merits of applicants. Analyses of notes, credentials, forms, and resumes are conducted. References are contacted if the candidate is being given final consideration. It is imperative that the prejudices and biases of the interviewer do not enter into the decision-making process. An emotional decision may well be an erroneous one.

To simplify matters during the selection process, it is usually easier to first eliminate unsuitable candidates. Next, a list—perhaps consisting of ten of the most viable candidates meeting the criteria for employment—is drawn up.

Employment interviews

It is a common practice in the business world to interview candidates for a position. It would be very unusual, indeed, for a company to employ a candidate for a position without first conducting an interview. When a business employs a person, a large expenditure of money is involved over the long run. Let us assume a junior executive is to receive a salary of twenty thousand dollars a year. In twenty-five years, not considering raises, the individual will have been paid a half million dollars! It is vital that the individual being interviewed be appraised objectively and accurately.

LEGALITY

The interviewer should review the legality of asking certain questions during an employment interview. There are certain pre-employment interview questions that are prohibited by federal law. The applicant can take legal action if asked questions concerning:

1. National origin
2. Race or color
3. Age
4. Religion or creed
5. Handicap or health conditions not job related
6. Credit rating
7. Type of military discharge
8. Organizational membership that reveals religion, race, ancestry, or color
9. Personal habits in private life
10. Arrests

11. Marital status (married, divorced, single, or engaged)
12. Parental status (age and number of children and pregnancy)
13. Personal character
14. Credit rating (charge accounts, and so on)

Questions may be asked in the following areas:

1. Academic, professional, and vocational education
2. Experiences in military service as it relates to job
3. Names and addresses of references
4. Organizational memberships associated with a job (professional, civic, and scientific groups)
5. Convicted of a crime (and disposition of case)
6. Handicap or health problems which may affect work performance or job placement
7. Names of relatives employed by the company

Your role as an interviewee

BEFORE THE INTERVIEW

We have considered the role of the interviewer; however, as a college student, you should be informed of the role you play in an interview. The following are suggestions for a campus recruitment or regular office interview:

Review Your Qualifications. It is wise to keep a record of your accomplishments. Include anything you do that is significant, such as club membership, civic participation, travel, and so on. A seemingly inconsequential fact may secure a position for you. During an interview, an interviewee mentioned that he delivered newspapers as a boy. The interviewer, a former newspaper boy, was very impressed by this fact and employed the young man!

Pre-Interview Planning. Do your "homework" by "boning up" for the interview. For example, determine what the salary being paid in the business world is for the position. Research the company you are applying for employment with. Your college placement and career planning office will assist you in this task. Go to the reference section of the library and look up the financial status and history of the company. Reference works such as the Dun & Bradstreet *Reference Book, Moody's Manuals,* and Standard & Poor's *Corporation Records* should provide you with valuable information. The company's annual report is another excellent source of information. A standard leadoff question during an interview is "Why do you want to work for our company?" The more "ammunition" you can gather, the better.

[handwritten margin notes: "Know exactly what your qualifications are"; "Do your homework"]

If you know someone who works for the company, ask questions. It may be helpful to stand in front of the company and watch the attire of employees. One major company prefers that its male employees wear white shirts. This can be noted while observing the attire of employees. If you went to that interview wearing a white shirt, you would make a favorable impression. Your college career and placement office may be able to provide you with additional information about the company.

Draw up two lists of questions:

Test question

1. Questions you anticipate will be asked, and
2. Questions you want to ask.

Try to formulate appropriate answers to the questions that you anticipate will be asked. Be sure that you have "touched all bases" during the interview. Don't accept a position without knowing the salary!

Some of the questions you may be asked are:

List of Anticipated Questions

1. Why do you want to work for our company?
2. What are your future career plans?
3. What is your educational background?
4. Have you had any work experience?
5. Have you ever assumed a position of leadership?
6. What are your interests? Hobbies?
7. Do you plan to go on for advanced graduate degrees?
8. What salary range do you have in mind?
9. Have you participated in extracurricular activities in college? Sports?
10. What is your major strength? Deficiency?
11. Do you have any special talents or abilities?
12. What magazines do you read on a regular basis?
13. Have you traveled? If so, where?

Some of the Questions You May Want to Ask

1. What are the opportunities for advancement in the near future?
2. What special or extra-hour duties does the position entail? Travel? Entertaining?
3. What is the salary range? Are there bonuses?

4. What are the working hours? Paid vacations?

5. What are the benefits? Insurance? Retirement? Medical? Dental?

Pay particular attention to your appearance. Dress tastefully and conservatively. You should be clean, neat, and well-groomed.

DURING THE INTERVIEW

As an interviewee, you walk a rather thin line. You must "sell" yourself; however, you will make a bad impression if you oversell yourself. If you are very modest and undersell yourself, you won't get the position.

Give Specific Answers. During the interview, be courteous, sincere, and forthright. Answer all questions truthfully. Be yourself. Be careful about rambling on. Answer questions completely, concisely, and accurately. Avoid giving simple "yes" and "no" responses. Provide pertinent details. For example, instead of saying, "I am a college graduate," say, "I hold my Bachelor of Science degree in Business Administration from the University of North Dakota."

If you do not know the answer to a question, tell the interviewer. Honesty is the best policy. The interviewer may purposely insert a question that cannot be answered to test your veracity. For example, "Have you heard about the research Howard Tinstil (no such person) conducted in the field of accounting?"

Nonverbal Responses. Try to avoid communicating a negative impression nonverbally. Your body language will be observed by an expert interviewer. Don't slump in your chair, tap your feet, play with your eyeglasses, or stare off into space. Maintain eye contact. Try to appear poised, confident. At the close of the interview, graciously thank the interviewer for conducting the interview.

POST-INTERVIEW PERIOD

Generally, if you have applied for a minor position, it is not necessary to write a follow-up, thank-you letter. However, if a great deal of time was spent during the interview or if you applied for a major position, a telephone call or a thank-you letter would be appropriate. If any special courtesy was extended during the interview period—as taking you to lunch—be sure to express your appreciation in the follow-up letter.

Follow-Up Letter. Also, a follow-up letter can be written to provide additional information requested during an interview. Or, you may wish to expand on an idea or question proposed.

```
May 1, 19XX

Dear Ms. DiMarci:

Thank you very much for interviewing me for
the position of accountant on April 15.  The
interview was a very pleasant experience.  It
was very considerate of you to spend so much
time reviewing my personal and professional
qualifications.

I am definitely interested in securing a
position with your fine company and would
appreciate your serious consideration of my
candidacy.

Since my interview, I have been awarded the
National Society of Accounting Award for a
college project completed this semester!

I shall be pleased to provide you with any
additional information you may need about
my qualifications.

Sincerely yours,

Rebecca O. Rich

Rebecca O. Rich
```

Sometimes they may not like this

FIGURE 18–2. An interview follow-up letter

Two additional letters can be written:

1. A letter accepting the position (see Figure 18–3).
2. A letter refusing the position (see Figure 18–4).

```
                                    April 30, 19--




        Dear Ms. DiMarci:

        I am delighted, indeed, to accept the
        position as accountant with Wilson &
        Baxter, starting on May 10 and look
        forward to my professional association
        with you and other members of the
        firm.

        Sincerely,

        Rebecca O. Rich
        Rebecca O. Rich
```

FIGURE 18-3. Letter of acceptance

```
                                           April 30, 19--




        Dear Ms. DiMarci:

        Thank you very much for offering to me
        the position of accountant with Wilson
        & Baxter.

        I must, of necessity, decline the position
        since it entails a great deal of travel.

        I am flattered that you have offered this
        position to me and appreciate the many
        courtesies you have extended to me.

        Sincerely,

        Rebecca O. Rich
        Rebecca O. Rich
```

FIGURE 18-4. Letter of refusal

should match companies

Good Grooming. Your appearance should be appropriate for the position. You should be neat, clean, and well groomed. During a recent lecture, a director of personnel for a major company was told by a male with hair down to his shoulders: "I have the right to wear my hair any way I wish." The director of personnel said, "Yes, you have the right; however, we will not employ you!"

Be Punctual. Be sure that you are on time for an interview. Personnel directors consider being late the most offensive thing an applicant can do, since this throws off the interview schedule for the entire day. Plan to arrive at least fifteen minutes before the interview. Don't be too early. This can also create an unfavorable impression.

Summary

An interview is a structured, formal face-to-face meeting at which purposeful information is exchanged and, on many occasions, evaluations are made. Many types of interviews are conducted in a business world: appraisal, counseling, disciplinary, employment, goal-setting, grievance, improvement, information, investigative, job analysis, news, orientation, problem solving, progress, promotion, retirement, sales, termination, training, and transfer.

There are three distinct steps in the interviewing process:

1. Preparing for the interview
2. The interview proper
3. The post-interview period

Preparing for the interview requires that attention be given to the following:

- Determining the purpose
- Establishing criteria
- Researching
- Drawing up a list of questions
- Scheduling the interview
- Inviting participants to the interview
- Planning the physical arrangements
- Recording the interview

The interview proper requires certain actions by the interviewer. First, the interviewer breaks the ice by exchanging social pleasantries. Next, the interviewer states the purpose and subject of the interview. The first question asked should be innocuous, to set the interviewee at ease. Both direct and open questions are asked. Direct questions require a specific response; open questions are generally used to gain insights into the personality of the interviewee. The effective interviewer is an experienced listener and observer.

The post-interview period is the time for making judgments about the relative merits of applicants. Analyses of notes, credentials, forms, and resumes are conducted. Unsuitable candidates are usually eliminated first; next, a list of viable candidates is drawn up.

Special expertise is required in conducting employment interviews, since there are certain pre-employment interview questions that are prohibited by federal law.

The interviewee should review personal and professional qualifications and conduct pre-interview planning. During the interview, the interviewee should be courteous, sincere, and forthright. Pertinent details should be provided. There are certain actions that the interviewee can undertake during the post-interview period, such as writing follow-up letters if special courtesies were extended. The appearance of the interviewee should be appropriate for the position. Also, the interviewee should be on time; tardiness is offensive to most interviewers.

Discussion

1. You are interested in working for a company. How would you research the background of the company to prepare for an employment interview?

Study questions

1. What is an interview?
2. What types of interviews are conducted in the business world?
3. List the three steps in the interviewing process.
4. List the questions that cannot be asked by an interviewer when interviewing a candidate for a position.

Activities

1. Assume that you are going to interview a person who has just graduated from college and holds a Bachelor of Science degree in

Business Administration. The person is applying for the position of junior executive.
- How would you prepare for the interview?
- What questions (list twenty) would you ask during the interview?
- What would your post-interview activities be?
2. Assume you are being interviewed for a junior executive position.
- How would you prepare for the interview?
- What questions (list ten) would you want to ask during the interview?
- What would your post-interview activities be?

ACHIEVEMENT OF LEARNING GOALS

Check the appropriate boxes to determine whether you have or have not achieved the learning goals of this chapter.

I Can:

	YES	NO
1. Recognize the many types of interviews conducted in the business world.	☐	☐
2. Prepare adequately for an interview, both as an interviewer and as an interviewee.	☐	☐
3. Explain effective interviewing techniques.	☐	☐
4. Describe the activities undertaken during the post-interview period by the interviewer and interviewee.	☐	☐
5. Identify the legality of certain questions asked during employment interviews.	☐	☐
6. Create a favorable impression as an interviewee during an employment interview.	☐	☐

If any of your responses were "no," it is suggested that you review pertinent chapter parts.

IV

ELECTRONIC/
TECHNOLOGICAL
COMMUNICATIONS

19

The Automated Office

LEARNING GOALS

1. Explain automation in the business office.
2. Describe the paperless office.
3. Identify the sophisticated electronic devices that have modernized communication systems in the business office.
4. Comprehend the new terms that are used in the new technology.
5. Understand the integration of office technologies.
6. List the subsystems of the automated office.
7. Recognize modern office communication systems.

mechanization – machinery, thats human operated.
automation – machinery that self efficent

Test question

The term *automation* defines a system in which processes or operations are automatically performed by electronic devices, sophisticated machinery, etc. Albert Kushner states that "automation refers to a substitution of machine labor for human labor. Either manual or intelligent labor may be automated, and the range of potential applications covers a wide field of activities in the factory and in the office."[1]

Simply stated, the purpose of office automation is to increase the productivity of clerical workers and managers by providing them with automated tools and efficient systems and procedures to alleviate the paperwork glut, sometimes called the *paper explosion.* Presently, attention is being paid to the automation of tasks performed by managers; previously, attention was focused mainly on increasing the productivity of clerical workers.

In a fascinating article about automation, "Fighting the Paper Chase," Christopher Byron states:

[1]H. B. Maynard, Editor-in-Chief, *Handbook of Business Administration* (New York: McGraw-Hill Book Co., 1970, p. 15–14.

372

Though office automation is already making large strides among clerical and lower-level administrative workers, the real gains seem destined to come from getting professional and management personnel to use the new equipment. And this is likely to take place before too long.[2]

A computer terminal or microfilm reader on an executive's desk may become as ordinary as a telephone or dictation machine is today.

Automation has had a major impact on manufacturing for decades. New automated tools are being introduced in factories in a major effort to increase productivity and reduce costs. For example, a *robot revolution* is presently taking place in industry. There are an estimated 10,000 robots in use in Japan. Some of these robots work ten times faster than humans.[3]

The business office is currently undergoing a dramatic change, an abrupt transition from antiquated procedures that have not evolved fundamentally for over a century to sophisticated, integrated systems incorporating electronic technology.

Advanced computerized devices and new administrative support systems have been designed to facilitate rapid communication, streamline text production, increase information access, reduce costs, and accelerate white-collar productivity. "Paper and pencil is being replaced by CRT and keyboard.[4]

Office automation involves the implementation of interacting systems. New assignments of tasks performed by machines and people is taking place. The automated electronic office is expected to replace the traditional office. To cite a specific example, in many offices the old "typing center" is being replaced by the word processing center or decentralized word processing units. Some of these word processing centers have telecommunication capabilities and are tied in with worldwide networks. Also, they may provide input for computers.

Advanced microcomputer technology has made this dramatic change feasible by reducing costs considerably. The first electronic digital computer was developed in 1946 at the University of Pennsylvania. This cumbersome machine weighed tons and consisted of 18,000 vacuum tubes.[5] It cost a half million dollars. Present-day microcomputers consist of silicon circuit wafers

[2]Christopher Byron, "Fighting the Paper Chase," *Time*, 118, no. 21 (November 23, 1981), 67.

[3]"The Robot Revolution." *Time*, 116, no. 23 (December 8, 1980), 72–83.

[4]Denise R. Guillet, "Augmenting Administrative Support," *Administrative Management*, XLI, no. 11 (November 1980), 38.

[5]G. B. Beitzel, "Computer," *Collier's Encyclopedia*, Volume 7 (New York: Crowell-Collier Educational Corporation, 1969), p. 122.

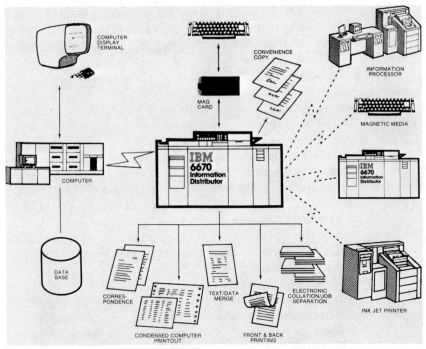

The IBM 6670 Information Distributor can play a central role in the communications of a business organization. (Courtesy IBM)

smaller than a fingernail, a quarter-inch-square, and each has more than twenty times the computational power of the 1946 monster. Perhaps more startling, each chip costs less than ten dollars!

Silicon chip technology has led to such dramatic developments as editing typewriters that can detect and correct spelling errors and dictation machines that can convert sounds (spoken words) into typewritten copy.

Whether hidden as a microprocessor deep in the workings of a word processor, or disguised as mainframes that run word and text processing software, computers are storming the office.

Mostly they don't look like computers—these intelligent typewriters, word processors, high function copiers, micrographics units—but they are its progeny, children of the semiconductor age.[6]

Paperless Office. In the past, information has been transferred and stored mainly on paper. As new electronic procedures and systems become more

[6]"Trends in Computing," *Fortune*, 101, no. 10 (May 19, 1980), 62.

entrenched in the automated office, the so-called *paperless office* becomes a near reality. A paperless office is one in which paper has been replaced by electronic digital and micrographic systems. Professor Perkins at Washington State University has stated:

> The office is now in a period of transition where more and more information processing functions are being automated through sophisticated electronic systems. The 'paperless' automated office is attainable today. Citibank of New York has designed a prototype office environment that replaces paper with an integrated electronic system, and Micronet, Inc., of Washington, D. C., is also experimenting with the paperless office concept.[7]

It should be noted that although paperwork can be decreased by 95 percent in the traditional office, some individuals believe that a completely paperless office will not be realized in the near future. William Benedon lists six major barriers to a totally paperless society: "traditional values, legal values, accounting and audit values, legislative values, societal values and procedural values.[8]

It must be added also that some of the electronic equipment in operation is designed to generate the creation of paper documents, such as intelligent copiers and text-editing typewriters. "But systems analysts, records managers and other information management professionals increasingly emphasize the high cost of creating, storing, retrieving, reproducing and disseminating paper documents.[9]

The automated office of Micronet, Inc. in Washington, D.C. is interesting to examine, for it is a model paperless office. The equipment, procedures, and systems instituted at Micronet, Inc. have improved management, communication, and the handling of data. Advanced electronic technology is used to eliminate unproductive paperwork. "The office converts all incoming and original data to either electronic form or microform, which can then be edited, indexed, stored, retrieved, or converted to paper."[10] At Micronet, the paperless office "integrates voice input, word processing, optical character recognition, electronic mail, calendars, message sending, filing directories and text editing, computer indexing and processing, COM, micrographics,

[7]Edward A. Perkins, Jr., "Executive Typing In the Age of the Automated Office," *Business Education World*, 60, no. 4 (March–April 1980), 30.

[8]William Benedon, "The Paperless Society: Fact or Fiction," *IRM*, 13, no. 4 (April 1979), 101.

[9]William Saffady, "The Automated Office: An Introduction to the Technology," *Journal of Micrographics*, 13, no. 8 (November–December 1980), 21.

[10]Rodd Exelbert and Bob Sample, "Micronet: *World's First Paperless Office Opens*," *IRM*, 13, no. 6 (June 1979), 55.

automated storage and retrieval, telecommunications and color graphics systems into a fully-automated office facility.[11]

Presently, most firms have scattered systems working independently throughout their offices, such as word processing, facsimile, TWX, telex, etc. "They have separate budgets, in many large companies, and even separate managers.[12]" The integration of office technologies will result in increased production and cost reductions. Data processing and word processing activities will merge in many offices.[13]

Slutzky contends that the integrated office will evolve into the "communicating integrated office." Office systems will communicate with each other by the use of satellites. The partnership of IBM, Comsat, and Aetna Insurance (Satellite Business Systems Inc.) provides us with a glimpse of the future. This company provides satellite communications, video teleconferences, electronic mail, and computer-to-computer hookups for intracompany use.[14]

New terms

The new technology has spawned many new terms that should be part of the modern manager's vocabulary.

Cathode Ray Tube (CRT). A vacuum tube with a fluorescent screen used for the visual display of data, information, letters, documents, graphics, and so on. A new 19-inch diagonal text-editing typewriter CRT screen displays up to 6,000 characters (two pages at a time). (*Note.* A CRT may also be used for entering data into a computer's memory.)

Communicating Typewriter. An editing typewriter with high-speed electronic communications capabilities that can send or receive messages over telephone lines. Communicating typewriters are linked to other communicating typewriters or suitably programmed computers. Computer information can be played out on a communicating typewriter. Communicating typewriter networks are used for the transmission of electronic mail.

Composer. A sophisticated typewriter that produces a variety of type styles and sizes that looks like professional print (camera-ready galleys).

Electronic Blackboard. Information written in chalk on an electronic blackboard appears automatically on a distant terminal TV monitor.

---

[11]"The Paperless Office—A Total Commitment," *IRM*, 14, no. 4 (April 1980), 24.

[12]"Office Productivity—Challenge of the 80s," *Business Week*, no. 2677 (March 2, 1981), 70.

[13]David D. Beebe, "Crossroads: The Merger of Word and Data Processing in Business Education," *Journal of Business Education*, 56, no. 7 (April 1981), 275.

[14]Joel Slutzky, "The Office of the Future & Beyond, *IRM*, 13, no. 4 (April 1979), 64.

Electronic Mail. Communications systems involving the electronic transmission of information or messages. Communication services such as facsimile (fax), communicating word processors (CWPs), computer-based message systems (CBMs), mailgrams, electronic computer originated mail (ECOM), Telex, and TWX are examples of electronic mail.

Facsimile. The exact transmission of graphics (pictures, text, diagrams, documents, maps, graphs, sketches, etc.) over regular telephone lines by the use of graphic transceivers. Facsimile is a form of electronic mail.

Microcomputer. A computer incorporating silicon circuit wafers. *circuit wafers*

Micrographics. The photographic process by which letters, documents, graphics, and so on, are reduced in size and recorded on film. Magnifying devices are required for reading film images.

Phototypesetter. A phototypesetter converts typewritten text from an editing typewriter to a typeset format. This permits high quality, in-house typesetting capabilities without chemical processing. *Printing done at home if you want.*

Printer. A machine that prints information from an editing typewriter or computer. New laser-based printers can print forty-three pages a minute. Also, by the use of communications lines, fifty pages can be sent cross country in a few minutes. This provides a high-speed manner of sending electronic mail. *43 pages a minute*

Reprographics. The reproduction of letters, documents, and graphics by photocopying or duplicating (stencil, spirit, offset) processes.

Telecommunication. Distant communication by telegraph, radio, television, cable, telephone, and facsimile.

Teleconference. Audio conference among company employees by telephone, conference calls. Also used in the business world interchangeably with the word "videoconference," entailing visual conferences by television, incorporating satellite hookups and large, wall-sized projection screens.

Text-Editing Typewriter. Highly sophisticated typewriter that has revision and storage capabilities. Earlier models employed magnetic tapes and magnetic cards; more advanced models have display (cathod ray tube) devices that reveal text in page format. Text-editing typewriters are also called *word processing typewriters* or *word processors*. These editing typewriters usually have automatic features and magnetic memory. *screen keyboard input*

Voice Recognition. The input of data by the human voice into a computer terminal.

Word Processing. A process or system for the expeditious production of typewritten materials, generally incorporating the use of sophisticated dictating machines and text-editing typewriters.

Subsystems of the automated office

Don Avedon lists the following subsystems that are interfaced and integrated in the automated office:

1. Voice systems
2. Word processing
3. Optical character recognition (OCR)
4. Data processing
5. Reprographics
6. Micrographics
7. Communications and facsimile
8. Graphic systems
9. Teleconferencing
10. Electronic mail
11. Photocomposition[15]

Some of these new tools of automation are too complex to be treated in depth in this chapter; therefore, other chapters of this text contain more detailed information about equipment, processes, and systems which are associated with these subsystems.

Modern office communication systems

A NEW ERA

The dazzling new technology, coupled with innovative systems and procedures, has created a new era of communication. Communications will be created instantaneously—from memory disks or by speaking to voice recognition computers—and travel over long geographic distances—assisted by satellites—in microseconds. The mailman walking through the rain and snow may well become an "extinct species" of the twentieth century!

As traditional work procedures and role change, new skills will be required. Personnel will have to be retained to fill newly created positions. A single multi-office system will be able to support satellite work stations, remote printers, and data storage units. The managing of communications in the automated office will require a specialist in managerial communications.

Office automation, the marriage of computer technology and office

[15]Don M. Avedon, "The Automated Office," *IRM*, 14, no. 7 (July, 1980), 10.

systems, has created a new structuring of the communications process. Previously, the communication function was performed by an office manager. Now, it also involves data processing and communications people, an equilateral triangle of involved participation. (See Figure 19–1.)

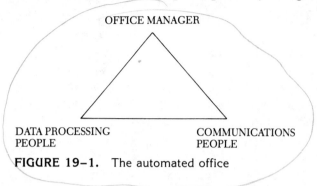

OFFICE MANAGER

DATA PROCESSING
PEOPLE

COMMUNICATIONS
PEOPLE

FIGURE 19–1.   The automated office

Summary

The term *automation* pertains to a system in which processes or operations are automatically performed by electronic devices, sophisticated machinery, etc. We are in a dramatic period of transition in office communication. Antiquated procedures are being replaced by sophisticated electronic systems. Advanced computerized devices have been designed to facilitate rapid communication, streamline text production, increase information access, reduce costs, and accelerate office productivity.

The so-called *paperless office* has become a near reality. The integration of office technologies will result in increased production. Eventually, the integrated office will evolve into the communication integrated office.

New terms associated with the automated office should be understood by the modern business manager. Also, the eleven subsystems that are interfaced and integrated in the automated office should be understood.

The new technology in communications has created new systems and procedures. Communications will be created instantaneously and travel long distances in microseconds. New skills will be required of personnel, and a restructuring of the communications process will take place.

Discussion

1. Explain what is meant by office automation.
2. Will the completely paperless office be realized in the near future?

Study questions

1. What is the simple purpose of automation?
2. What is replacing the old "typing center" in the modern office?
3. What new technology has made the automated office possible?
4. Does the paperless office exist? If so, where?
5. What do the letters CRT represent?
6. What do you call an editing typewriter with high-speed electronic communications capabilities?
7. Highly sophisticated typewriters that have revision and storage capabilities are called by what name?
8. The exact transmission of graphics over regular telephone lines by the use of graphic transceivers is called?
9. Communications systems which entail the transmission of information or messages in electronic form are called?
10. What is another term used for "micrographics"?
11. What is the blackboard called that is used to transmit images to a distant terminal TV monitor?
12. What is the term used for the reproduction of letters, documents and graphics by photocopying or duplicating?
13. What is the process or system for the expeditious production of type-written materials generally incorporating the use of sophisticated dictating machines and text-editing typewriters called?
14. What machine converts typewritten text from an editing typewriter to a typeset format?
15. What is distant communication by telegraph, radio, television, cable, telephone, and facsimile called?
16. Office automation has created a new structuring of the communications process—an equilateral triangle of involved participation. List the people involved.

Activity

Assume that you are going to automate communications in your business office. Explain what new equipment you would order.

ACHIEVEMENT OF LEARNING GOALS

Check the appropriate boxes to determine whether you have or have not achieved the learning goals of this chapter.

I Can:

	YES	NO
1. Explain automation in the business office.	☐	☐
2. Describe the "paperless" office.	☐	☐
3. Identify the sophisticated electronic devices that have modernized communication systems in the business office.	☐	☐
4. Comprehend the new terms that are used in the new technology.	☐	☐
5. Understand the integration of office technologies.	☐	☐
6. List the subsystems of the automated office.	☐	☐
7. Recognize modern office communication systems.	☐	☐

If any of your responses were "no," it is suggested that you review pertinent chapter parts.

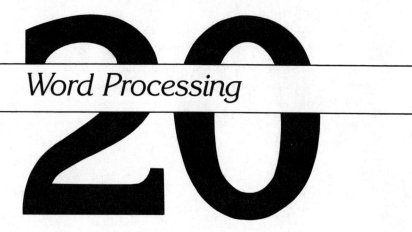

Word Processing

1. Explain word processing concepts.
2. Understand the restructuring of employees in a word processing system.
3. Identify the new equipment used in word processing.
4. State the managerial considerations when word processing systems are implemented.

Test Question data Proc.
Info Proc.
Word Proc.

Much attention in the business world has been given to *data processing*, the expeditious handling of data typically through computers. Recently, attention has been given to *information processing*, the storage and rapid retrieval of textual and numerical information via computer, and to *word processing*, the efficient management of typewritten communications through the use of highly technical office equipment and computers. The term *Textverorbeitung* (word processing) was coined by Ulrich Steinhilper, a German employee of IBM, in 1965. Presently, word processing is a multibillion-dollar industry. It is anticipated that the market for word processors will have an annual growth rate of 32 percent![1]

The paper explosion

As business expands in the twentieth century, it is being paralyzed by the so-called *paper explosion*. The quantity and the cost of written communication is

[1]Aimee L. Morner, "Personal Investing," *Fortune*, 100, no. 13 (December 31, 1979), 76.

The IBM Displaywriter System is a modular, software-based word processing system that can be customized to suit particular applications.
One of its features: an electronic dictionary that checks the spelling of about 50,000 words. (Courtesy IBM)

soaring as antiquated methods prevail, methods that cannot cope with a multitude of forms, increased verbal communication, and masses of data generated by electronic equipment. In the 1980s, the cost of a business letter is estimated to be between $6 and $13, depending upon the method of computation. (This figure includes the cost of postage, stationery, salaries of secretary and administrator, typing supplies, typewriter, office overhead, and so on.) The accelerating volume of paper work, coupled with the escalating cost, makes it critical to create new procedures and technology to manage the transformation of ideas into typewritten communication and, thereby, increase office productivity.

Word processing concepts   *Started over 20 years ago in Germany.*

The key to the smooth operation of any business or organization is communication. It is essential that office managers be familiar with word processing concepts, so that the business communication process can be accurate, efficient, and rapid.

The Wang Office Information System/140 is a large-volume word processing and office automation system. This system consists of a printer (leftmost), a CRT terminal, a floppy disk drive (to right of operator), and a disk drive (rightmost). (Courtesy Wang Laboratories, Inc.)

Word processing facilitates the conversion of thought into typewritten expression. It entails the integration of new technology—dictating systems, sophisticated editing, typewriting systems, reprographics—improved work flow procedures, and specially trained personnel in the communications process. Simply stated, ideas or thoughts are transferred expeditiously and rapidly, by a systems approach, into typewritten form.

In a word processing system, the person who formulates the thoughts or ideas to be communicated, the encoder of the message, is called the *author, word originator,* or *principal.* The principal initiates the message to be expressed in typewritten form. In a traditional office system, this person is commonly called the dictator.

[handwritten: Test question]

[handwritten: euphanism — word that makes something sound better than what it really is.]

The traditional office

ANTIQUATED PROCEDURES

First, we will examine a traditional communication system (Figure 20–1). The dictator speaks directly to the secretary, who writes the message in shorthand, a rapid, symbolic way of writing. In a shorthand system, words are written phonetically, by sound. The dictator and the secretary are both involved in this relatively slow processing of communication at the same interval of time; therefore, two salaries are being paid simultaneously during the dictation period. Ideally, the secretary should be in a mode of output productivity—reducing the "in basket"—during work hours.

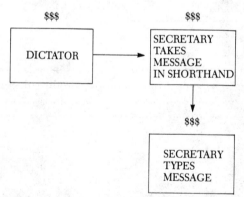

FIGURE 20–1. The traditional dictation system

Secretary as Transcriber. After writing the message in shorthand, the secretary assumes the role of typist, moving to a typewriter and transcribing the message from shorthand symbols into typewritten form. The typing process is relatively slow; originals or carbons must be assembled, errors must be erased—

it takes about one minute to correct an error on an original and two carbon copies—and proofreading must be done. The document is then presented to the dictator for signature; however, if errors are found, or if the message is changed, the document usually must be retyped. This is a slow, painstaking, inefficient procedure. IBM has estimated that the *production rate* of a secretary in a traditional system is a mere eight words a minute! This figure is all the more surprising when we realize that the *copy typing rate* of a typist upon completion of training may be 40 to 60 words a minute.

Increased Efficiency. Word processing is geared to reducing this cost by making the process more rapid and efficient. For the most part, shorthand is eliminated. Even though shorthand is more rapid than traditional handwriting, word processing systems require that the time of secretaries be more productively used.

A traditional office system may employ highly skilled, highly qualified secretarial personnel who are inefficient because of the system. A multitude of tasks are required and performed. Duties range from taking dictation, answering the telephone, filing, being a receptionist, typewriting, to making coffee and watering plants. No matter how much energy is expended, communications productivity is generally minimal. The traditional secretary is a generalist.

New secretarial procedures

Word processing evolved in the early 1960's as a result of the quest to improve the efficiency of the office communication process. New secretarial procedures were devised in office environments to match productivity improvements offered by word processing. The duties of secretaries were restructured. Two classifications of secretaries, based on work specialization, evolved: *Correspondence secretaries,* type from dictation, proofread, and edit; and *administrative secretaries,* perform clerical and administrative tasks.

Another term commonly used to identify the correspondence secretary is *word processor.*

In the traditional office, the secretary usually performs many diverse tasks. In a word processing system office, correspondence and administrative secretaries may support many individuals. In a very large office, there may be additional positions (other than administrative and correspondence secretaries) created, such as proofreaders, schedulers, and supervisors. It should be noted that in a small office, where word processing equipment exists, a single secretary may fill the roles of both an administrative and correspondence secretary. Equipment and procedures determine the increase in overall productivity.

In a word processing center, highly sophisticated electronic office communication systems are used. The principal dictates via an electronic dictation system where input is accomplished at the principal's work station and received at the secretarial work station. (See Figure 20–2.)

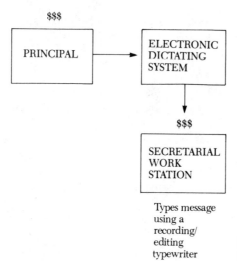

FIGURE 20–2. The traditional system plus word processing capability

This procedure reduces costs considerably because the secretary is engaged in more productive activities while the principal is dictating to a machine. The structure of word processing systems can vary from office to office. A common structure is depicted in the following chart (Figure 20–3).

New equipment

Two types of equipment are essential: dictating machines and automated typewriters. However, other kinds of equipment (copiers, composers, telecopier, facsimile machines, communicating typewriters, shared logic systems, high-speed printers) may be integrated within the system.

Input equipment

DICTATING MACHINES AND SYSTEMS

Electronic dictation is the third rung of an evolutionary ladder. (See Figure 20–4.)

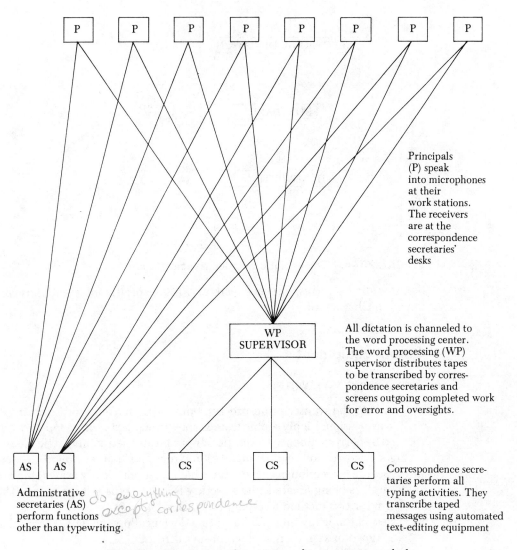

Principals (P) speak into microphones at their work stations. The receivers are at the correspondence secretaries' desks

All dictation is channeled to the word processing center. The word processing (WP) supervisor distributes tapes to be transcribed by correspondence secretaries and screens outgoing completed work for error and oversights.

Correspondence secretaries perform all typing activities. They transcribe taped messages using automated text-editing equipment

Administrative secretaries (AS) *do everything except correspondence* perform functions other than typewriting.

Note: The ratios of principals to correspondence secretaries and administrative secretaries vary from office to office. Usually an administrative secretary supports two or more principals. Administrative secretaries may be word originators in some offices.

FIGURE 20–3. A word processing system

The principal dictates into a microphone or into a telephone receiver. Machine dictation is six times faster than handwriting; twice as fast as shorthand. Later, the message on disk, tape, or belt is transcribed by a transcrip-

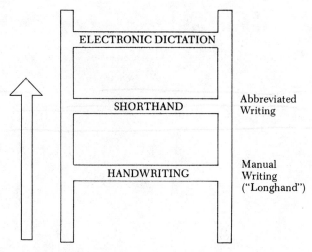

ELECTRONIC DICTATION

SHORTHAND — Abbreviated Writing

HANDWRITING — Manual Writing ("Longhand")

FIGURE 20–4. The evolution of electronic dictation

tionist, called a correspondence secretary. More specific information is contained in Chapter 16.

Output equipment

TEXT-EDITING TYPEWRITER

To speed up the transcription process, converting spoken words into typewritten expression, highly sophisticated typewriters, *text-editing typewriters*, are used by correspondence secretaries. Input is recorded on magnetic media. Changes or corrections can be made by retyping, without erasing (the operator types the correction over the error which is automatically erased. Since a rough draft is being created, the secretary is free to type at high speed. The new term for this method of typing is *keyboarding*.

New cathode ray tube (CRT) editing devices allow the typist to see what is being typed or stored on a television-like screen.

Some editing typewriters have a *green-on-green screen*; other models have a *black-on-white* screen that appears like a regular full sheet of typewriting paper. Mistakes are rapidly and easily corrected, facilitated by the visual aid of the screen. Once the first input is complete, the screen permits further visual editing and verification of the text prior to final-copy printout. These editing typewriters are also called *word processing typewriters* or *word processors*.

Easy Corrections. Corrections, revisions or the updating of previously typed and recorded documents are executed by the correspondence secretary with ease. The magnetically recorded input can be changed without necessitating

What looks like just an electronic typewriter is the Intelligent^tm Typewriter from Exxon Office Systems. This unit has a number of text-editing features (note the special keypad on the right of the board) that typewriters do not have. (Courtesy Exxon Enterprises)

the entire retyping of a document. Materials can be merged; additions and deletions can be accomplished electronically. Also, the entire document need not be proofread, only the sections containing changes.

Other Capabilities. Newer editing typewriters can automatically justify the right margin, move entire columns, assemble documents from stored information, center, tabulate, search the copy for errors and correct them, space vertically, adjust margins, number pages, allow the insertion of footnotes, and so on. A magnetic memory disk can store one hundred letters. These memory disks enable the secretary to recall documents to the screen instantaneously. Specially programmed disks can be used to handle accounting tasks, prepare payroll, keep inventories, prepare ledgers, and so on.

Push-button Response. By pressing a button, the final draft can be printed at 150 to 600 words a minute. Magnetic cards may be coded for future output or revision. Repetitive typewriting tasks can also be accomplished automatically by the mere pushing of a button!

COMMUNICATING TYPEWRITER

Communicating typewriters are used for machine communication or to gain access to a computer system. Information can be transmitted over ordinary telephone lines at 240 characters per second to another communicating typewriter. The use of the computer by either a communicating typewriter or terminal is called a *shared logic system*. Information from a computer can be played out on a communicating typewriter to create letters, complex documents, mailing lists, and so on.

COMPOSING TYPEWRITER

Test question

Composing typewriters are used to produce camera-ready copy for publication in varied type styles and sizes as commonly seen in books, periodicals, and newspapers. The right margin can be justified, made even, as in the case of this text so that high-quality textual material can be produced quickly.

The advantages of these text-editing typewriters are as follows:

1. Input is accelerated, since erasures are eliminated. Correspondence secretaries can type at rough-draft speeds.
2. Revisions can be made easily, without retyping an entire document.
3. Entire documents need not be proofread when returned for correction or change, only the specific sections that were revised need be reviewed.
4. Automatic features, such as automatic centering and tabulating, accelerates typewriting input.
5. Copy can be stored for future playback requirements.

Considerations    *Dehuminzation taking place today*

Although word processing accelerates the communication process and, thereby, saves important budget dollars, there are some managerial considerations which must be made. A secretary in a traditional office may resist the introduction of word processing systems which do not require shorthand skills. Learning shorthand requires intensive study and hours of repetitive drill. Secretaries may be reluctant to diminish or give up this specialty.

In a traditional office, the typical secretary is a generalist performing a variety of tasks, from taking dictation to answering the telephone. In moving to a word processing structure, some traditional secretaries may fear this change. Executives, aware of the human factor associated with change, have upgraded secretarial positions and pay scales as incentives. New titles have evolved, such as "supervisor of word processing." This has provided the incentive of promotion that was lacking for secretaries in the traditional office structure.

In some organizations, the one-to-one executive–secretary relationship commonly found in the traditional office diminishes with the introduction of word processing. In a word processing system, a correspondence secretary may serve many principals but be physically isolated from them.

The implementation of word processing systems is a challenge to creative management, for the efficient management of written communication is vital in the communicative process. Word processing concepts should be flexible and open to change as newer technologies emerge. Many companies have entered the field and are producing sophisticated word processing equipment.

Summary

Word processing facilitates the conversion of thought into typewritten expression. It entails the integration of new technology, improved work-flow procedures, and specially trained personnel.

In the traditional office, the dictator speaks directly to the secretary, who writes the message in shorthand. The secretary transcribes the message from shorthand symbols into typewritten form. This is an expensive process, for it may cost $6 to $13 to produce a letter.

Word processing is geared to reducing this cost by making the process more rapid and efficient. Two classifications of secretaries based on work specialization has evolved: *correspondence secretaries* (who type from dictation, proofread, and edit) and *administrative secretaries* (who perform clerical and administrative tasks).

In a word processing center, highly sophisticated electronic office communication systems are used. The principal dictates via an electronic dictation system. To speed up the transcription process, highly sophisticated editing typewriters are employed. New cathode ray tube editing devices allow the correspondence secretary to see what is being typed or stored by viewing a television-like screen. These editing typewriters are also called *word processors*. Corrections, revisions, or the updating of previously types and recorded dictation are executed by the correspondence secretary with relative ease. New editing typewriters have automatic features that expedite the production of textual material. Repetitive typewriting tasks can be accomplished automatically.

Communicating typewriters are used for machine communication or to gain access to a computer system. *Composing typewriters* are used to produce camera-ready copy for publication in varied type styles and sizes.

The implementation of word processing systems is a challenge to management, for the traditional secretary may resist the introduction of word processing systems which do not require shorthand skills.

Discussion

1. Explain why word processing has been received so widely in the business world.

Study questions

1. Explain the concept of word processing.
2. Define the following terms in relation to traditional office systems:
   - dictator
   - shorthand
   - secretary
   - transcribe
3. Define the following terms in relation to word processing systems:
   - principal
   - correspondence secretary
   - administrative secretary
   - text-editing typewriter
   - keyboarding
4. List two words synonymous with "principal" used in word processing systems.
5. Contrast the traditional office communicating system to the modern office system employing word processing systems.
6. Relate some of the managerial considerations concerning the new roles of the secretary in word processing systems and what managers are doing to combat this.

Activity

If possible, visit an office that has word processing systems and procedures. Describe your observations (note personnel, equipment, procedures).

ACHIEVEMENT OF LEARNING GOALS

Check the appropriate boxes to determine whether you have or have not achieved the learning goals of this chapter.

I Can:

	YES	NO
1. Explain word processing concepts.	☐	☐
2. Comprehend the restructuring of employees in a word processing system.	☐	☐
3. Identify the new equipment used in word processing.	☐	☐
4. State the managerial considerations when word processing systems are implemented.	☐	☐

If any of your responses were "no," it is suggested that you review pertinent chapter parts.

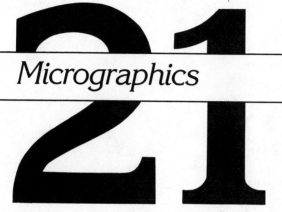

Micrographics

LEARNING GOALS

1. Recognize the role micrographics plays in the communications process.
2. Identify the equipment and basic microfilm formats used in a micrographics system.
3. Understand the applications of microphotography in the business world.
4. State the benefits of microfilming.
5. Know the basic operations of microfilm systems.

Information processing

The terms *data processing* and *word processing* are familiar to most business students. This chapter concerns micrographics, which play an important role in information processing systems. If a business organization is to function efficiently, it is essential that it manage its communications expeditiously. Micrographics facilitates the storage and retrieval of written communications (memos, letters, reports, various documents, publications, etc.).

The term *micrographics* refers to microfilm record-storage processes. A *microphotograph* is a reduced scale or miniature photograph of an object. Images on 16mm black-and-white film are 1/50 the size of the originals. This photoreduction ratio is commonly expressed as 50:1. Other ratios (40:1, 32:1, 20:1, 5:1) are also employed.

Microfilm is film containing microimages, miniature photographic images of records. The size of the reduction is relative to the size of the lense in the microfilm camera, called a *microfilmer*.

The microfilm is viewed on a standard microfilm reader, since the microimages are too small to be read by the naked eye. The microphotograph is enlarged by the use of a lense and projected on the back of a lit screen. To

396

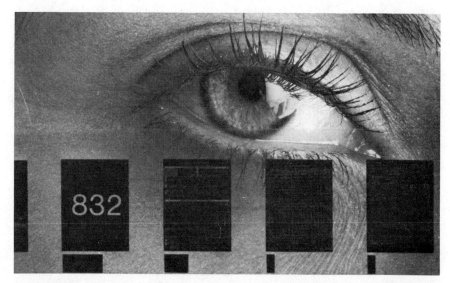

Each frame on this microfilm contains one document page. The marks below the frames are indicators to the Kodak IMT microimage terminal. When the proper number of each size of mark has passed through, the terminal automatically stops and displays the image of that document. (Courtesy Eastman Kodak Company)

produce a *hard copy* (paper copy) of the projected image, a *microfilm reader-printer* or *high-speed printer* is used.

Photomicrography is a process that is the opposite of microphotography. A photomicrograph is an enlarged photograph of a minute object. For example, microbiologists take photomicrographs, photographs through microscopes of microorganisms. (See Figure 21-1.)

History of microphotography

Miniature photographs were taken as far back as 1852; however, the outstanding example of textual microphotography occurred in 1870. During the siege of Paris, René Dagron, a reknowned French photographer, prepared micro-dispatches that were flown by carrier pigeons from Tours to Paris. Although the Prussian army sharpshooters and hunting falcons killed some of the carrier pigeons, several hundred thousand messages were delivered. At first, messages were projected on a screen and secretaries transcribed them; later on, as technology improved, the making of enlarged prints on paper was achieved. It is interesting to note that many of these messages from the Franco-Prussian War have been preserved and may be read today.

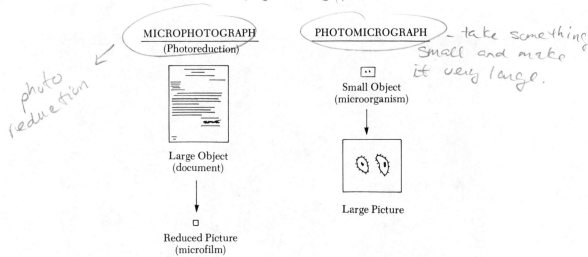

Test Question (handwritten)

MICROPHOTOGRAPH
(Photoreduction)

Large Object
(document)

Reduced Picture
(microfilm)

photo reduction (handwritten)

PHOTOMICROGRAPH

take something small and make it very large. (handwritten)

Small Object
(microorganism)

Large Picture

FIGURE 21-1. Comparison of microphotography and photomicography

After the Franco-Prussian War, microphotography was too expensive for general use. The advent of the motion picture industry in the early 1900s gave impetus to microphotography. A combination of advances in photochemistry and optics made practical applications of microphotography financially feasible.

Applications of microphotography

Test question (handwritten)

wasn't used until 1800 (late) (handwritten)

The practical business applications of microphotography can be traced to the late 1920s when George McCarthy, a banker, invented the first practical microfilmer. Other inventors soon developed the technology of a new industry, new equipment and microformats. Banks made the first applications of microfilming systems. Soon, government and business followed. Modern microformat and retrieval techniques have made microfilm more efficient than many paper and computer-based methods. V-Mail during World War II is a commonly known application of microphotography.

Microphotography is commonly used in the business world for processing information; however, some uninformed individuals associate microfilming exclusively with spy stories. We have all seen espionage movies in which a spy, using a miniature camera, takes pictures of top secret documents. The pictures are reduced to a microdot, the size of the period at the end of this sentence.

Business and industry have employed microfilming in many diverse ways to maintain and control records. Banks commonly keep a microfilm record of all checks, Master Card and VISA transactions. Department stores

Advantage: access to account very quickly (handwritten)

use microfilming in their accounting systems. Voluminous documents, such as catalogs, are often microfilmed.

Accounts payable and receivable files, customer files, personnel files, purchasing records, legal documents, planning records, graphs and drawing, marketing records, and quality control records can all be placed on microfilm.

Although the microfilming process is expensive, the many savings enumerated in subsequent parts of this chapter more than offset the cost. An effective microfilming system should be custom-tailored to fulfill the specific needs of a business or industry. There are a variety of microfilm information handling systems to choose from.

Benefits of microfilming systems

In the past, information processing was based primarily on paper, records systems. Today, microfilming and/or computer systems have replaced or supplemented paper systems. There are eight significant benefits from the use of microfilming systems:

1. Space Saving *92% of space is saved*
2. Security
3. Permanency
4. Legality
5. Speed of Entry and Retrieval
6. Computer Capability
7. Dimensional Uniformity
8. Mail Savings

SPACE SAVING

Information on microfilm requires as little as two percent of the space required by conventional paper records systems. For example, a cartridge of microfilm holds as many documents as a standard file cabinet drawer. Four cartridges are the equivalent to a four-drawer filing cabinet. (See Figure 21-2.)

An excellent example of the benefits of space saving is the microfilming of the *New York Times*. The *New York Times* is published daily and there is a voluminous Sunday edition. The *New York Times* is considered to be an excellent source of information by researchers; therefore, librarians consider it essential to store copies. If microfilming were not available, a large building, perhaps even a skyscraper, would be required for storage. It is interesting to note that libraries have subscriptions for microfilmed copies of the *New*

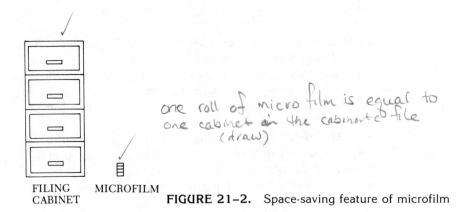

one roll of micro film is equal to
one cabinet in the cabinet file
(draw)

FILING   MICROFILM
CABINET   **FIGURE 21–2.** Space-saving feature of microfilm

York Times and other important newspapers. This liberates them from the
task of microfilming newspapers.

SECURITY

Because of the space-saving benefits of microfilming, it is economically feasible to store a duplicate microfilm file. Duplicate microfilm records off the
premises provide protection against the destruction of vital, irreplaceable
documents. Also, it is a sound precaution to microfilm records that are
handled a great deal or transferred.

Vital Records Preserved. Napoleon said, "An army moves on its stomach." We
can say, "A business moves because of its records." A classic example of the
crisis caused by the destruction of vital records took place in Hartford, Connecticut. In January, 1917, the G. Fox & Co. store, the largest department
store in New England, was completely destroyed by fire. Not a wall was left
standing. All of the financial records of the company were ruined. Tables were
set up on the sidewalk and customers volunteered to pay their bills. Because of
the honesty of the people in Hartford, the store survived. Today, in a more
complex business world where a large percentage of the business is conducted
by credit, a similar disaster destroying vital records could end a business.
Warfare and atomic attack could destroy the economic fabric of our nation;
therefore, many companies have found it prudent to store duplicate microfilm records in underground vaults secure from atomic attack.

 To protect important documents, a master set of microfilm records
should be stored in a fire-resistant security vault or central file off the
premises. For example, the G. Fox & Co. now keeps a duplicate set of its
records on microfilm in Silver Spring, Maryland.

 Only duplicate microfilm files should be circulated. Original copies
should be removed only when revisions are essential.

PERMANENCY

Archival microfilm lasts longer than paper—indefinitely. Natural deterioration is minimal. Microfilm is composed of cellulose acetate, less inflammable than paper. Microfilm is more durable than paper and is unlikely to wear out, smudge, wrinkle, fade, or tear.

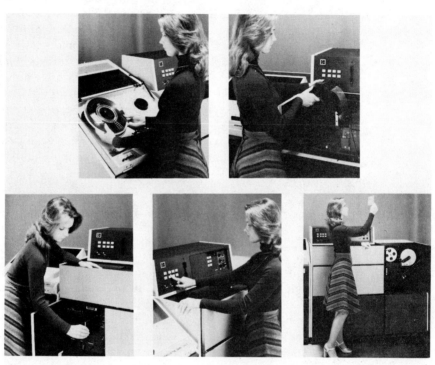

The operator uses a Kodak Komstar microimage processor: (1) Load the print image tape; (2) Load the film cartridge; (3) Insert the form slide (if necessary); (4) Push the start button; and (5) Collect the finished fiche. (Courtesy Eastman Kodak Company)

Important historical documents in the Vatican, Tokyo, and Jerusalem have been microfilmed to preserve them. Scholars can have access to textual material without directly handling fragile, priceless documents. In the business world, too, it is also critical at times to protect original copies of important documents from excessive handling.

LEGALITY   *advantage to microfilming*

Under federal and state legislation, microfilmed business records are admissible as court evidence. Microfilmed records are admissible as primary

evidence when the original documents are lost or destroyed. The Internal
Revenue Service also permits microfilmed reproductions of records.

SPEED OF ENTRY AND RETRIEVAL

Microfilming systems save many of the hours required in conventional paper
systems for the sorting, filing, and retrieval of information. In seconds, a
sought-after document can be speedily and conveniently retrieved from
millions of documents searched by the use of electronic equipment. This rapid
accessibility to documents is one of the outstanding features of micrographics.
Relatively little physical effort by a seated operator using automatic readers
and sophisticated electronic circuity reader-printers is required. This
liberates office workers from tedious hours spent locating and refiling papers
in conventional paper filing systems. Misfiling is not a concern, since microfilm images are locked in a permanent sequence. Paper copy can be speedily
reproduced from microimages. Also, if desired, economy half-sized copies can
be reproduced.

COMPUTER CAPABILITY   *Electronic images recorded into microfilm*

Computer generated data files can be converted to microimages, *Computer
Output Microfilm (COM)*. Data can be converted from magnetic tape to cathode ray tube, then photographed on microfilm; the use of paper can be by-
passed completely! High resolution, full-page imagery can then take place if
desired. A large portion of the microfilm material in use today is generated
from computers. Two thousand computer print-out pages may be contained
in as few as ten microfiche. (A "microfiche" is a sheet of film, usually four by
six inches, containing numerous microimages.)

dimentional uniformity   ✳

DIMENSIONAL UNIFORMITY

Although original documents may vary in size, microfilm images are uniform
in dimension. This expedites and facilitates the handling of documents.

MAIL SAVINGS

Microfilm can be mailed less expensively than heavy, voluminous paper
documents. For example, a microfilmed set of encyclopedias can be mailed in
a tiny package. Ten microfiche containing the 2,000 pages can be mailed using
a first-class postage stamp. Also, within a company, it is easier to move tiny
packages of film, rather than moving larger file folders and paper documents.

The microfilm system   How it works

PHOTOGRAPHING

A *microfilmer* (a special microfilming camera) takes miniature pictures of hard-copy (paper) information. Some microfilmers double film; that is, they make a duplicate roll of film while making the original. Papers should be in the correct sequence before being photographed. Index signals are photographed as guides for conventional filing systems. In a minute, hundreds of objects can be microfilmed; thousands of pictures can be taken on a roll of

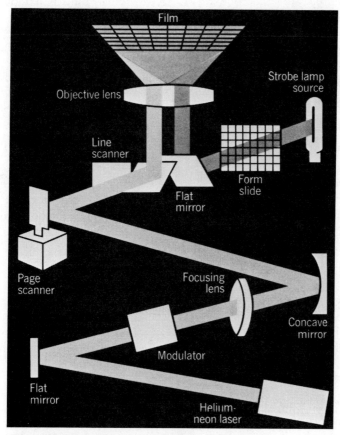

Data recording can be accomplished by advanced laser technology on a dry laser film.
(Courtesy Eastman Kodak Company)

microfilm. Computer output microfilmers can translate data onto microfilm at speeds up to 18,000 pages per hour.

PROCESSING

The film from the microfilmer is processed in a *microfilm processor*. Film processing can be done in an office or, in some instances, the film is sent to a laboratory for processing. An in-house microfilm processor is easy to use and does not require a darkroom. A duplicate copy is often made for storage in a protective vault. Photographing and processing can be joined by using a *camera/processor*, which exposes and develops the film automatically. After film processing, it is common practice to destroy the original, paper records to conserve space.

INDEXING *marking the film*

A microformat is selected (roll film, magazine, jacket, microfiche, film folio, aperture card) and the microforms are indexed.

RETRIEVAL

Retrieval techniques depend on the microformat selected. Automatic retrieval systems make access to documents fast and convenient. A *microfilm reader* magnifies the microfilm for viewing. In seconds, the desired micro-image can be located and presented on screen for viewing. A *microfilm reader-printer* or *high-speed printer* is used to produce enlarged hard copies. Single or multiple copies of a document can be made inexpensively. Also, a reader-printer permits viewing on a screen.

Microforms

Six basic microfilm formats, called *microforms*, are in use. The type selected depends on the need for flexibility in updating, speed of retrieval, and the size and length of the document being recorded.

ROLL FILM

When microfilming began in the late 1920's, almost all microfilm was on small reels of 100 foot (30.5 metre) lengths of 16mm or 35mm film, plus a short leader and trailer. Each roll of film contained as many as 5,000 images. Roll film is placed in cartons for filing and storage.

FIGURE 21–3. Roll film (Courtesy of 3M Company Microfilm Systems)

Initially, all microfilm is in roll form. The roll film can be converted to other microforms. Roll film is particularly useful for sequential records; for example, a newspaper file.

MAGAZINES

When roll film is placed into a plastic housing or cartridge, it is called a *magazine.* This magazine is similar to a tape recorder cassette. There are advantages to placing roll film in magazines: the film is protected by the

The Data Search System 1000 micrographics system
(Courtesy Bell & Howell)

cartridge, and it is self-threaded for microfilm readers. Magazines are used for convenient, automated retrieval, high-speed programs.

FIGURE 21–4.   Magazine
(Courtesy of 3M Company Microfilm Systems)

JACKETS   *a micro film format*

Microfilm jackets are made of clear acetate and contain transparent chambers in which strips of 16mm and/or 35mm film are inserted. There are three sizes of microfilm jackets: one size accommodates 16mm film; another 35mm film; and a third is a combination of 16mm and 35mm film. A typical microfilm jacket is 4 by 6 inches, containing up to 70 microimages of documents. Strips of film can be changed in a jacket.   *made from clear acitape*

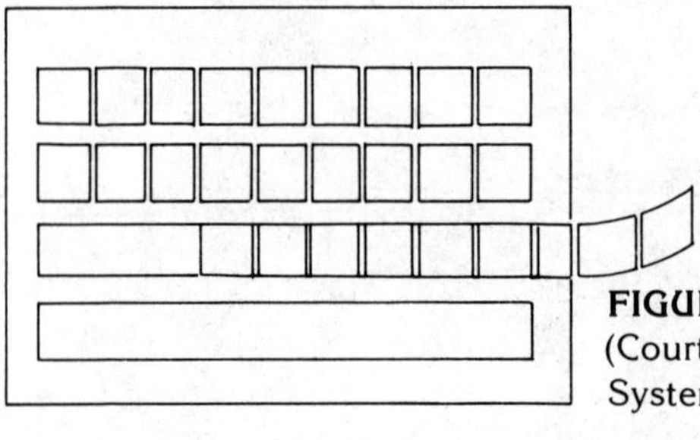

FIGURE 21–5.   Jacket
(Courtesy of 3M Company Microfilm Systems)

MICROFICHE   *– sheet of film 98 – full-color*

A microfiche is a sheet of film containing up to 98 full-color or 300 black-and-white microimages. Microfiche is usually 105mm by 148mm.

FILM FOLIOS

Film folios are usually 105mm by 148mm in size. They have chambers for microfilm and space for notations. They are compatible with microfiche files.

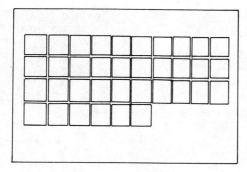

FIGURE 21–6. Microfiche
(Courtesy of 3M Company
Microfilm Systems)

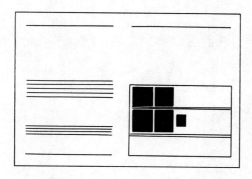

FIGURE 21–7. Film folios
(Courtesy of 3M Company
Microfilm Systems)

APERTURE CARDS Key punch card

Aperture cards are data processing cards that can be automatically indexed. They have openings for microfilm insertion—by hand or automatically—and spaces for notations. Duplicate cards can be created in seconds. Aperture cards can be processed as regular punched cards in a data processing system.

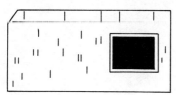

FIGURE 21–8. Aperture card
(Courtesy of 3M Company Microfilm Systems)

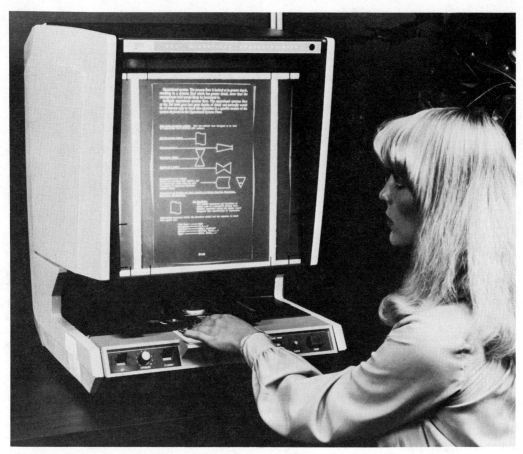

The 3M 800 Reader/Printer (Courtesy 3M Corporation)

Kodak

Summary

Micrographics facilitates the storage and retrieval of records. The benefits of microfilming are as follows:

- Space saving
- Security
- Permanency
- Legality
- Speed of entry and retrieval

File-search reader/printer (Courtesy Bell & Howell)

- Computer capability
- Dimensional uniformity
- Mail savings

The basic operations of a microfilm system are described in the following four steps:

1. *Photographing.* A *microfilmer* takes miniature pictures of hard-copy information.
2. *Processing.* The film from the microfilmer is processed in a *microfilm processor.*
3. *Indexing.* A microformat is selected (roll film, magazine, jacket, microfiche, film folio, aperture card) and the microforms are indexed.
4. *Retrieval.* A *microfilm reader* is used to magnify the microfilm for viewing. A *microfilm reader-printer* or *high-speed printer* is used to produce enlarged hard copies.

A microfiche housing frame book (Courtesy Connecticut General Corp.)

Discussion

1. Describe the role micrographics plays in the communications process.
2. Describe the equipment used in a micrographics system.

Study questions

1. Explain the eight benefits of a microfilming system.
2. Define the following terms:
   - Microphotograph
   - Microfilm
   - Microfilmer
   - Microfilm reader
   - Microfilm reader-printer
   - Micrographics
   - Photomicrography

- Microphotography
3. The history of microphotography is very interesting. Tell some of the highlights of this history.
4. Explain how microphotography is commonly used in the business world.
5. What are the four basic operations of a microfilm system?
6. What is COM?
7. List the six basic microfilm formats.

Activity

Visit your library and determine how microfilming is used. In writing, describe the equipment, microforms, and procedures.

ACHIEVEMENT OF LEARNING GOALS

Check the appropriate boxes to determine whether you have or have not achieved the learning goals of this chapter.

I Can

	YES	NO
1. Recognize the role micrographics plays in the communications process.	☐	☐
2. Identify the equipment and basic microfilm formats used in a micrographics system.	☐	☐
3. Understand the applications of microphotography in the business world.	☐	☐
4. State the benefits of microfilming.	☐	☐
5. Explain the basic operations of microfilm systems.	☐	☐

If any of your responses were "no," it is suggested that you review pertinent chapter parts.

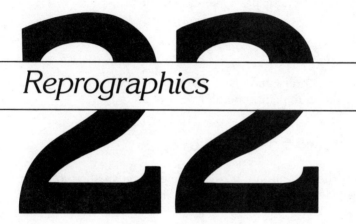

Reprographics

1. Understand the need for reprographic systems in the communication process.
2. Explain the two basic reprographic processes used in the modern office.
3. Know what factors should be considered when instituting reprographic processes for a company.

reproduction of graphics

The word *reprographics* is derived from the words "reproduction" and "graphics;" therefore, reprographics involves the copying of graphics. In the modern business world, the term is broadly interpreted to include such diverse copying activities as the typing of carbon copies to the running off of thousands of copies on an offset printer.

Littlefield et al state:

> Reproduction is indispensable to an efficient office for several reasons: (1) paperwork plays a vital role in communications; (2) wide distribution of information is required; and (3) there has been a substantial increase in the volume of paperwork in most businesses.[1]

Business executives should be familiar with reprographic systems in order to make intelligent decisions regarding the best processes for the communication tasks of their companies.

New technologies have made in-house copy-making efficient and rela-

[1]C. L. Littlefield and others, *Management of Office Operations* (Englewood Cliffs, N.J.: Prentice-Hall, Inc., 1978), p. 144.

tively inexpensive. Copying machines are standard equipment in both small and large offices. Years ago, many reproductive tasks were performed by private, commercial printing firms. The ever-increasing volume of paper-work in modern offices has made the use of reproduction equipment absolutely essential in the communication process.

It is very common in the business world to make multiple copies of written communications for two major reasons:

1. File copies are made of important papers, and
2. Multiple copies are often distributed internally and/or externally.

The major advantage of written communications is that there is tangible evidence, a record of the message. In the traditional office, the making of carbon copies and the use of stencil and fluid processes were the mainstays of reproduction processes. In the modern office, these processes have been supplemented by highly sophisticated copying and printing processes.

Reproductive equipment is used singly or in combination; for example, a photocopy machine making masters for a fluid duplicator. There are two basic reprographic processes used in the modern office: photocopy and duplicator.

Photocopying requires no intermediate master or stencil to produce copies. Duplicating necessitates an intermediary step, the replication of the original document by producing a master or stencil.

Photocopying — *replaced carbon copy*

Of the two processes, individual copies are generally more expensive to produce by the photocopying process. However, since a stencil or a master need not be created, it is comparatively less expensive to make photocopies when a small number must be produced. It would be uneconomical to make photocopies when a large number is needed. Duplicators are used for long runs.

Photocopying machines, commonly called *copiers*, make exact images of original documents being reproduced. Some reproductions are of such fine quality that it is difficult to tell a copy from the original. Photocopying equipment is particularly useful when complex originals, such as diagrams, legal documents, tabulations, tables, graphs, artwork, maps, plans, financial statements, and so on, must be reproduced. Not too long ago, for example, typists spent an incredible amount of time laboriously typing copies of college transcripts; students spent countless hours in libraries copying information from books and reference works; secretaries in business offices typed letters, forms, memos, and reports repetitiously. Now, these reproductive tasks can be com-

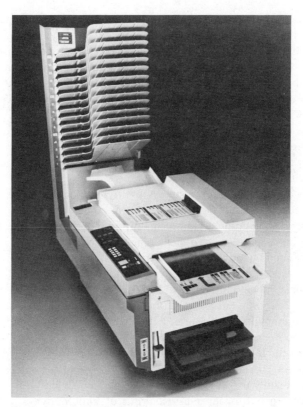

Royfax 130R photocopier, with document feeder and
15-bin sorter (Courtesy Royal Business Machines, Inc.)

pleted in seconds at tremendous savings in time and energy on high-speed
copying machines which can produce as many as forty copies a minute.

It is unusual, indeed, to find a modern office, large or small, that does
not have a copier. Desk and floor models are strategically dispersed throughout most modern offices. Since an intermediate master or stencil is not required, the process is direct, rapid and easy to operate. The operator needs no
special training. To make a copy, the original is placed on or into the machine,
a dial is set for the number of copies needed, a button is pressed, and an exact
copy is made when the original is scanned. Some copiers can make two copies
a second.

Photocopy machines with a flatbed are used when pages from bound
material, such as books or magazines, must be reproduced. The original is
placed face down on the machine.

Other copiers permit the original to pass through the machine. These
copies are used solely for reproducing single sheets of paper. A passthrough

copier works this way: the original is fed into the machine, passes along on rollers, and is ejected from the machine with the copy.

Due to the high cost of individual copies, managers must keep a tight reign on the use of photocopying equipment, for employees may make copies of personal papers. Also, copiers should be used when a limited number of copies is needed, usually up to ten. If large quantities are needed, duplicating equipment should be used. A secretary may be tempted to use a copier for long runs, since there is no need to prepare a master. Since the cost-per-copy is much higher on a photocopying machine, this could be very expensive. A duplicated copy usually costs less than one cent per copy; a photocopy can cost two to seven cents per copy.

Some executives assign a supervisor to control the use of photocopying machines. All work must be submitted for approval to the supervisor before it can be reproduced. A log is kept of the number of copies made and by whom. Some copying machines have locks placed on them. A "key" is required for operation. The key may have a counter on it.

Generally, typists should make carbon copies of all short letters and all nontechnical typing. However, in some cases when the typist is unskilled, it may be more economical to make photocopies. Some of the manufacturers of photocopying equipment contend that it is generally more economical to make photocopies than to make standard carbon copies.

One of the major advantages of using photocopying equipment is that it is easy to make corrections on the original. If corrections are carefully made, they will not show up on the copies.

There are two broad classifications of photocopying machines: those that use *plain paper* and those requiring *chemically coated paper*. Plain paper copiers are increasing in popularity, since copies can be made on paper similar to the original (even letterhead stationery). Also, copies can be made on both sides of a sheet of paper.

Colored Copies. Photocopying machines can offer distinctive features, such as enlargement or reduction in size of the original. Also, copiers can reproduce color. It should be noted that it is considerably more expensive to make colored copies.

Legal Restrictions. The manager should be aware of the legal implications concerning the reproduction of certain documents and the penalties imposed for copying them.

Do Not Copy:
- Drivers' licenses
- Automobile registration
- United States currency

The Ektaprint 150PS copier-duplicator automatically feeds documents onto the copier platen and returns them after copying. The sorter provides up to 15 sets of jogged and collated copies. Such features are the result of microprocessor circuitry within the copier. (Courtesy Eastman Kodak Company)

- Gold and silver certificates
- Certificates of deposit
- Bonds
- Paper money
- Postage stamps
- Passports
- Draft cards
- Citizenship papers or naturalization papers
- Immigration papers
- Copyrighted material, as limited by the doctrine of fair use (a copyright notice appears on all copyrighted material)

417

The reproduction of copyrighted material without the permission in writing from the publisher can result in legal problems. To cite a specific example, a teacher in charge of a school play purchased one copy of a script from a publisher, made a photocopy of each page, ran the photocopies through a thermofax machine to make fluid duplicator masters, and then duplicated thirty copies of the script. The publisher discovered this infringement of the copyright law and sued the teacher and the school system!

It is especially hazardous for an executive to copy any material from copyrighted publications without permission. The executive and the company can be sued for large sums of money. The prudent thing to do is to receive written permission before copying copyrighted material.

Photocopies also have important ancillary uses, such as making transparencies for overhead projectors and creating masters for other duplicating processes (offset mats, stencils, fluid masters).

When a photocopy is made, "copy" can by typed at the bottom of the correspondence rather than "cc" (carbon copy). For example:

Copy to Judith Maddock;
Copies to Howard Greene, Mark, Jones, Melanie Rosen.

One of the most expeditious ways to answer correspondence is to write responses directly on the original. The original with the handwritten responses is photocopied for office records and the original is returned to the correspondent. This is an informal manner of corresponding and is used with reservation.

TYPES OF PHOTOCOPIERS

Photocopiers may use one of two methods of reproduction:

1. Electrostatic process
2. Thermographic process

Electrostatic Process. In an *electrostatic copier*, a light source "reads" the image on the original and recreates the image on the copy paper. The surface of the copy paper representing the image becomes electrostatically charged, and it draws ink onto the copy paper in either powdered or liquid form. In this manner, the image is transferred from the original to the copy.

Thermographic Process. The *thermographic process*, also known as the "thermal" or "infrared" process, was developed by Carl S. Miller of the Minnesota Mining and Manufacturing Company. Copies are created when infrared light strikes heat-sensitive paper. Only carbon (print, lead pencil, and the like) images can be reproduced. Some colors on the original will not copy.

The machine is relatively easy to operate. A "sandwich" is made of the original and specially treated paper, which is fed into the machine. Both the original and the copy emerge after exposure to heat for a brief time. Since copies are not of high quality, thermographic copies are generally used within a company; the low quality precludes external use. Thermographic copiers are commonly used to produce transparencies for the overhead projector and stencils and masters for duplicating machines.

Duplicating

There are three basic classifications of duplicating processes:

1. Stencil duplicating process (mimeographing)
2. Fluid duplicating process (spirit process)
3. Offset duplicating process (lithography)

The three processes require the creation of an intermediate master (called a "stencil," "master," or "offset mask").

Selection process

MANAGEMENT DECISIONS

The business manager should realize that the photocopying or duplicating process selected is relative to immediate, specific needs. No simple answers exist for deciding what process to use. Most companies, large and small, require an array of photocopying and duplicating equipment. The following factors should be considered when instituting reprographic processes for a company:

1. Number of copies required
2. Use of color
3. Quality of copies needed
4. Cost per copy
5. Reproductive speed
6. Cost of purchasing or renting equipment
7. Training of operators
8. Office space requirements
9. Individuals who will be using the equipment

F.L

10. Maintenance and repairs
11. Cost of supplies
12. Controlling the use of copy and duplicating equipment
13. Reduction or enlargement needs
14. Preparation of masters

The manager generally must make reprographic decisions such as:

- What process is justified by cost?
- What process is qualitatively best for the situation?
- Is it necessary to prepare a master, original, or stencil?
- What process is required from a time standpoint? How much speed is required?

Selection Guidelines. These are nine guidelines that may assist you in selecting a reprographic process to use for a specific job:

1. The better the quality of copies, the more expensive the process.
2. Copies from fluid duplicators and thermographic copies should not be used for external communications. The quality of copies ranges from fair to poor.
3. Copies from stencil duplicators are good, and the cost is moderate.
4. Photocopies and offset copies are of excellent quality and remain the same the entire length of the run.
5. Photocopying is most economical for short runs, one to ten copies, since an intermediate master or stencil is not required. It is relatively expensive for long runs.
6. The duplicating process is more economical for long runs; however, it is more expensive for very short runs since intermediate masters must be made.
7. Photocopying machines are easier to operate than duplicating machines. Some duplicating machines require trained operators. No training is required to operate photocopying machines.
8. No masters are needed for photocopying machines; masters are required for duplicating machines.
9. For very short runs, use photocopying. For runs up to 300 copies, use fluid duplicating; up to 10,000 copies, use stencil duplicating; up to 50,000 copies, use offset duplicating.

Summary

Business executives have to make intelligent decisions regarding the best processes for the reproduction of various business documents used for communication tasks. To do this, it is vital that they be familiar with various reprographic systems.

New technologies have made in-house copy-making efficient and relatively inexpensive. There are two major reasons for making multiple copies of written communications: 1. File copies are made of important papers, and 2. multiple copies are often distributed internally and/or externally. There are two basic reprographic processes used in the modern office, photocopy and duplicator.

The two most common photocopying processes are electrostatic and thermographic. *Photocopying machines*, commonly called copiers, make exact images of original documents. There are two, broad classification, of photocopying machines: those that use plain paper and those requiring chemically coated paper.

There are three basic classifications of duplicating processes: stencil, fluid, and offset. *Stencil duplicating* is also called *mimeographing*. Stencil duplicators are used for long runs, the making of thousands of copies. *Fluid duplication* is commonly referred to as the spirit process. This process is usually used for short runs, up to 300 copies. *Offset duplicating*, originally known as lithography, is used when many high-quality copies are needed.

There are many factors which should be considered when instituting reprographic processes, such as the number of copies, use of color, quality, cost, speed, training of operators, space requirements, individuals who will be using the equipment, maintenance and repairs, controlling the use of equipment, reduction or enlargement needs, and preparation of masters.

When selecting a process to use, the manager should consider cost, quality, the need to prepare a master, and speed.

Discussion

1. Explain the implications of reproducing copyrighted material without permission.
2. Explain the factors that should be considered when instituting a specific reprographic process.

Study questions

1. Describe the two basic reprographic processes used in the modern office.
2. What are the advantages of photocopying? Disadvantages?
3. Explain how the misuse of photocopying can be controlled.
4. What is the thermographic process?
5. List some items that cannot be legally copied.
6. List some of the ancillary uses of photocopying machines.
7. List the three basic duplicating processes.

Activities

Assume you are an executive. Make determinations concerning the duplicating process to use:

1. You need five excellent copies of a map in a hurry. Cost is not a factor.
2. Fifty thousand excellent copies are needed of a report.
3. You need two hundred copies of a directive for in-house distribution. A reprographic process providing fair copies at a low cost would be ideal.
4. Five thousand good copies of a proposal are needed. Limited cost is preferred.
5. You need a transparency master.
6. You need a reduced copy of a graph.
7. An enlarged copy is needed of a financial statement.
8. You want to make copies on both sides of five sheets of paper.

ACHIEVEMENT OF LEARNING GOALS

Check the appropriate boxes to determine whether you have or have not achieved the learning goals of this chapter.

I Can:

	YES	NO
1. State the need for reprographic systems in the communication process.	☐	☐

2. Explain the two basic reprographic processes used in the modern office. ☐   ☐

3. Identify the factors to be considered when instituting reprographic processes for a company. ☐   ☐

If any of your responses were "no," it is suggested that you review pertinent chapter parts.

Radio/Television

LEARNING GOALS

1. Understand the advantages of radio and television communications in the business world.
2. Learn the basic equipment used in radio and television communication systems.
3. Describe radio and television systems used in business.
4. Explain satellite communication networks.

424

Radio communications

Radio communication makes possible instantaneous oral exchanges between individuals working within a company unit or in the field. Sales representatives are an excellent example of *mobile personnel* that can benefit from radio communications.

Communicating by radio entails the converting of sounds into electro-magnetic waves and transmitting these signals, without wires, to a receiving set where they are converted to sound.

Communication by radio is usually a bilateral system; the receiver is able to transmit a response to the message sent. Radio communications should not be confused with radio broadcasting, where transmitted signals are received by the general public. Businessmen use radio communications for the exchange of ideas, information, data, and so on.

These are some of the advantages of mobile radio communication in the business world:

1. Mobile personnel can be controlled efficiently by management.

2. There are many savings, such as labor, mileage, and telephone bills, that offset the cost of radio communications.

3. Service to customers is improved. It is possible to respond rapidly to customer needs.

4. Communication is instantaneous.

Radio communicating equipment has improved considerably from the large, unwieldly walkie talkies of World War II to present-day compact, lightweight models. Frequency modulation (FM) provides quality reception by reducing interference considerably. Most radio units are solid state and have a high degree of reliability. (See Figure 23–1.)

FIGURE 23–1.   Mobile radio (Courtesy of Motorola)

Mobile radio communications can be subdivided into two broad systems: one-way and two-way.

ONE-WAY SYSTEMS

In a one-way mobile radio system, the receiver is alerted but does not transmit instantaneous feedback by radio. For example, an executive may be inspecting a plant carrying a receiving device called a *beeper*. If the executive is needed, his beeper will emit an alerting noise. Usually, the executive will go to the nearest telephone and call a predesignated person.

Radio paging equipment comes in three models:

Tone and Voice Receiver. First, an assigned tone code is received, then the voice message follows.

Tone Receiver. An alert tone only is received. The tone is quieted by pressing a "silence" switch.

Voice Receiver. No tone is received; therefore, every voice on the channel is received. Voice squelch controls facilitate clear reception of messages.

Pagers are small, lightweight, and compact. They have no protusions and slip easily into a pocket or handbag. Some people prefer to clip them to a belt. They are made for rugged treatment. Some models have solid-state circuitry and rechargeable batteries. Lapel loudspeakers and earpieces are available as accessories. (See Figure 23–2.)

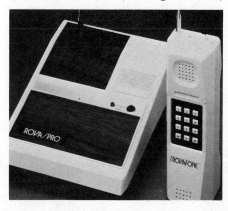

FIGURE 23–2. Pager

Another type of one-way system combines a loudspeaker with a radio. It is commonly used for paging individuals that are not easily located. An employee working in a large storeroom or fileroom may be difficult to find. Paging the individual by loudspeaker saves a great deal of time and effort.

TWO-WAY SYSTEMS

A two-way mobile radio system permits a response by the receiver of the message. Instantaneous feedback from a person in the field is, at times, very important when conducting a business.

Components of a two-way mobile radio communications system are shown in Figure 23–3:

1. *Base station.* Located at an office or point of dispatch.
2. *Mobile unit.* Located in a car, truck, or carried by an individual. The mobile radio is compact, lightweight. It is either carried in hand or worn on the person.

Repeater Service. To extend the range of communciation, repeater service can be used. A conventional non-repeater system has a limited range. Also, quality antenna sites extend radio range. Special repeater channels are not as crowded as lower frequency channels. Repeater stations provide around-the-clock service. They have channel guard tone modules that reserve a channel from intrusion by other users.

For example, in an actual situation, a typewriter broke in a college classroom. A note was handed to the department secretary requesting the repair of the typewriter. The secretary telephoned the service department of a typewriter company and requested a service visit. Within five minutes, the service representative arrived, repair bag in hand. Startled, the instructor asked how the representative got there so rapidly. Coincidentally, the repairperson was driving past the college when the dispatcher radioed that a typewriter was broken. If the service representative had not received the communication by radio, he (in this case) would have returned to his company in another town, only to drive back to the college the next day. In this admittedly simple example, the time and gasoline saved were considerable. Also, students did not suffer the loss of the use of this typewriter for so much as a day. Many other activities in the business world can be expedited by the use of the two-way radio.

The equipment used by the person in the field is a portable, *two-way radio*. Motor vehicles can be equipped with under-dash and transmission hump two-way radios. The dispatcher at the base station has fixed station equipment. The equipment is either desk-top, wall-mounted, or floor-mounted. (See Figure 23–4.)

Radio Data Terminal. It is possible to link a mobile person by radio to a computer. This is how the system works:

1. A mobile person, in the field or any other location, holds a portable data terminal and portable radio.
2. The operator enters information in the data terminal by punching alphanumeric keys. This information is transmitted by radio to a base station.
3. At the base station, a computer interface unit interfaces to a host computer.
4. Messages sent back to the operator from the computer are displayed on the portable data terminal.

MOBILE TELEPHONE SERVICE

Mobile telephone service is based on radio communications. You may have seen automobiles and trucks equipped with telephones. With a mobile phone, it is also possible to communicate by telephone from aircraft in flight and ships at sea. Mobile telephones are interconnected by radio. You can call almost anywhere with a mobile phone: your office, customers, personnel, and so on.

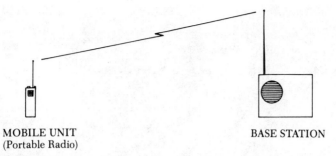

MOBILE UNIT
(Portable Radio)

BASE STATION

FIGURE 23–3. Components of a two-way system

FCC Regulations. The Federal Communications Commission regulates radio communications, since the number of channels is limited. Businesses are designated lower-power radio channels; and, therefore, the area of coverage is limited or confined. Some businesses operate on overloaded channels. To help relieve the spectrum saturation problem, new radios have been devised that operate on various frequency bands. This permits more channel availability and increased air time. For example, some companies operate solely within the 800 MHz band, rather than using several bands.

It is interesting to note that the federal government is, perhaps, the largest user of mobile radio equipment. The Bureau of Narcotics and Dangerous Drugs, Department of Defense, and Treasury Department make widespread use of radio communications.

Television

Television entails the electronic transmission and reproduction of visual images, together with sound, through space or by wire. Any intelligent discourse relating to modern business communications must, of necessity, include this relatively new communication system.

There is no one person who can be credited with the invention of television, for it developed from a series of discoveries in the fields of electrochemistry, electricity, and magnetism. The first home television receivers were marketed in 1939. Color television is relatively new; experimentation began in 1940. Presently, a technological revolution is taking place in the field encompassing such developments as satellite transmission, computer linkups, and cable networks.

Various television systems are finding their way into the business world. Business executives are finding video equipment as important as audio equipment.

Teleconferencing (Courtesy Aetna Life & Casualty)

CLOSED-CIRCUIT TELEVISION

Closed-circuit television refers to a local or private television system connected by a coaxial cable. Today, many businesses have video systems for inter-office communications, reporting, training personnel, safety, and information. Also, closed-circuit television is used for many industrial and educational purposes. Banks use closed-circuit television to help tellers verify signatures. The main office records room televises a picture of the signature card to a teller at a branch office. Some stock brokerage firms are tied in with Wall Street by closed-circuit television. Instantaneous information about stocks, bonds, and commodities can be transmitted. Airline ticket offices have been leaders in the use of closed-circuit television.

Hazardous Conditions. Closed-circuit television is used in conjunction with computerized robots in industry when there is a danger to personnel; for example, handling radioactive materials. Personnel can remain at a safe distance from hazardous conditions, yet observe and manipulate operations.

Security Systems. In addition, closed-circuit television is used in security systems. A television camera or cameras can be installed for surveillance in a department store or bank. Bank cameras shoot a picture every fifteen seconds.

Closed-circuit television can be used for close-up observation. Television and microscopes combine to observe minute objects.

Employee Communciations. Information can be easily and quickly dispersed by television information systems within a business. Pratt & Whitney Aircraft uses a closed-circuit television system to convey in-house messages to employees. Monitors are scattered throughout the company for viewing by personnel.

Hoise and Mayer tell about the diverse uses of closed-circuit television in business:

> Closed-circuit television has been used successfully at large conventions to address all the people in separate rooms together when there is no single room large enough to accommodate the entire group. It is even possible to hold a convention in several cities at once. Closed-circuit television is also used for demonstrations to large groups. The large screen enables everyone to see the demonstration clearly. With an audio hook-up, it is possible for the audience to ask the demonstrator questions and be answered immediately. Occasionally, closed-circuit television is used by companies to keep in contact with salesmen scattered over the country.[1]

VIDEODISCS

The *videodisc player* "is the visual equivalent of the phonograph; it plays discs prerecorded with television signals much as a turntable spins audio records."[2]

Video Sells. Videodiscs are used successfully to sell products in the business world.

> On a busy Saturday afternoon in a Chevrolet showroom, a young couple accompanied by two lively children seek out a free salesperson. Unable to find one, the young couple decide to leave, when an alert salesman spots them and approaches. "What particular model are you interested in?" he asks. The salesman then ushers the family over to a television and selects the videodisc for the Chevy Citation. Assuring the

---

[1]William A. Hoise and Barbara Mayer, "Which Audiovisual Aid for Which Situation?," *Public Relations Journal*, XIX, no. 12 (December 1963), 6.

[2]"Technology-Videodiscs: A Three-way Race for a Billion-dollar Jackpot," *Business Week*, no. 2644 (July 7, 1980), 72.

family that he will only be a few minutes, the salesman returns to his first customer...

This scene could have happened in any one of the 10,000 General Motors showrooms across the United Sates and Canada.[3]

The videodisc is used for imparting information. The operator has random access. This makes visualization of specific segments of a disc possible. Also, freeze frame is another important feature.

As a Training Tool. The videodisc is a valuable device in a company training program. Rather than having to repeat the same activities for training purposes, they can be recorded on discs and viewed in a "theater" situation or conference room. A videodisc player may have interactive capability. The viewer can respond to questions by pressing a digit on a keypad. If the response is correct, the viewer proceeds; if not, the viewer reviews the section of the disc providing the correct answer.

VIDEOCASSETTES

Videocassettes are gaining in popularity in the business world, for they are easier to use than 16mm films.

In many companies, videocassettes have become as popular as 16mm films for the small sales meeting. Meeting rooms are equipped with TV monitors. Snapping in a videocassette is actually less trouble than setting up a movie and screen. Some firms with a central closed-circuit TV system, like the Xerox Training Center, actually convert films into videocassettes and send the program by wire to the meeting room when the instructor calls for it. Now that the smaller half-inch videocassette is gaining in popularity for home use, we will undoubtedly see a wider use of that videocassette in business training programs.[4]

VIDEOTAPE RECORDERS

Videotape recorders are in sharp competition with videodisc players. In addition to playing prerecorded television tapes, videotape recorders can record television signals. Executives in the office of the future may consider video equipment to be as indispensable as audio equipment is considered to be today.

---

[3]Joanne Aidala, "Videodiscs: A Vehicle for Selling Cars," *Videography*. 6, no. 1 (January 1981), 40.
[4]Homer Smith, "Keep Your Eye on the Visuals," S&MM [Sales & Marketing Management], 119, no. 8 (December 12, 1977), 57.

Replaces Briefing. Important business activities such as meetings, interviews, and conferences can be videorecorded for future reference. For example, rather than being briefed on an important meeting an executive missed, the meeting can be seen (and heard) on a television screen.

Portable, battery-powered videorecorders are now available (called portapaks). Also, companion video color cameras have been lightened to permit convenient and easy taping.

Performance Evaluation. Videotaping can be of particular value in evaluating performance. A salesperson can tape and observe himself or herself in action. Personnel interviewers have also found this performance self-appraisal of particular value.

In an effort to communicate effectively, the Emhart Corporation has a videotaped version of its annual report for stockholders.

TELECONFERENCING

Personnel in a company can confer visually over teleconferencing networks. If the conferees are long distances apart, satellite transmission is used. Reception is made in a teleconference room on wall projection screens. Please refer to Chapter 15 for more details about televised conference meetings and video-phones.

SATELLITE COMMUNICATION NETWORKS

Satellite communication is used in business for the transmission of television broadcasts, as well as computer data, facsimiles, telephone calls, and other communications.

Western Union was first in space with Weststar I and II in 1974. RCA has Satcom I and II in orbit. Satellite Business Systems Co., owned by International Business Machines, Comsat General, and Aetna Casualty & Surety Co., has entered the communciations satellite industry too. Presently, there are eleven communications satellites orbiting the earth.

TELEVISION-COMPUTER COMBINATIONS

Business persons in the future will exploit television-computer technology:

- To transmit electronic mail
- To view electronic newspapers
- To schedule travel
- To receive information and research problems
- To order merchandise
- To activate alarm systems

Roof-top satellites may become as familiar as television antennas in the not-so-distant future (Courtesy IBM)

- To manage systems (such as energy or maintenance)
- To bank electronically
- To "talk back" or respond to programming by pressing buttons
- To inventory goods

Summary

Radio communication makes possible instantaneous oral exchanges between individuals working within a company unit or in the field. Communication by radio is usually a bilateral system. The advantages of mobile radio communication follow:

1. Mobile personnel can be controlled.
2. There are many savings.
3. Service to customers is improved.
4. Communication is instantaneous.

In a *one-way mobile radio* system, the receiver is alerted but does not transmit instantaneous feedback by radio. Usually, a beeper will emit an alerting signal and the executive will go to the nearest telephone and call a

FIGURE 23–4. Various components of radio repeater service system

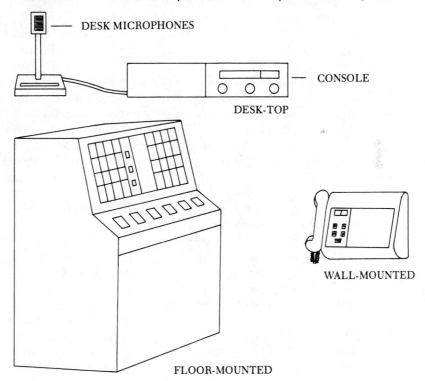

DESK MICROPHONES

CONSOLE

DESK-TOP

FLOOR-MOUNTED

WALL-MOUNTED

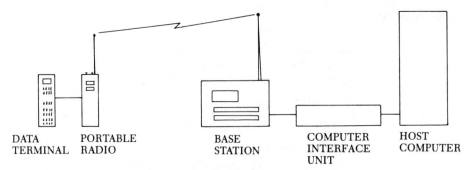

DATA   PORTABLE   BASE   COMPUTER   HOST
TERMINAL   RADIO   STATION   INTERFACE   COMPUTER
                                              UNIT

FIGURE 23–5. Linking a mobile radiotelephone to a computer

predesignated person. *Radio paging* equipment comes in three modes: tone and voice receiver, tone receiver, and voice receiver. Another type of one-way system combines a loudspeaker with a radio.

A *two-way mobile radio* system permits a response to the message by the receiver. The two basic components of a two-way mobile radio communications system are: 1. base station and 2. mobile unit. To extend the range of communication, repeater service can be used. Motor vehicles can be equipped with two-way radios. The dispatcher at the base station has fixed station equipment. This equipment is either desk-top, wall-mounted, or floor mounted.

It is possible to link a mobile person by radio to a computer.

Mobile telephone service is based on radio communications. The Federal Communications Commission (FCC) regulates radio communications.

Modern business executives are finding video equipment as important as audio equipment. Today, many businesses have video systems for communications, reporting, training, safety, information, and verification. *Closed-circuit television* is used in conjunction with computerized robots in industry.

The videodisc player plays discs prerecorded with television signals. *Videocassettes* are gaining in popularity, for they are easier to use than 16mm films. *Videotape recorders* are in sharp competition with videodisc players. In addition to playing prerecorded television tapes, videotape recorders can record television signals.

Personnel in a company can confer visually over teleconferencing networks. If the conferees are long distances apart, satellite transmission is used. Presently, there are eleven communications satellites orbiting the earth. Television-computer combinations will be used in the future to transmit electronic mail, view electronic newspapers, schedule travel, receive information and research problems, order merchandise, activate alarm systems, manage systems, bank electronically, respond to programming, and inventory goods.

Discussion

1. Explain how radio and television are used in the business world.

Study Questions

RADIO COMMUNICATIONS

1. What kind of personnel benefit most from radio communications?
2. Differentiate between radio communications and radio broadcasting.
3. List four advantages of mobile radio communications in the business world.
4. What are the two broad systems that mobile radio communications can be divided into?
5. In a one-way mobile radio system, does the receiver who is alerted transmit instantaneous feedback by radio?
6. What are the three modes of paging equipment?
7. What are the two basic components of a two-way radio communications system?
8. What function is served by repeater stations?
9. List the three kinds of radio equipment found at base stations.
10. Explain how data are transmitted from the field to a computer.
11. What agency regulates radio communications?
12. Who is the largest user of mobile radio equipment?

TELEVISION COMMUNICATIONS

1. Who can be credited for the invention of television?
2. What is closed-circuit television?
3. Tell how closed-circuit television is used in security systems.
4. What is a videodisc player?
5. Does a videodisc player have interactive capability? If so, how?
6. How does a videotape recorder differ from a videodisc player?
7. What are portable, battery-operated videorecorders called?
8. What company has videotaped its annual report for stockholders?
9. What companies own Satellite Business Systems Co.?

Activities

1. Visit a company that uses radio and/or television communications. Write up your observations of the visit (equipment, procedures, functions served, etc.).
2. If you have a CB radio in your car or if a friend has one, describe in writing how it operates, how to speak on a CB, popular CB terms, etc.

ACHIEVEMENT OF LEARNING GOALS

Check the appropriate boxes to determine whether you have or have not achieved the learning goals of this chapter.

I Can:

	YES	NO
1. State the advantages of radio and television communications in the business world.	☐	☐
2. List the basic equipment used in radio and television communication systems.	☐	☐
3. Describe radio and television systems used in business.	☐	☐
4. Explain satellite communication networks.	☐	☐

If any of your responses were "no," it is suggested that you review pertinent chapter parts.

Prentice-Hall College Division Guidelines On Sexism

Sexism in books includes sins of omission as well as of commission and bias in thought and concept as well as in language. Those who write and edit textbooks need to be particularly sensitive to both areas, for the portrayal of roles and life situations as exclusively masculine or exclusively feminine or the more subtle omission of women as participants in the action is just as much bias as is the general use of *he* or *man* to characterize all human beings. The purpose of establishing guidelines for nonsexist language is to help remove the conceptual and linguistic barriers that now artificially divide many aspects of life and work by gender. They are intended to sensitize both authors and editors to the many ways in which sexism may be expressed and to give them some tools with which to attack the problem.

These guidelines therefore contain "checklists" of things to look for in reading or in editing a manuscript as well as specific kinds of expressions to change or avoid. Eliminating sexism requires as much attention to thought and attitude as it does to pronouns and occupation titles. Much in the same way as one can observe the letter but not the spirit of the law, one can carefully use *he or she* or *they* and yet have a book that in fact ignores women as equal partners in the enterprise of transmitting or expanding human knowledge.

Striking a balance is tricky; women in many cultures and in many eras have been treated as second-class citizens, and certainly the laws and rhetoric of recent years have yet to become part of everyday reality. But to recognize the contributions of women, past and present, is not only to correct the record; it is to make the facts available to those who will create and live out new social realities. And to treat people as human beings, as members of a common group, without identifying them by gender is to promote changes in attitude that can liberate both men and women and allow society to take advantage of each individual's full potential.

Bias in concept and coverage

OMISSION

Check the descriptive and illustrative material—the examples used to illustrate concepts, and the descriptions of processes, social structures, and typical situations: Are women simply ignored? Are they treated as exceptional cases or, on the other hand, as part of the landscape or the baggage? Are the subjects of studies all male? Is the work of women scholars cited? Certain subjects—history, the sciences, and business—are special candidates for careful scrutiny. The argument usually advanced—that there are no women involved or that women did not play certain roles in certain periods or cultures—does not justify ignoring women altogether or mentioning them only as auxiliaries or oddities.

Here and on the following pages are some examples of what to look for, accompanied by some possible unbiased alternatives.

Biased	*Unbiased*
The pioneers crossed the desert with their women, children, and possessions.	Pioneer families crossed the desert carrying all their possessions.
The slaves were allowed to marry and to have their wives and children with them.	Slave families were allowed to stay together. *or* Married slaves were allowed to live with their families.
Radium was discoverd by a woman, Marie Curie.	Marie Curie discovered radium.
When setting up his experiment, the researcher must always check his sample for error.	When setting up an experiment, a researcher must always check for sampling error.

Reprinted with permission from Prentice-Hall, Inc.

As knowledge of the physical world increased, men began to examine long-held ideas and traditions with a more critical eye.	As knowledge of the physical world increased, old ideas and traditions were examined with a more critical eye. *or*. . . people began to examine long-held ideas and traditions with a more critical eye.

EQUAL TREATMENT

Check the use of adjectives and modifiers: Do those used for women consistently create a negative impression or betray a patronizing attitude? Are women mentioned consistently as an afterthought? Does the inclusion of women seem like a conscious effort or a concession on the part of the author? An attempt to be trendy or up-to-date? Are women consistently described in physical or sexual terms that are never used when describing men? Is a woman's marital status always mentioned even though the context does not require it?

Biased	Unbiased
The poor women could no longer go on; the exhausted men. . .	The exhausted pioneers. . . *or* The exhausted men and women. . .
There were also some women painters in this period, most of them daughters or wives of painters.	The women painters of this period were. . . **or** worked primarily in. . . *or* Among the painters of this period, X, Y, and Z [both men and women] worked primarily in. . .
Though a woman, she ran the business efficiently.	She ran the business efficiently.
Mrs. Acton, a statuesque blonde, is Joe Granger's assistant.	Jan Acton is Joe Granger's assistant.
The little girls played with the boys.	The girls played with the boys; the children played; the little girls played with the little boys.
The line manager was angry; his secretary was upset.	The line manager and his secretary were both upset by the mistake.
All the strong young men of the village took part in the festival, as did the young girls.	All the young people of the village took part in the festival.

STEREOTYPING

Check the portrayal of roles, the description of jobs and skills, the treatment of life styles and life situations: Are people treated as human, or are all the por-

Reprinted with permission from Prentice-Hall, Inc.

trayals done in male or female terms? Does the reader get the impression that only men to X and only women do Y? Are men portrayed one way and women another? Are all people in positions of authority or trust (the therapist, the politician, the scientist, the philosopher, the leader, the historian) male? In an education text, are all the teachers female and all the professors and administrators male? How is the family described and analyzed? Do "mommies" always stay at home? Does the author imply they should? What are the role models for children? How are recent changes in the family power structure treated? In a business text, are all the executives male and all the secretaries and assistants female? Can the reader instantly infer that all the participants in a meeting or conference are assumed to be male? Do examples of human behavior always reinforce the stereotyped idea that women and men are totally different kinds of creatures?

Biased	Unbiased
As a child, she was a tomboy; sports and not dolls were her main interest.	She was actively interested in sports as a child.
Most of the men in this plant are married heads of household.	In this plant, most of the married heads of household are men.
Current tax regulations allow a head of household to deduct for the support of a wife and children.	Current tax regulations allow a head of household to deduct for the support of a spouse and children.
The line manager is responsible for the productivity of his department; his foremen, for the day-to-day work of the girls on the line.	The line manager is responsible for the productivity of the department; the supervisors, for that of the workers on the line.
The secretary brought her boss his coffee.	The secretary brought the boss coffee.
The teacher must be sure her lesson plans are done well in advance of the day she plans to teach the material.	The teacher should prepare a lesson plan well in advance of the day the material will be taught or The teacher must be sure his or her lesson plans . . .

Completing this "awareness checklist" should give an editor (or an author) a good idea of whether or not a particular manuscript needs more than the adjustment of pronouns or changes in language to make it unbiased or non-sexist. At this point the editor or the copy editor can evaluate the scope of the problem and make recommendations for substantive work in addition to changes in language and expression. It is the overall presentation, not so much the occasional lapse in language, that can give a book a bias the author may not have intended.

Bias in language and expression

PRONOUNS

The use of *he, his, him* to denote any person in general is the most common problem in editing language for bias, simply because English has no neutral pronoun in the singular. If there is no way to reword a passage or a sentence to avoid unnecessary pronouns or to change to the plural, the best current solution is to use *he or she, his or her.* Coined terms, such as *(s)he* or *she/he,* should be avoided; they are usually distracting to the reader and annoying to the author. In citing examples, individuals in the examples may sometimes be male, sometimes female. If this alternative is chosen, avoid stereotyping male and female roles (see page 4).

None of these suggestions—removing pronouns, changing to the plural, alternating examples, or substituting *he or she*—should be followed blindly as immutable rules. Context and clarity of expression are important considerations in a text and should not be sacrificed merely to ensure that every pronoun has been changed. The constant use of *he or she* leads to clumsy, repetitious phrases and sentence structure. A change to the plural may be wrong in a given context—for example, when the discussion is of one-to-one relationships such as that between parent and child. Alternating the *he* and *she* examples does not work well in many contexts. Both author and editor need to use a variety of approaches in sensitive, appropriate ways. It is advisable for the author to include a note in the preface to the book explaining what approach has been taken to avoid stereotyping and sexism.

Biased	*Unbiased*
A person's facial expression does not always reveal his true feelings.	Facial expression is not always an indicator of a person's true feelings.
Sometimes a doctor will see his patients only in a hospital.	Sometimes a doctor will see patients only in a hospital.
The clinician must take his measurements accurately and carefully.	The clinician must take accurate and careful measurements.
The typical child does his homework right after school.	Most children do their homework right after school.
A good lawyer will see that his clients are aware of their rights.	A good lawyer will see that his or her clients are aware of their rights.

HUMAN, NOT MAN: DESCRIBING THE WORLD

One way to establish an unbiased tone that treats people as individuals who share universal human characteristics and traits is to avoid the use of the word *man* to mean all people and the use of -*man* words in general. If such words must be used, they should be accompanied by an explanation or be set in a context that clearly does not exclude women.

Biased	Unbiased
man, as in when man first walked upon the earth	human beings, humans, human race
mankind	human race, people, humankind, humanity
primitive man, early man	primitive people(s), primitive men and women
man-made	manufactured, made, synthetic, artificial
manpower	labor, workforce
the common man, the man in the street, the layman	the average citizen, the layperson, the nonspecialist
wise men	wise people, elders, leaders
Stereotyped Expressions	*Alternatives*
The committee decided he was the right man for the job.	The committee decided he was the person for the job. *or* . . . was right for the job.
The teacher must always remember that her role in the learning process is a vital one.	Teachers must always remember that their role in the learning process is a vital one.
Research has shown that the smart shopper knows what she wants before she enters the store.	Research has shown that smart consumers know what they want before they enter the store.
One new specialty at which she may aim is that of nurse-practitioner.	One new specialty at which he [*or* he or she, the student] may aim is that of nurse-practitioner.
Mary is an extremely accurate typist; Alice is not.	Jack is an extremely accurate typist; Mary is not.
Some chimpanzees in the experiment received no mothering.	Some chimpanzees in the experiment received no parental care [*or* nurturance].
Children need someone to mother them.	Children need a parent[*or* parental care, nurturing].
I'll have my girl call him.	I'll have my secretary [*or* assistant] call him.
girls' basketball team	women's basketball team
ladies' room	women's room
career girl	[give the occupation]

Reprinted with permission from Prentice-Hall, Inc.

Parallel Treatment	Alternatives
The men in the office took the girls to lunch.	The men in the office took the women to lunch.
This is my secretary, Mrs. Smith and my aide, Jack Green.	This is my secretary, Alice Smith and my aide, Jack Green.
Dr. Jones and his wife Diane	Dr. and Mrs. Jones, Jack and Diane Jones
man and wife	husband and wife
co-ed	student
college men and girls	college men and women
the men and the ladies	the men and the women, the gentlemen and the ladies
at a meeting between President Nixon and Indira Gandhi [or Mrs. Gandhi]	at a meeting between President Nixon and Prime Minister Gandhi [or Richard Nixon and Indira Gandhi, Mr. Nixon and Mrs. Gandhi]

Avoid using cliches such as the following:

the woman driver	boys' night out
the nagging mother-in-law	dizzy blonde
the little woman	catty women
the henpecked husband	female gossip
gal Friday	man-size job

OCCUPATIONS AND TITLES

Naming a person's occupation has been an editorial problem, simply because so many job titles and occupations were themselves gender-linked terms. Many alternatives are now available, so that it is usually easy to use descriptive words that can apply to any person, whether male or female. Unnecessary gender identification can also be deleted.

Biased	Unbiased
actress	actor
authoress	author
businessman	businessperson, executive, manager
chairman	chair, chairperson
cleaning lady	household worker, cleaner
congressman	member of Congress, representative
foreman	supervisor
fireman	firefighter
houseboy	servant
housewife	homemaker, consumer
mailman	mail carrier, letter carrier

policeman, policewoman	police officer
salesman, saleswoman	sales representative, salesperson
stewardess	flight attendant
woman doctor	doctor
male nurse	nurse

Index